BE HERE NOW

The Great Oasis Reunion Gig of ~~2025~~ 2029

Paul Carroll

This edition is published in 2025 by DreamEngine Media Ltd.

ISBN 978-1-915212-20-7

Email: publishing@dreamengine.co.uk
Website: DreamEngine.co.uk
Social Media: @DreamEngineuk

Printed in Great Britain by Biddles Books Limited, King's Lynn, Norfolk

For Grace

"The only reason why Oasis will come back is when we're fucking skint and I'm far from skint as you can tell and I won't be skint for a long, long fucking time. Believe me, it ain't gonna be happening."

Liam Gallagher, 2010.

MAYBE…

Oasis to reform?

They said it could never happen.

Just imagine it didn't, and we had to wait a little bit longer to see our heroes together on stage again.

Not in a series of stadium shows, but in a one-off gig.

At a festival, the likes of which has never been attempted before.

Taking place exactly twenty years after plums flew in Paris.

Welcome to 2029.

Welcome to Be Here Now.

CONTENTS

1

DON'T BELIEVE THE TRUTH

Rachel's mind is racing as she squeezes her bag onto the back seat of Justine's Fiat 500. Will this rust bucket even get them to Hull and back? The car's not the only thing looking mean and small this morning – Justine is already sporting a face like a wet weekend, which is hardly a good portent for their girls' trip out. Girls? Well, scrub that. Middle-aged women to be more accurate, but who'd willingly own up to that? Not Rachel, for one.

Justine looks on blankly as Rachel fumbles with the passenger seat to fold it back into an upright position. It would have been more sensible to put her bag in the boot, but Justine has already filled that to overflowing. Didn't she read the detailed 'what to pack' guide she'd sent her? Obviously not. She's equipped for a polar expedition by the look of it. Rachel swallows her irritation and clambers in – it's not a good start.

There is no one to wave them off from the Batley cul-de-sac as her son Tim is already at his dad's flat, where he will be spending the weekend while she's away. She feels, not for the first time, a twinge of remorse that her estranged husband, Matthew, is missing out on this once-in-a-lifetime, bucket list dream: *the* comeback gig of the century. The reunion they said could never happen. She concedes Matthew is a much bigger fan than she is, and by rights deserves to be there more than her, but a separation is a separation, and she must stand firm – there's more to life than going to gigs, regardless of who's playing. What's more important is deciding if the next thirty or forty years has more to offer than mute acceptance of stale domesticity. If anything, this weekend will be a further opportunity to find herself and prove she's right to question her marriage before it's too late.

No sooner do they turn at the end of Rachel's road, Justine signals a left and pulls into the petrol station. To fill up. They're only going one hundred miles there and back; would it really have been too much trouble to have done that yesterday? She carefully dispenses the fuel, squirt by squirt, until a round £20 clicks up on the display. Rachel takes in her friend's North Face jacket, elasticated jeans and red-laced hiking boots as she disappears into the forecourt shop and suppresses an inward sigh. She could at least have made an effort. They're going VIP yet Justine looks like a volunteer steward on the local fun run. She sneaks a guilty peek at her bag – she's spent weeks perfecting a capsule wardrobe to channel a nineties vibe and reddens slightly at the thought she might have overdone it. Justine is taking an age to pay, and not for the first time Rachel ponders her choice of companion for the weekend. The greatest money-can't-buy experience of all time, and this is who she's ended up taking. Has she done it to rub Matthew's nose in the dirt even more? No, it's not even that. Justine was third choice as two other friends turned it down, one citing she was 'a bit past festivals', and the other she'd love to come but her husband was away on a golfing trip that weekend so she was looking after the kids. It summed up exactly why Rachel was determined not to be thwarted – she wasn't dead yet. Justine clinched the position on the grounds of being available – she's unattached and has a whole six weeks off from her primary school teaching duties for a start – and by offering to drive. She mutters under her breath as her companion for the weekend makes her way back to the car holding two polystyrene cups: *well, it's too late now.*

They finally get going again, heading out to the M62. Justine clicks on the radio. It's Woman's Hour, examining this morning: deepfake pornography; do women really swear less than men; and is it time to lower the age of consent? Should Rachel ask Justine to put some music on, help get them in the mood? She looks across at the driver, who is gripping the steering wheel and straining through her varifocals as if trying to read the bottom line on an eye chart, and thinks better of it. Instead, she takes a sip of the molten coffee only to discover it contains sugar. She quietly slips the cup into the drinks carrier.

Half an hour into their journey, Justine suddenly switches the station to Radio 2. A wish to duck the debate on the age of consent? No, time for Pop Master now Ken Bruce has returned to his natural home. Rachel relaxes slightly – perhaps she's being a bit hard on Justine and needs to lighten up. She needs to remember it's not all about her, despite what she's going through. Plenty of marriages break up – it's hardly new. This is her decision, which places her in an altogether stronger position than many women who are suddenly dropped by their husbands for a better offer. She's the one who has called for the time-out, the trial separation, and she'll be the one to decide at the end of it what's best for her.

She has no desire to be defined by the man in her life – she's her own woman. Starting her dog walking business is the best thing she's ever done. Fetch has gone from strength to strength in the past three years, and she recognises its success has done much to fire her independence. Ultimately, it's made her question whether she's outgrown Matthew. She's still young, not unattractive, earning decent money – why, she's not begun to scratch the surface of possibilities the world offers. Is Matthew the worst husband in the world? Probably not, but he isn't the man she married – the sort of man who'd have swum the Channel to see a gig like this back in the day, the sort of man who'd have scaled mountains just to spend an evening with her. Now he was set in his ways – boring. Unambitious, stuck in a rut – football, pub, mates. Let's face it, he'd lost interest in her, she'd become invisible. God, he'd been shocked when she told him she'd had enough – he hadn't seen that coming. The memory of him pleading, sobbing for her to change her mind was painful, but she steeled herself not to buckle – she had to find out if there was more to life than this. It had been hard on poor Tim, who simply couldn't understand why Mum and Dad were taking time apart. For what reason? For how long? When would they be getting back together? It was hard to explain to a fourteen-year-old, but she tried, despite knowing her answers were competing with Matthew's twin mantras of 'I can't work your mum out at all' and 'It's a phase she's going through'. Tim was her priority still – another two years older and he might possibly have been making this trip with her. He continued to live with her, of course, but she was determined he should see as much of his dad as possible. They would have lots of time together this weekend, which was good. She nods to herself – she's doing the right thing. It's the only way she can find out for sure. It has taken guts to do this, and she's proud of her resolve in the face of all the surprised and questioning faces once people learned the news. A six-month separation. Then she'd decide.

And four months in up pops this stroke of good fortune. Deep inside, she knows this is the moment of truth.

Justine takes the exit slip as the Ferrybridge services come into view. She's stopping again. Toilet break. At least they'll be able to get a decent coffee. Justine insists on taking turns to go inside so the bags aren't left alone in the car. At least that's sensible, thinks Rachel, especially as it's her bag on the back seat. Ten minutes later, she's beginning to suspect Justine has been kidnapped – where is she? She sighs. Is this what it's going to be like all weekend? No, she chides herself – be pleasant, be positive. Remember what you've got lined up this weekend. You're one in a million. No, you're one in ten million. Don't be a mardy arse. When Justine finally strolls into view, Rachel gives her a rictus grin and shoots off inside. Won't be a jiffy.

There's only a Costa in the service station, so it will have to do. Fortunately, not a big queue, just four men who seem to be together. The men are laughing and joking and teasing the poor girl behind the counter who is getting flustered as they constantly change their order. Intentional, and not funny at all. Rachel tuts to herself and begins to regret her caffeine craving. They really are loud and obnoxious. That's when she notices the one at the back, a pasty-faced beanpole who looks like the love child of John Cooper Clarke and Olive Oyl, quietly slipping an array of sandwiches, cake and biscuits into his voluminous window cleaner-size pockets. She stares open-mouthed at the brazen audacity of it all. He turns to her, winks, and strolls for the exit. His three friends collect their drinks and amble after him, mission accomplished. As a responsible citizen Rachel's first instinct is to dob the light-fingered twiglet in, not least because the perpetrators have now left the scene and can't threaten her. She takes one look at the red-faced girl behind the counter, reminds herself she's on her way to the best weekend ever in the history of the world, and offers up a meek 'Skinny latte with oat milk, please.' Costa, she reasons to herself, must build leakages like this into their cost base. Will she mention this incident to Justine once she's back in the car? Maybe later, when the driver won't be able to insist on the full force of the law being involved, which would only delay them even further.

***

Despite their Toyota Land Cruiser being parked opposite the front door of the service station the Costa Four appear to be in no hurry as they prepare to divvy up their booty. Nobody can see them through the blacked-out windows anyway. There is considerable hilarity at the ease with which their lunch has been acquired, although not everybody shares the joke. The driver nervously keeps his eye on the building as a game of bagsy develops over their swag. 'Can we try to stay out of jail this weekend,' he chides. He's greeted with a collective shrug. 'Do you think anybody saw?' They ignore him as they rip away at the wrappers. He gives up. 'There's a bag to put the rubbish in,' he reminds them. The car is spotlessly clean, inside and out, and sports a brand-new air-freshener with the legend *My Car. My Music. My Rules* hanging from the rear-view mirror. The man at the wheel has imposed a strict no-smoking ban on his passengers that has already led to protests from the most nicotine-dependent member of the quartet (the accomplished petty-thief, although his kleptomania has nothing to do with his craving for tobacco). They tuck into their food, and the driver can't help but notice the mess they're making.

He doesn't want to be a wet blanket, but it's no good. 'Careful with those crumbs, lads. I've just had it valeted.'

The chubby occupier of the passenger seat produces a half bottle of whisky and offers to top up their coffees. The two in the back enthusiastically proffer their cups, while the driver covers the top of his with his hand. 'Come on, Dave. Don't be a wuss,' fat boy chides. 'We're on manoeuvres, right?' He's vociferously backed up from the rear seat.

Dave thinks about it, and not wanting to be a party-pooper removes his hand. 'Just a drop mind, Ent,' he says to the self-appointed barman. Just in case they think he's going soft he adds a defiant, 'Don't worry, I'll catch up as soon as we get there.'

The fourth occupant of the car scratches at his beard before launching a point of order to the passenger seat. 'That's your second muffin, Ent. There's only one each.'

'No, it's not,' comes back the injured reply. 'I've had one muffin and this…' he says, stuffing the remnants of a pastry into his gob, '… is a cinnamon bun.'

'Trust you to be counting, JJ,' sneers the pipe cleaner next to him. 'I'm the one who half-inched them, and I say Ent can eat what he likes.'

'Fuck off, Stoggy,' is all JJ can muster in reply.

The four form an unlikely looking unit. All middle-aged and white, but there the uniformity ends. Dave, the driver, is well-scrubbed and groomed and, obviously no stranger to a strict gym routine, in considerably better nick than the other three. He's decked out in designer casual gear, although no amount of premium brand shopping will ever deliver the laidback vibe he's so clearly aiming for. He gives the impression he's been dressed by his wife – one who had a pristine Ken Doll look in mind but ended up with lawyer-on-holiday instead (which, coincidentally, is exactly what he is). That suspicion is reinforced by his accent, which is clear and enunciated when he wants it to be but slips when he's drunk or trying to be one of the lads. It's his car, of course it is, because he wants to be in charge at the same time as appearing democratic.

Ent – short for Entwistle – has let himself go a bit. A type 2 diabetes case-in-waiting, he maintains he just needs to lose a few pounds to knock himself back into shape. Ent's done all right for himself with his small building business (extensions a speciality). Everybody says the trade is a goldmine, that you can't go wrong given the lack of competition and the desperation of punters to source a reliable builder (as if such a thing exists), but Ent doesn't agree. He finds it almost impossible to hire craftsmen or labourers these days, juggling jobs on a daily basis is stressful, and that's nothing compared to handling disgruntled customers. Take, for example, Dave's missus – he's not expecting a glowing testimonial from her any time soon after they botched the kitchen at their new home. And he'd given them a special mate's rate for the job as well (twice the price of anyone else).

JJ, on the other hand, is serious, focused, exact – entirely suited to his job as a traffic and transportation manager. This ginger-bearded wonder could help you fill in a tax return, download the latest software upgrade to your phone, or mend a fuse. Dry, precise and slightly uptight, he's not known for letting his hair down, but can hold his own with the best of them in his head. If only he didn't suffer from a few minor health problems. Most are hypochondriacal fancies, but his IBS isn't and is a major cause of concern and anxiety for him, not least in social settings. Ever evaluative, JJ looks up to Dave, is smart enough never to use Ent's building firm, and is wary of Stoggy who he considers a loose wheel.

Ah – Stoggy. Mr Whippet, in every sense. Stoggy has been of interest to the police on occasions too numerous to mention, yet remains resolutely irresponsible. His criminality extends to supplying drugs (occasional transactions with Dave and Ent convince them they still have street cred, although he never deals them the good stuff). When times are leaner, he might be found working for Ent as a labourer (unbeknown to Dave, he's the main reason the underground heating in his new kitchen cracked the floor the first time it was turned on).

The four travelling companions don't work together, aren't bosom buddies, and have little in common. There are but two things uniting them. First, shared school days at Parrs Wood Comprehensive where they spent years 7 to 11 coming to terms with puberty, discovering their educational potential and adjusting their sights for life as a consequence.

The second thing they have in common? Oasis, innit?

2

HALF THE WORLD AWAY

The sea is like a millpond as the launch circumnavigates the island. Given the lack of wind, the thousands of turbines towering above stand almost motionless, casting the impression of a ghostly forest onto the surface of the blue water. Bernard Roscow shivers slightly, despite the temperature being in the high twenties on this gorgeous summer's day. 'Ross' has headed the production for numerous large events – festivals, global mega tours, even the coronation party for King William. He's the go-to man, the cool head who never drops the ball, the martinet who makes everything run to order and on time. So why the glum expression?

His companion, Matthew Salt, notices his introspection and jovially slaps him on the back: 'I don't know about Be Here Now, Ross, you look like you'd rather be anywhere but here.'

Ross shakes his head at Salt's poor riff on the festival title, his upper lip curling upward in a resigned scowl. Wouldn't he just?

Salt, the only music promoter people know the name of, had no such qualms when offered the gig of the century. Was he up for it? You bet. The only man who could make it happen. After a career spanning fifty years this is how he wants to go out – with a bang. The biggest, most innovative, ground-breaking and sensational live music event ever. And he's staged quite a few already. There was the prestige of doing this, of course, but Salt recognised early on he'd met the perfect sponsors too – where their lack of experience was in inverse proportion to the endless pots of money at their disposal. Their requirements were ambitious in the extreme but Salt, reasoning saying no never made a buck, breezily reassured them that nothing was impossible. As long as the price was right. The budget has tripled since the first negotiations, and he's full of self-congratulation as to how far he's pushed it. In fact, he personally stands to make more money this weekend than over the first forty-five years of his glittering career. Probably get a gong thrown in as well. All that's left at this juncture is to get it over the line. And with Ross at his side, surely nothing can go wrong.

The pair are conducting a final inspection of the island before the crowds arrive. Their course will take in the various landing points for the different categories of guest, the offshore perimeter security and the registration gates, before a final check of the site. An idea that started out eighteen months ago is about to come to fruition, the culmination of thousands of man hours and hard work. Ross swears by the maxim, 'If it's not done by the eleventh hour, it's not going to be done at all' which is why Salt instinctively knows this inspection will turn up no problems. All is ready and prepared. Shipshape and Bristol fashion, albeit in the North Sea rather than facing west.

'Looking good, Ross,' says Salt as he flicks his cigar stub into the briny.

Ross raises his eyebrows. 'That's not very environmental. You'll have Eclipse on your back for endangering the fish.'

Salt laughs. 'God, give me strength. That bloody woman. Just tell her it's my smoked herring recipe if she asks.' The head of production looks unamused.

Appointing Eclipse as the event's eco-warrior was very much the idea of the sponsor. Salt indulged this tangible commitment to ecology, sustainability and the environment as a marketing gimmick pure and simple but soon learned that the green goddess got to call far too many shots for his liking. While he was perfectly happy to say one thing and do another, poor old Ross had to deal with Eclipse on every aspect of the logistics to ensure they met the planet's approval. He'd almost walked off the job when she banned the use of helicopters at the site. On that same matter, Salt recalls the terse interchange with the band's representatives who were adamant their boys 'weren't going to paddle to the gig'.

As they near the end of their circuit the promoter is upbeat. 'Told you there was nothing to worry about. All in hand. You've done a great job.'

Ross accepts the praise lightly. 'I still think it's bloody stupid putting on a gig like this on a floating turd in the middle of a shipping lane.'

Salt has heard much of this before. 'It's not a…' He stops and draws himself up: 'Holm Island is a state-of-the art Eco Island, designed to deliver renewable green energy to meet the nation's future needs,' he recites.

'Bollocks,' comes the reply.

'An outstanding example of British ingenuity and world-beating scientific leadership, initiatives like Holm will help the UK achieve full energy security by 2050.'

'Or so it says in the press release.'

A wide grin spreads across Salt's face. 'It would have been easier to say: "You just can't miss with wind and piss".'

'They didn't have to actually do the gig here though. They could have done it anywhere, and got thousands more people in.'

'True, Ross, true. But our friends at British Energy want the world to see what bright sparks they are. And let's face it, the whole world will be watching.'

Ross has other things to think about than the sponsor's commercial aims. 'Well, I still think it's a risk. Limited capacity, ferrying people in and out, tight accommodation and facilities, a band that hasn't played for twenty years, VIP, VVIP and VVVIP guests playing one-upmanship, interference every time I do something…'

'Bloody hell, chill out, Ross,' Salt teases, 'you'll give yourself a thrombie.' Of course, Ross is right, but every change to a conventional – safe – approach to an event of this scale has been an opportunity for Salt to add a few more zeroes to the cost.

Ross is on a roll now. 'And using the term BRITEPOP. How shite is that? Who came up with that?'

It certainly wasn't Salt, but it was a cue the British media were only too happy to adopt once they'd had it fed to them. 'Come on, it's not that bad. British Energy – BRITE – riffing on Britpop. And who do we have playing? Yes, it's simple, but often the most memorable things are.'

Ross remains unimpressed. 'As long as they keep out of my hair for the next couple of days, I'll count it as a win.'

Their boat pulls in and berths. Salt is about to remind his friend he doesn't have any hair but swerves at the last second. 'What's next?' he asks.

Ross checks his iPad. 'Just stage, lighting, sound, dressing rooms, security, catering, first aid, eco-camping, boutique camping – oh, and the low water consumption vacuum toilets specified by the queen of the eco-warriors. As if I didn't have enough to do.'

Salt looks at his watch. 'I can skip that bit, can't I? A few people to gladhand. I enjoyed the boat trip though.'

Ross sticks the iPad in his backpack and prepares to disembark. From the jetty the overhead wind turbines appear even taller and more imposing, a surrounding army laying siege, squeezing the small floating footfall in a vice-like fist. He has one more item for Salt before he departs. 'How's the weather looking?'

Salt peers at him over his Ray-Bans and chuckles. 'You can see for yourself – cracking the flags as they say. I must remember my Factor 50.'

Ross wearily shakes his head. 'The forecast. Tomorrow and the day after. I don't need to remind you how important it is.'

Salt is only joshing. BRITE have had the British Meteorological Office working overtime on this, including an in-depth analysis of weather precedents on the same weekend over the years. 'The latest news is set fair, all the way. You just worry about the things you need to deal with and leave the rest to me.'

***

The processing plant deep in the heart of the island is a hive of activity but that's all about to change. At the given signal from BRITE's Martin Grundy, the master control panel is to be put on standby for the next three days, a health and safety requirement given the thousands of people who will be occupying Holm that weekend. Enough energy has been stored to maintain all functions and services – and uphold the energy company's sustainability credentials – until the last punter is clear on Sunday afternoon.

Martin has been central to Be Here Now happening since being appointed to the new energy concern two years before. The head of marketing job spec was pretty basic: put us on the map, make us famous. On being shortlisted, Martin calculated his fellow candidates for the post would focus on the technological and engineering aspects of the new man-made energy island or work themselves into an excited state over the role Holm would play in the nation's long-term energy and environmental strategy – all very worthy, but rather dull. He buttered up the CEO's PA to nab the last interview slot, his logic being he'd stand out like a breath of fresh air at the end of a tedious day for the panel. His opening gambit was to present each of them with a BRITE business card he'd had made up with 'Martin Grundy, The Genie of What If' printed on it. That got their attention. His mantra – 'think big' – was the only way to go in his opinion and nobody else stood a chance after that. But how big could he take it, really? It was a reasonable interview question, and one that had him essaying examples he appeared to make up on the spot: 'Oh, you know, something like a round the world race using renewable energy, or building the world's biggest kite, or powering the floodlights of every club in the European Super League'. Encouraged by positive nods to these suggestions, he found himself adding another one off the cuff: 'Or what if we got Oasis to reform to do a gig on the island itself.' He'd laughed gleefully at the time, to emphasise that the sheer implausibility of an idea was merely the gateway to making it happen. Little did he imagine which idea the panel would warm to most.

At four o'clock on the dot the giant turbine blades make one final slow rotation and fall silent. The low hum that almost nobody notices after a day on the island is now pronounced by its absence, succumbing to the sound of seagulls. But it's not only the turbines that are to be shut down because as well as being a state-of-the-art wind farm, Holm Island's second claim to fame is its sustainable bioenergy plant, converting millions of tonnes of raw wastewater per year into a renewable low carbon form of biomass fuel. Converting sludge, that is. Sewage sludge. Martin's name for it – 'Poo Power' – has struck a chord with the Carry on at Your Convenience British public, who might otherwise have shown little interest in the onward journey of their number ones and twos (now they know they're doing their bit for the planet every time they pull the chain). Two huge underwater pipelines carry the sludge from the east coast of England to the island, where it is separated in a giant centrifuge, the solids being processed into dry fuel pellets while the cleaned water by-product is returned to the mainland through a third pipeline.

As soon as the turbines and the centrifuge power down, Martin makes his way to ground level, fresh air, and the office he's requisitioned for the duration, the nerve centre of Be Here Now. The chief engineer of Holm Island was less than pleased to be temporarily turfed-out but bowed to the instruction from above that whatever Martin wanted he was to get. History was in the making, and The Genie of What If was the man helping to make everybody's wishes come true.

There are a hundred and one messages for him, but he isn't interested in dealing with any of these until after his scheduled call in five minutes' time. He slumps into his chair and pulls open the desk drawer. There, beneath the 'Holm from Home' sign he removed from the office door on moving in, is his Eco water bottle, made of recycled stainless steel and ocean bound plastic. He takes a deep draught of its contents and lets out a sigh of satisfaction. Nothing hits the spot like a Screwdriver. He shakes the bottle – about a quarter left – and decides he'll reserve that for after his call. BRITE has a zero-tolerance policy towards alcohol at work but, as far as Martin is concerned, nobody at BRITE is coping with anything like the responsibilities he has to handle. Besides, a drink makes him more creative – he has all his best ideas when he's in a relaxed state. In fact, in his view, the consumption of alcohol should be compulsory in all marketing departments (although he's not gone as far as suggesting this to his current employer). For now, this is his little ritual. Nobody is being harmed, nobody can smell it and, if anybody remarked, he's drinking orange juice. And, Christ, does he need a shot or two of his special OJ ahead of speaking to Amanda.

Whether Martin likes it or not, Be Here Now would be nowhere without Amanda Teale, the government minister for CLEAN (Climate, Life, Ecology and Nature). After all, she's the one who's come up with most of the money for it. Nobody wants to openly acknowledge that fact, not least the Treasury, because it wouldn't look good spending millions of pounds of taxpayers' money on something as non-essential as an Oasis gig. Amanda, however, sees it differently: their undeclared investment is vital to underlining the lead the nation is taking in saving the planet. Not by booking Oasis, of course, but via a unique public and private joint venture forged to help the country achieve energy self-sufficiency.

Martin's role in all of this is either 'genius' or 'coincidental' depending on how you view the role of marketing. A daft idea that had little prospect of success suddenly takes off with two phone calls. Martin calls Matthew Salt and asks him if he can get a price on Oasis. After he stops laughing, he puts out feelers, and eventually pitches an amount that could interest the boys. A stupid price no one in their right minds would contemplate, and way out of BRITE's budget. But if – phone call number two – the government could underwrite the venture, then look at the undoubted benefits and value for all. Martin doesn't even make the second call – he leaves it to their public affairs director, who has an 'in' with CLEAN. Is funding BRITE to put on Be Here Now a better return for the UK taxpayer than, for example, filling potholes, improving coastal and flood defences or stocking up on PPE? Despite that, it takes less than three months for Amanda to greenlight it – she can justify it to herself, she'll have a great story to tell at next year's COP 35, plus she might get to meet Liam Gallagher. It's on. But as Martin has discovered, she who pays the piper calls the tune. And she's been making his life hell ever since. He eyes the flask again but his phone rings to hijack that thought: Amanda Teale's office for him. The first thing she will want to know is if he's managed to get her an exemption on the helicopter ban.

Whoever thought marketing was a glamorous profession should try walking in his shoes for a few hours.

3

D'YOU KNOW WHAT I MEAN?

'This is a bit more like it,' says Rachel as she's handed a glass of Champagne (the real stuff, not Prosecco) from the waiter at the entrance to the lounge. They've finally boarded the ferry that's to transport them to Holm Island and the gig. Justine, too, allows herself a small squeal of delight – this is really happening. Even with their unscheduled stops they made it to Hull with plenty of time in hand to park, gather their bags and get in line to register.

'Told you we were travelling in style,' Rachel crows as they find a seat next to the panoramic window. 'VIP all the way.'

The lounge begins to buzz as more and more people arrive – the sense of anticipation is high, and there doesn't appear to be a limit to how many glasses of fizz each person can have. Justine spots there's a buffet laid out – is that free as well? Despite not knowing for sure, Rachel nods casually and points to the laminated 'Supersonic' guest pass dangling from her neck. 'All-inclusive,' she says triumphantly. 'I could get used to this.' They chink glasses, not quite believing their luck.

That's when Rachel sees the Costa Four sweeping in, each relieving the waiter's tray of two glasses each. Her jaw drops, causing Justine to remark, 'What's wrong, Rach? Do you know them?'

Before she can reply, her mouth gapes wider still as the four make a beeline in their direction and plonk themselves down heavily on the banquette seat beside them. 'Don't mind if we sit here, do you, girls?' says the chubby one. He drains one of his glasses, points at the other, and adds: 'Great cure for seasickness, you know. It's the bubbles.' Justine stiffens at the greeting 'girls' and shrinks into the upholstery while shooting panicked looks at her companion. The skinny one – the thief – is the last to sit down. Recognising Rachel from earlier he nods silently in her direction, a smirk spreading across his face.

Halfway down his second glass the overfed one lets out a huge burp. 'Whoops,' he says by way of an apology. 'Better out than in, though.' The four men dissolve into laughter. 'Like I said,' he adds, 'it's them bubbles.' Rachel searches desperately for an escape route – a spare table, a party of women they can attach themselves to – but is too slow as the Belch ploughs on seamlessly. 'Ent,' he says, offering his hand. 'Short for Entwistle.' Both Rachel and Justine allow him to administer a limp handshake. He indicates the other three in turn. 'Dave. JJ. Stoggy. Fellow travellers all.'

They meekly acknowledge them and offer a weak *Rachel* and *Justine* in return.

'Right,' says Ent, rubbing his hands before pointing at each of the women in turn. 'First time – go.' He's met with puzzled looks. Surely, he can't mean…

'Oasis,' explains the one who is dressed more smartly than the others. 'The first time you saw Oasis.'

'I've never seen them before,' Justine volunteers.

There is a sharp intake of breath. 'What, seriously?' says an incredulous Ent. 'You having us on?'

Justine shrugs her shoulders. Why would she joke about something like that? Her expression suggests she thinks there's more to life than Oasis, which seems to momentarily stun the four men.

The one with the ginger beard breaks the silence. 'And what about you, er, Rachel? You must have seen them?' he almost pleads.

Rachel imagines this is what it must be like being on Mastermind. Two minutes on a specialist subject. Only not on a topic of your choosing. 'Yes,' she assures them. 'A long time ago, though.'

There's a palpable sense of relief around the table. Thank goodness for that. 'Well, it was a long time ago for everybody,' Dave gallantly offers. But her time isn't up yet – *I've started so I'll finish*. 'Where?'

She hesitates. What was the name of it? 'It was at a festival in Spain.'

'Benicassim?' JJ pipes up. 'You saw them there? Nice one. 2000, 2005 or 2009?'

They played there three times? *Think*. No, she can discount the first two – she'd been there with Matthew, footloose and fancy free before marriage, parenthood and wage-slavery intervened in her life. '2009,' she confirms, 'definitely the last one.'

'Pretty bum gig by all accounts,' Ent recalls. 'Noel said it was a waste of time 'cos of the shite sound. The PA blew up during "Wonderwall" and Liam did one of his disappearing acts halfway through the set.'

She can't be sure if he's being sympathetic or scornful.

JJ has a supplementary question: 'Was it you that started the fire then?'

Rachel is mystified. What on earth is he talking about?

JJ eyes her suspiciously. 'There was a big fire at the site that night – caused carnage. Punters evacuated, the lot, then the winds blew out most of Friday. Are you sure you were there?'

Rachel rankles, her cheeks starting to flush under the weight of interrogation. 'Why would I say I was if I wasn't?'

Dave rides to her rescue. 'Bloody hell, lads, give her a break.' He flashes her a wide smile. 'At least you saw one of the final shows. That's something.'

Rachel doesn't respond directly. Benicassim. Twenty years ago. They'd only gone for the day because she didn't fancy camping. Matthew had been so desperate to see Oasis they'd interrupted their Spanish holiday and hired a car to come up from Valencia. She'd driven so Matthew could have a few beers – a few too many as she recalls. They'd had an almighty argument before the band came on because he wanted to go to the front, and she said they'd get crushed. They ended up watching from miles away, Matthew resenting every minute – *we may as well be in the bloody car park* – before legging it early to beat the crowds. Not very rock 'n' roll. It had been loud – she remembered that much.

'And what about you?' she counters, throwing a bone to the four hungry hounds to scrap over. 'How many times have you seen them?'

Her enquiry is met with a fresh outburst of mirth. 'Now that,' says Dave, 'is a very controversial question. I've seen them the most times, but I find my record is challenged, without any clear evidence, by some of my companions.'

'Rubbish.' It's JJ, who knows a thing or two about stats. 'You include the times you've seen High Flying Birds, Beady Eye and Liam in your tally, and that's plain wrong.'

Dave brushes off the accusation. 'Fifteen times – I may even have underestimated there.'

Ent isn't having any of this. 'You need to forgive Dave, girls – he's a lawyer and used to making things up. In any event, the earliest gigs count more, so you'll find Stoggy here is the champion. He was at the Nynex in '95 and he's still got his Bank of Burnage refund cheque from Heaton Park.'

Stoggy just smiles and says nothing. It strikes Rachel he hasn't uttered a single a word yet – he just watches on; with the gang, but not part of the gang.

'Hang on,' JJ protests. 'You can't add arbitrary weightings to gigs attended. Each one counts as a single unit, so I think you'll find I've seen them the most times on that solid mathematical basis.'

Ent leans in towards the two women. 'Except none of his really count, do you know why?' He doesn't wait for them to guess. 'Because he's a Rag, that's why.' Rachel and Justine are clearly at a loss as to what a Rag is, so he enlightens them. 'A Salford Red.'

Ent, Dave and Stoggy launch into an impromptu chorus of "Blue Moon" while playfully battering JJ over the head.

JJ bristles with indignation. 'It isn't mandatory to be a Man City supporter to like Oasis.' It's not clear if he's trying to explain the distinction to the two women or attempting to console himself. 'And what about Bonehead? He's a Man United fan too.'

Dave mediates once more. 'Come on, lads. He can't help it.'

Rachel shoots a sideways glance at Justine, her signal they should make a run for it. In unison they deftly drain their drinks preparatory to making their excuses.

In the same moment Ent spots the waiter has recharged his tray and jumps up to relieve him of his load. 'Another one, girls?' he shouts over his shoulder. They shake their heads, but regardless he plonks two glasses down on the table before returning for more. 'We'll have them if they're still going begging.'

Trapped. Not that there's anywhere else to go in the rapidly filling lounge.

Justine voices the very thought on Rachel's mind at that point. 'How long is it until we get there?'

Ent is apologetic. 'Did you want me to get you a double?'

Dave interprets. 'I think she wants to know what time we're getting to Holm Island, Ent. Not how many she can get down her neck in the meantime. Not everybody is on a mission like you.'

Ent takes this admonition in good grace. 'Dickhead.'

Dave turns his attention to Rachel, as if weighing up the budget potential of a new client. 'Ignore them, Rachel. Just high spirits. We've been waiting twenty years for this so we're a bit pumped.'

The image of Matthew, weeping uncontrollably as he begged her to give him one more chance, pops into her mind. God, what would he have given to be on this voyage now, probably loving this sort of banter. She shifts guiltily. 'Oh, I get it. Don't mind me.' Remembering Justine she adds, 'I mean us.'

Ent looks from one to the other. 'So, are you two, like, friends, or what?' It's an enquiry that, as far as Rachel can divine, is dripping with innuendo and accusation. Cheeky sod.

'Yes. Friends. Catching up. A weekend break.'

Stoggy scoffs. 'I thought people went to the Lake District for a weekend break – not the gig of the century.'

Oh, it speaks. 'We can do both, can't we?' says Justine sharply. 'Have a weekend of relaxation as well as watching the concert.'

Dave jumps in again. 'Er, to answer your question, we leave here at one and disembark at Holm around four. Still on UK time you see. Induction, orientation and accommodation in that order, and the welcome dinner tonight. Assuming...' he holds up his Supersonic laminate, '... you've got the same package as us.'

Rachel nods. She supposes everybody on the boat has the same package. Everybody in this lounge at least.

Now JJ is curious and can't stop himself asking aloud: 'I'm not being funny,' he says, 'but a trip like this is an awful lot of money. I mean, if you're not, like, madferit Oasis freaks.' He realises that came out more bluntly than he'd intended so adds, 'I mean, you could have gone first class to Barbados for a fortnight on what it's costing.'

Justine doesn't miss a heartbeat in replying: 'Oh, we're not paying,' she gloats. 'Rach won this in a competition.'

Four pairs of eyes pop out of their heads at the news. *A competition. Free*?

Ent is the first to respond. 'You won it?' he exclaims. 'Who bloody with?'

Rachel gives Justine the death stare at being outed. Nobody needed to know that particular detail, but too late now. 'British Energy. BRITE. They had a draw for new account holders – I switched my account to them three months ago.' They stare at her, dumbfounded. She shrugs. 'Well, somebody had to win it.'

Stoggy shakes his head in disbelief. Silent, yet speaking volumes at the same time: *A real Oasis fan somewhere has been denied this weekend as a result. There's no justice in the world.*

JJ has a more practical thought at this revelation. 'You could have sold it for a fortune.'

Rachel is getting sick of this. Why is she not allowed to be here while they are? Why are they so bloody entitled? 'I wanted to come, thank you very much. And I don't see why we shouldn't,' she adds tartly. 'And, besides, it was a non-transferable prize.'

Ent is still in shock. 'You lucky, lucky…'

He's cut off. 'Well, well done you and welcome to the party,' says Dave, raising his glass. 'We fortunate few.'

Rachel reaches for her glass – she feels she needs it after that exchange. But she's curious too – how come this lot can afford the weekend? Maybe the lawyer one who clearly fancies himself, but the other three? The pudgy one looks like the sort of person you'd find with his elbows out at an all-you-can-eat buffet, the beardy one like he's still got a coin purse in his back pocket, while the pipe cleaner is surely on weekend release from prison. Not exactly the types she'd been expecting to meet on this trip.

'So, what bank did you lot rob to be here?' she says, suppressing a giggle.

There's an awkward silence, until Stoggy steps up to the plate with a pithy four-word answer: 'The Bank of Dave.'

Ent and JJ exchange embarrassed looks. It's official – they're freeloading too. No need for Stoggy to cough to that. After all, they could have made this weekend if they'd had to pay for it themselves. Maybe. Well, maybe not.

Now it's Rachel's turn to be surprised. 'You're kidding?' she exclaims. 'You could buy a small family car for what it costs to come here, and you've stumped up for four? That's incredibly…' she searches for the right word but settles on '… generous.'

Dave has already had to deliver a similar explanation to his mistrusting missus (although he'd halved the actual amount it was costing in that version). He's the very model of modesty. 'It's my fiftieth, see. And this came up and, well, mates are worth more than gold, aren't they? Oasis – it was meant to be. And it's only a loan – the guys will pay me back when they can.' His three companions shuffle uncomfortably, as if unwilling to discuss the small print. 'Plus, I had a little windfall at work – you can't take it with you, can you?'

Ent perks up once more. 'Ill-gotten gains. Told you he was a lawyer,' he jokes. 'Where there's blame there's a claim and all that. We're just helping him to ease his conscience.'

JJ is altogether more beholden. 'A very thoughtful gesture and appreciated by all.'

Stoggy, however, posits another view. 'Plus, he had no one to go with.' *Ouch*. Nobody laughs. Rachel decides she prefers him with his mouth shut.

A loud exclamation from Justine spares Dave any further embarrassment. 'Oh my God,' she yells, pointing east. They spin around to look. There, in the distance, looms their destination, a city emerging from the waves: Atlantis (albeit encircled with what appears to be a high white picket fence). They stand and crowd the panoramic window to get a better look.

'I have never, ever seen anything like that,' coos JJ. 'It's like a sci-fi film. Blade Runner or something.'

As the ferry inches closer and closer, the angular lines of Holm Island sharpen into focus, the towers, the buildings, the sheer scale of this man-made edifice in an unlikely setting taking their breath away.

'I don't know about Blade Runner,' Justine counters. 'It's more like Emerald City to me. The Wizard of Oz.'

Ent, unsurprisingly, has a different take. 'Nah. Skull Island, I reckon. I hope King Kong's had his dinner.'

As they pass between the outer circle of columns and lose sight of the turbine tops, there is a palpable air of excitement and expectation on board. A thought flashes through Rachel's mind: *Love Island?* She doesn't share it with the others.

4

ACQUIESCE

Salt and Martin watch as the first eager passengers disembark and are shepherded into the holding area for their briefing.

'Here we go,' says Martin, his fingers twitching nervously at the enormity of it all, and the knowledge of where the axe will fall if anything goes wrong.

Salt is altogether more sanguine. 'Here we go indeed, Martin. History in the making.'

The Supersonic punters are generally middle-aged, with an unmistakable bearing of self-assurance – and self-entitlement – stamped across their lined faces. They strike Martin as the type of people who post one-star reviews on Tripadvisor and Amazon, or endure a courier service's holding music for sixty minutes to moan about a late delivery.

Supersonic is the top category of ticket available to the public for Be Here Now. The industry gasped when they went on sale at twelve and a half grand a pop, but they sold out in less than an hour. Salt immediately regretted not charging fifteen thousand a go. The Supersonics are staying on Holm for three nights, whereas the bulk of this weekend's crowd, the Supernovas, will be shuttled to and from several liners moored off the island. While the Supersonics consider themselves the bee's knees, they're not, at this juncture, aware of the corporate and guest arrangements that will have them eating their hearts out when they discover somebody is having it larger than they are.

On a given signal the lights go down and all eyes turn to the spotlit stage as two figures charge out to the opening bars of "Hello". One is a wiry septuagenarian with a chiselled face, greying mullet and tinted glasses, the other a lissome and stunning babe at least fifty years his junior. 'You're here. It's now,' he exclaims, punching the air. 'Yes, folks, it's happening, really happening,'

'Who's mad for it this weekend?' trills his counterpart. There's a half-hearted cheer from the audience. 'I said who's mad for it this weekend?' she repeats, thrusting the mic towards the crowd. This time the response is louder.

Martin grimaces at the panto *shtick* and looks nervously towards Salt who's beaming widely. It was the promoter's idea to hire Jez Moss and Cleo Benjamin to act as hosts for the weekend. *Old and new,* he'd insisted, *then and now.* Jez, a Mancunian radio presenter who'd made a career out of claiming he'd been the first to play Oasis, and Cleo, fresh from her first solo tour after leaving girl band Vix, to appeal to a younger audience. The unlikely duo is to front the presentation of the entire weekend and add much needed vitality, glamour and musical insight at the same time as delivering practical information such as where the emergency exits are.

The whole idea of briefing guests on arrival has been a bone of contention between promoter and sponsor. Salt wanted to avoid heavy-handedness – these are paying guests, after all – whereas BRITE'S Health and Safety team remained steadfast that, as the event is taking place on an actual work site, people shouldn't be allowed free range. Rules must be followed. Hence the idea of using Jez and Cleo to lighten it up.

Once numerous engineers and lawyers had inputted into the script it was in danger of lasting longer than the Gallagher brothers' feud. Martin worked valiantly to reduce it down to a manageable length, not that you could tell from the growing restlessness among the audience as Jez and Cleo attempt to make the small print sound fun. It doesn't matter how many times they proclaim 'We are our own exclusive community' and 'We will be the centre of the world on Saturday', the house rules regarding site safety, no-go areas and zero-tolerance to drug use begin to sound increasingly intrusive and controlling. When Cleo informs the crowd they're shortly to be taken to their accommodation there's an audible sigh of relief, only to be dashed seconds later when Jez announces, 'But first, let's hear from our own eco-warrior, Eclipse, to share with you what Be Here Now is doing for the environment this weekend.'

While Salt was forced to concede people could do with 'a few useful facts' on arriving at the island, he'd been totally opposed to the idea of BRITE showcasing its green credentials at the same time. 'People don't want corporate bullshit; they want to party,' was his not unreasonable view. However, this was another area where BRITE, as hosts and sponsors, got their way.

Salt yawns and throws a 'told-you-so' shake of the head at Martin as Eclipse enters the stage to a deafening silence. Despite her name and title, Eclipse wouldn't look out of place in the latest series of The Apprentice. Petite, brunette hair swept back into a simple low bun and smartly dressed in a dark blue trouser suit; she doesn't look the type to be gluing herself to Monet's The Water-Lily Pond at the National Gallery any time soon.

Her opening line, 'Every single person in this room is guilty of killing the planet,' hardly lifts the vibe. Several audience members bristle at this accusation as she surely can't be talking about them – many subscribe to The Guardian and replaced their boiler with a heat exchanger years ago. Luckily, it's not all bad news: 'But this weekend, we can all do something to atone.'

Atone? Salt and Martin visibly wilt as she continues.

'This weekend, as well as having a good time, we can learn there are better ways to live our lives in harmony with our environment.' Sniggers break out from some of the crowd. She ignores them and carries on. 'And when you leave Holm Island, you can help convey that message to the world, because where does the world start? It starts at your doorstep.' By now there is a palpable air of confusion among the audience – what's this got to do with Oasis? With them?

Salt can't take it anymore. He glares at Martin and spits out his two-word assessment. 'Fucking disaster.' With that he turns on his heel and heads out into the sunshine. Martin wants to follow, but is glued to the spot, a powerless eyewitness to a multi-car pile-up.

***

One hour later, the Stratford Bar – Supersonic badge holders only – receives its first guests: Dave, Ent, Stoggy and JJ.

'Fuck me sideways,' Ent complains. 'That was like being back at school.'

'How would you know,' JJ snipes. 'You were always wagging it.'

Dave ignores their childish prattle and marches straight to the bar. 'What are we having?' he wants to know.

They peruse the large chalkboard listing the bill of fayre – many of the drinks naff puns on Oasis songs. Stoggy takes command: 'Gin and tonic. Four double doubles,' he declares. Nobody objects: *that'll do.*

Dave shouts up the order to one of the waiting staff. 'Thought you'd be busier than this,' he offers by way of small talk as the optics are pressed into service.

The young man fixing the drinks in the special 'You Are Here' commemorative recyclable glasses smiles. 'We weren't expecting anybody for another half an hour. They said everybody would be unpacking and sorting their accommodation first. You must have been quick.'

Ent chuckles. 'Plenty of time for that later. Priorities first.'

They grab their drinks as the barman offers up the reader to Dave. All transactions and on-site access are secured by a (strictly non-transferable) wristband containing the holder's biometric data. The RFID (Radio Frequency Identification) technology of the wristbands not only enables the attendee to go cashless and keep track of spending, but it also allows Salt (and BRITE for a small fee to Salt) to data capture and target punters during and after the event. Dave, expecting a heavy weekend and feeling a moral obligation as unofficial host, has opted for the automatic top up option, where another one thousand pounds will be loaded as soon as his balance falls to fifty. Not wishing to appear cheap, Ent and JJ have opted for a fixed payment (the minimum suggested amount) and the hope of a bad WIFI connection. Stoggy also sports the mandatory wristband but has neglected to introduce any funds to his account yet. (Unluckily, he's to be dogged by technical problems in relation to it during their visit.) Dave hovers his arm over the reader and they hear the first 'ping' of the weekend. 'You'll find the receipt on the account page of your festival app,' says the barman, already guessing it's going to be quite a long list.

Dave raises a toast: 'To the regiment. I wish I was there!' as they salute the real start of their adventure.

'There was no need for all that save the whale guff, though,' says Ent, picking up from his earlier comment. 'It's a gig, not a spiritual retreat. We could have skipped Greta Gunboat or whatever she's called and come straight here.'

JJ isn't as quick to condemn. 'I get that they had to go through the health and safety bit though – we are on an actual working plant when you think about it.'

'Yeah – exactly,' agrees Ent. 'All the more bloody reason they should have just done ten nights at the Etihad. Sixty thousand a night – six hundred thousand in total. No need for all of this messing, and a tram ride home.'

'You're missing the point here,' counters Dave, who knows a thing or two about business. 'This is a one-off gig, so has a certain cachet. You can't have a unique event if it's just a run of the mill stadium show, so holding it here – it's genius. Adds to the magic, adds to the appeal.'

Ent isn't convinced. 'But they could have made more money doing ten nights at the Etihad.'

Dave, however, has been doing the math. 'Not so. There's ten thousand people here – that's all. Two thousand Supersonics and eight thousand Supernovas. Happy to pay daft money, glad they could get in. Then you've got the corporates, sponsorship, concessions, merchandise on top, and that's before you get to the worldwide simulcast and the movie. They say it's going to gross around two hundred mill – bigger than ten nights at the Etihad even if you charged an average of two hundred and fifty quid a ticket there, and the lads are only going to be on stage, for what, less than two hours for their share. It's genius. It was an offer they couldn't turn down – nobody in their right minds could.'

Ent can't quite get his head around all the figures (a common problem with builders at the best of times). 'Yeah, but I still think it would have been better if more people could have got to see them.'

Stoggy jumps in at this expression of solidarity from his friend. 'Is that why you've been showing off to everybody you meet that you're going, and they aren't?'

'Sod off. You know what I mean,' is all Ent can muster in reply. He changes tack. 'What do you think the staging will be like? It's got to be special for something like this, don't you think?'

JJ isn't so sure. 'Oasis aren't particularly renowned for their stagecraft or staging, are they? And it is only a one-off. The economics don't really stack up for anything outlandish.'

That prompts Dave. 'Remember Coldplay at the Etihad? What an experience that was. Real theatre, pushing the boundaries of live shows. They…'

His flow is cut short by Stoggy. 'Fucking Coldplay? Seriously? How can you mention that bunch of poshos in the same sentence as Oasis? Fucking pop group. Kiddies' entertainment.' He shakes his head sorrowfully and puts it to Dave straight. 'Oasis will keep it simple. And loud. It's all about the music, not the gimmicks. Rock 'n' roll, man. Fuck the fireworks.'

Nobody was expecting Stoggy to have quite so much to say for himself. There's a temporary lull before Ent circles back to the environment. 'Anyway, what about that poo power? At least I'm doing my bit for the planet. Two shits a day – I must be powering all the streetlights in Heaton Mersey by now.'

They laugh out loud, causing the bar staff to look in their direction.

'You have to admit, though,' says JJ, 'it is pretty impressive that this single artificial island can generate enough renewable energy to power the whole of Yorkshire.'

His observation is met with a chorus of catcalls. 'Bollocks to that,' Ent jeers. 'You're only saying that 'cos you fancied Miss Carbon Neutral. I'll give her that, though, she's a looker. I thought most of that lot had tatts, piercings and dyed dreads. They must be doing university degrees in it now.'

JJ sighs. It's almost impossible to get an intelligent conversation out of Ent when he's had a few. Hard when he's not. 'It doesn't matter what she looks like, Ent, she spoke a lot of sense is all I'm saying. As for fancying anyone, you didn't exactly make a big impression on those two women on the boat, did you? They couldn't wait to get away from us when we docked.'

'Whoa there,' Ent protests. 'I think you'll find it was Dave who was coming over all Mr Smoothie Chops.'

Dave gives it a pained, 'What, me?' shrug, but doesn't deny the charge.

'Granted, the blonde one wasn't bad,' Ent concedes. He takes a sip of his gin. 'But I didn't like the look of yours, JJ. Velma from Scooby Doo. You want to be careful there.'

JJ has heard all this before. 'Both of them seemed perfectly nice to me. And don't you think we're a bit old to be on the hunt?'

'Talking of which,' Stoggy pipes up, 'What about Jez Moss being let loose? Now there's a man who had trouble guessing a girl's age.'

'Yeah, but got away with it long enough,' Ent says.

They nod sagely. 'Somebody should warn that young bird he's with,' deadpans Stoggy.

That prompts Dave. 'Yes, who is that girl? I couldn't quite work out what she was supposed to be doing here. Are we supposed to know her?'

JJ does. 'Showing your age, Dave. Cleo Benjamin is massive, a mega-star. It's a really smart move having her to appeal to younger viewers who think Oasis is a soft drink.'

'Get JJ. Down with the kids,' Dave jests as he drains his glass. 'Right, you lot, let's get organised, shall we? Find our digs, drop our bags, a quick dab under the armpits and back here in half an hour.' He consults his phone. 'The app says Digsy's Dinner starts at eight. We don't want to miss that.'

5

THE MASTERPLAN

The bigwigs have gathered in the green room preceding the arrival of Amanda Teale. However, the atmosphere is far from relaxed as Salt is letting rip with his views on Eclipse's presentation. It bothers him not one jot that the eco-warrior is standing right in front of him. 'Why are we persisting with all this greenwashing guff when punters just want to get smashed and re-live their youth?' He really doesn't mind who he insults – he didn't get where he is today by calling a spade a useful implement for turning soil.

Eclipse isn't prepared to have her endeavours put in the shade by the irritable impresario. 'This greenwashing guff as you call it, is – despite your disparagement – the main reason we're here. Not some nostalgia trip for a load of old farts.'

'Well, that's news to me,' Salt sneers. 'And news to ten thousand punters who've paid top whack to be here.'

Eclipse shakes her head. He really doesn't get it. 'You seem to forget that the planet is in peril. Yet, here we are, on the threshold of reversing some of the damage we've inflicted. In twenty years from now the entire country should be self-sufficient on the back of renewable energy generated from developments like Holm. I'm not going to apologise for pushing that message. It's why I'm here.'

Salt rolls his eyes. 'There's a time and place for everything though, isn't there? And this isn't it if you ask me.'

'Well, luckily, nobody is asking you.'

Salt feels his hackles rising. The cheeky mare. 'Like nobody asked me to make all this possible. To make it happen. You want to be careful who you're insulting, love.'

She ignores the 'love' and strikes back. 'There are millions of lives at stake due to climate change – we need to address the problem head on, not pretend it doesn't exist. If one of your venues was burning down, would you keep it quiet and tell the band to play on, or would you trigger the alarm? Well, I'm the alarm.'

Salts sniggers. The alarm? She's not wrong there.

Martin finally summons up the balls to intervene. 'Can everybody calm it, please? This isn't helping.'

Salt petulantly announces he has things to do, leaving an awkward silence in his wake as he departs. Eclipse shoots Martin a withering look and goes off to convert somebody new.

Despite his smooth, self-assured air, his 'think big' mantra and his undeniable creativity, The Genie of What If is finding himself paddling increasingly hard beneath the surface. It's one of the reasons he seeks a little help from his special flask. As Be Here Now has got closer he's taken to thinking how some of his better ideas have rebounded on him. Take Eclipse, for example.

The idea of bringing an environmental expert and spokesperson on board to validate BRITE's green credentials and to endorse the technological breakthrough Holm Island represents was a no-brainer. Standard PR practice. The edgier the expert, the harder won the conversion from opponent to backer, the better. Finding a credible advocate, however, had been a nightmare as everybody they approached turned out to be a fully signed-up member of the awkward squad, either dismissing BRITE's overtures out of hand, or making so many demands regarding 'transparency' it was impossible to proceed. Then they find Eclipse. In fact, it was Amanda Teale who recommended Eclipse. Her background was reassuring – the daughter of a member of the House of Lords, privately educated, Swiss finishing school, and very easy on the eye. She'd already made waves appearing at a Parliamentary select committee examining whether the country was on track to reach net zero by 2050 and had become the go-to commentator on the environment for the major news channels (more relatable in their view, not that they had anything against crusties). This was how the climate argument was to be won – by reaching into people's homes and hearts, not by tunnelling under construction sites and obstructing traffic. Education versus activism. And there was no doubting her sincerity – changing her name from Charlotte Cholmondeley to Eclipse was only part of her commitment to the cause. As Amanda Teale attested, she'd be perfect for BRITE, and surely 'onside'. The minister was so pleased with her own recommendation, she offered to sort it out for the energy company. Eclipse knew exactly how they anticipated using her and laid down stern conditions before accepting. Teale, without consulting anybody else, promptly gave her *carte blanche* – and it soon became apparent to everyone at BRITE that Eclipse fully intended to use it. From the outset she insisted all facilities had to pass her approval before being specified. Take, for example, the modular Oasis village housing the Supersonics this weekend. The one thousand flat-pack geometric pods are constructed from seventy-five per cent recycled water bottle plastics and are to be donated to an international disaster relief charity the following week. Now that is exactly the sort of positive association the environmentally minded, renewable energy company wants out there, but then the ideas – the demands – started to become more extreme and difficult. Her low water consumption vacuum toilets were approved despite costing three times the standard festival unit, which was fine until Eclipse insisted they be connected to the island's biomass system for the weekend, despite being standalone. Next, she upset the caterers and concession holders by introducing a no-food-waste policy – *it's impossible* they cried, but she faced them down. Ross had his first heart attack when Salt informed him there were to be no reserve generators employed on the island, the standard industry insurance to ensure the show will go on. Eclipse's logic was inarguable as far as she was concerned: if we don't trust our own renewables, what sort of message does that send?

Martin knew it made sense in terms of image projection, but also that there are limits. He was the one dealing with her, and the one dealing with the myriad complaints about her undue influence and escalating demands. Finally, under pressure from colleagues, he tentatively raised the issue with Amanda Teale. Would it be possible to rein Eclipse in a teeny-weeny bit? Mistake. The minister for CLEAN reminded him in no uncertain manner whose gig this was. And it wasn't BRITE's. The British taxpayer was footing the bill here, to showcase the government's delivery on its renewable energy pledges and (despite the new oilfields recently opened up a few miles north) meeting its international commitments. Without the fifty million pounds (announced as a research and development grant) she'd given BRITE this show would never have got off the ground. The initiatives Eclipse was setting forth were minor in the scale of things (but useful to cite when pushed for examples of how they were getting it right). In other words, stop bellyaching and get on with it.

Martin came out of that meeting feeling six inches tall. Teale was a harridan, but it was undeniable she was right about the funding and was intent on getting her money's worth. And it would help polish the government's image (far more cost-effective than knocking a few pence off people's electricity bills). Eclipse was untouchable and he was now reduced to the role of apologist: *I know, but there's nothing we can do about it.*

His mood only lightened a week later when Eclipse banned the use of helicopters and refused to make an exception for government officials.

***

Salt makes his way to the arena to find Ross. The first time the punters will be allowed in here is tomorrow evening, and the site has thrown up several challenges and exhausting wrangles for the impresario. Essentially, it's a rectangle with a stage at one end, temporary stands hired from the British Open forming the other three sides, and a standing area smaller than a football pitch in the middle. Surprisingly, there's no super pit, as BRITE felt there shouldn't be too many price categories given what they were already charging. Salt considered this a missed opportunity to gouge a few extra quid. He was even more put out when the health and safety police, citing fire limits, proposed splitting the standing area into four strictly controlled access zones. He drolly asked, 'Why not just paint a numbered square for everyone to stand on?' At least he prevailed on that one. It got more heated still when Eclipse tried to insist that the area directly in front of the stage should be designated for those with accessibility requirements. Yet another stand-off ensued, resulting in another victory for Salt when he insisted Oasis (not that he asked them) wouldn't want to perform to a frontline of wheelchairs, crutches and amputees. In fact, he argued, given the gig was on an island, shouldn't they ban anyone who couldn't make their own way down a gangplank? In the end, a small symbolic access deck was agreed upon (and stuck in the rear corner of the temporary arena).

He spots Ross sitting on the back row of the tallest stand directly opposite the stage. He waves, but instead of coming down to him, Ross just waves back. Bugger. Salt starts the climb and is sweating profusely and out of puff by the time he reaches the top. 'Christ on a bike, I hope the punters sitting up here are fitter than me.'

'So do I,' Ross says, eyeing him with concern.

Salt gulps in the helpful ozone and recovers his breath before taking in the panorama spread before him. 'That is one hell of a view,' he says in genuine awe. He's not wrong. The whole island can be seen from this bird's nest vantage, the arena neatly fitted in between the processing plant and admin offices, the Supersonics village shoehorned into the park area created for staff recreation. It's what lies beyond though that truly catches the eye – the sight of hundreds of white wind turbines standing silently to attention like headstones in a military cemetery.

Ross, who comes up here to worry mostly, has never really considered the true beauty of this outlook. 'I suppose so. Still a bloody stupid place to have it.'

Salt laughs. 'Come on, Ross. Just look. This is beyond perfect. The turbines, the water, the sky, the sunshine – "This precious stone set in the silver sea". This is why it's so special. It's unique.'

'If you say so.'

The promoter scans the horizon. 'Is Norway that way?' he asks, pointing vaguely into the distance.

'No. Behind us. We're looking west – England. Just use the stage as a compass pointer.'

The position of the stage was yet another bone of contention. The meteorologists advised the stage be positioned at the north of the island as the best protection against prevailing winds common in this location. However, as soon as Amanda Teale saw the blueprints, she demanded the stage be placed on the west side of the island, facing east: *The UK proudly proclaiming itself to Europe.* All practical considerations were kyboshed, and everything rotated ninety degrees.

'Ah, yes,' Salt remembers, wishing he'd not brought it up now. He returns to surveying the arena below. 'Still, if this is the furthest seat from the stage, nobody will be able to moan.'

Ross laughs at that. 'Not that it will stop some of them.'

Salt smiles. He's not wrong there. Another thought strikes him. 'And the sound, it's going to be loud enough up here?'

Sound. Now there's a question. Unsurprisingly, Oasis have laid down strict specifications for the gig and no one, in particular the head of production, wants to screw up, especially on sound. Given they're only playing live to ten thousand people this should be easy enough to plan and deliver – after all, he's done shows with audiences of a quarter of a million – but there are always variables; they are in an unusual location, and preparation is everything. Plus, there's something else, a deep-seated memory he's been trying to forget for thirty-six years: The Duchess of York, Leeds, September 1993. Ross couldn't believe his luck when he somehow hustled a try-out as a sound engineer at the pub running the coolest gigs in town at the time. He'd mixed sound at the Uni a couple of times, but this was the real world. Could he try out on Wednesday? You bet. Who's on? Some band called Oasis. Ross had attended numerous gigs at the venue as a student and relished the opening. The room officially held two hundred and fifty, but he'd been at gigs when there was, at a guess, double that number squeezed in there. But on the night in question there were only two people in the audience, and even they left early. Despite this, the band played a full set, including encore, and appeared entirely relaxed about it. At least no one could criticise the sound. Or could they? Making the mistake of asking the band what they thought afterwards, Ross has never forgotten Noel's brusque assessment, along the lines of *It should have been louder, man! Slide the fuckers up – it's not going to give you an electric shock.* When Oasis returned to The Duchess the following April people were climbing through windows to get in, and Ross' services weren't called upon. Despite all he's achieved in his subsequent career (he's never done an Oasis gig since and has never met any of the band) Ross still feels the older Gallagher brother's invisible presence nudging his elbow upwards whenever he grabs the faders. *Louder, man*! Annoyingly, it's almost always the right solution. (He's not planning to mention any of this to anyone this weekend.)

At least he can put Salt's mind at ease on this one. 'Is it going to be loud enough up here? Salt, they're going to be able to hear it in bloody Bergen.'

That's good enough for the promoter. He nods his approval, then checks his watch. 'Are you coming to the dinner tonight, Ross? I'll go insane if I'm within a nautical mile of Teresa Green.'

Ross knows exactly who he's talking about and shakes his head. 'Would love to, Salt, but things to do and all that.'

'You don't know what you're missing, that's all I'm saying.'

'I'll get over it.' He has a better idea. 'Listen, why don't you just stay here and watch the sun set instead. It's serene up here, away from the mayhem.'

Salt dismisses the suggestion out of hand. 'What, and have them all bitching behind my back? No – going to have to dive in and do my stuff.'

Ross gets it. No arguing with that. 'Well, you're the master at it. And you enjoy it really.'

The impresario chuckles and starts to make his way down the long flight of stairs. When he's halfway, Ross shouts after him. Salt turns to see him standing with his arm outstretched, palm turned towards the heavens. 'Did you just feel a drop of rain?'

Salt gives him two fingers. 'Very funny. Now fuck off.'

6

SOME MIGHT SAY

Justine's face falls on viewing their home for the next three nights – their exclusive 'Bed Here Now' pod. 'It's a bit small, isn't it?' is the most positive thing she can find to say about it.

Rachel sniffs back this loss of face but finds she must agree. In her imagination she'd envisaged a Yurt, or a fancy bell tent at least, with rugs, fairy lights and throws to lend a bohemian vibe. But this is utilitarian at best. A plastic cube, with barely enough room to swing a cat. Two wide shelves provide the base for a mattress and a sleeping bag and that's about it. 'It's like one of those Japanese capsule hotels,' Rachel says, trying to remain positive. 'Cosy.'

'Or a prison cell,' Justine replies. 'There's even a pod on top of us – it's a tenement.' In fact, Justine is correct, because hundreds of the interlocking pods have been stacked up into a 'festival village' to maximise space. Despite being garishly wrapped in a green and white outer skin bearing the message 'A gift from the UK government', the overall appearance is reminiscent of a shanty town.

Rachel is determined to not let this get her down. 'Well, we're not paying for it, and we won't be spending much time in here, so it's fine. We've somewhere to sleep and that's all that matters. The people having to overnight on the boats would kill for this.' Signalling that's the end of the topic, she adds, 'Do you want to sleep on the right or the left?'

They creep awkwardly around each other as they unpack their bags, the contents of which mainly end up on the floor under the bed shelves. Within minutes they hear heavy footsteps overhead as new guests check in to their accommodation; neither of them comments, but each makes a mental note to dig out the earplugs they've brought as part of their toiletries checklist.

'According to this,' says Rachel, consulting the festival app, 'the Supersonic welcome dinner starts at eight. Dress code for us is "dirty shirt". Did you bring anything to wear?'

'Well, yes,' says Justine hesitantly. 'But it's fresh washed.'

Rachel lightens at that (and doesn't admit she had to Google it herself). 'It's supposed to be a joke, silly. From one of their songs – "The Girl in the Dirty Shirt". You can wear what you like. Come on, let's get ready and enjoy ourselves. That's why we're here.'

This reminder seems to have the desired effect on Justine – she squeezes her friend's hand. 'You're right, Rach. I think those dreadful men on the boat must have rubbed me up the wrong way.'

'The Mancs. Talk about full on. But we escaped, thank God.'

'Do you think they'll all be like them this weekend? Like members of a religious cult, crazy Oasis worshippers. Scary.'

'I don't think they were scary – just daft,' Rachel reasons. A picture of Matthew flashes into her head. 'You know how childlike grown men can be at times. Off the leash for the weekend, acting the goat. But I think you can relax about there being too many like them here – look at the price of tickets, that is if you could get one.'

'And he paid – sorry, funded a loan he'll never get back – for all four of them. Do you believe that?'

'Hmmm. The one who fancies himself?'

'The one who fancied you, more like, Rach. Didn't you notice how he was ogling you?'

Rachel ducks that. 'Lawyers aren't normally renowned for their generosity – maybe he's terminally ill and this is the final item on his bucket list.'

Justine laughs. 'Rach – don't be so wicked.' Now she has a question. 'So, what's their dress code, if we're dirty shirts?'

'Parkas, I would have thought. Seriously, I think the chances of bumping into them again are pretty remote.' Matthew comes to mind again. 'They look the type who'll spend the entire weekend in the bar and then miss the actual show.'

Justine is rummaging under her bed for her newly pressed button-through midi dress. 'Do you think we'll see any celebrities tonight?'

'I'm counting on it,' Rachel says. 'We need to be able to show off a bit when we get home. Shoot some sneaky snaps off on zoom.' She checks the time. 'Right, you go and use the pamper salon first and I'll work out how to lock this bloody pod when we go out. Let's not be late on our first night.'

Justine heads out with her washbag under her arm, leaving Rachel to catch up with herself for the first time that day. They've made it. They're here. The weekend is all lined up so why is she feeling antsy, like a reluctant bride? Was it those Mancs implying she had no right to be here, because that's what they were doing. Well, sod them, she has every right to be here – just as much as they do. Just because they saw Oasis in bloody Timbuktu or somewhere before she was born means nothing. Bloody trainspotters. Is it Justine winding her up? She feels a tinge of shame at the idea – if she hadn't come with her, then who would have? She's been a real cow towards her companion, and knows it. She determines to make an extra special effort to be nicer to her from now on. She takes in the plain white walls of the pod closing in on her. Justine is right – perfect accommodation for the man in the iron mask. This is definitely a let-down, but then all the other Supersonics have the same. Meanwhile, millions of people wish they were here instead of her: *get a grip, Rach,* she tells herself. But she can't let that thought go. Millions, yes, but one in particular: Matthew. He'd be in the small rented flat now, making his special tea for Tim. Toad-in-the-hole, made with pre-bought Yorkshire puddings and chipolatas. Disgusting, but they both loved it. He'd be wondering how she was doing out here on the island. She has to admit Matthew could have been as horrible about her being here as those loudmouths on the boat. But no, he'd been very supportive: *What a stroke of luck. Have a brilliant time.* Not once had he shown any resentment towards her good fortune or tried to suggest he had a superior claim on going. That must have taken a lot. Had she been too rigid in denying him this weekend? Didn't he deserve it after all the years they've spent together, despite their uncertain future? Well, too late now. And in any case, the whole point of the separation is to find themselves. Well, find herself. Who's to say she won't meet the man she's to spend the rest of her life with this weekend? Not that she's looking, of course, but as a *for instance.* For some inexplicable reason, lawyer Dave pops into her mind. She squirms. No! Not someone like him! Oh, it's all so complicated, she doesn't want to think about it.

Thankfully, Justine re-appears at that moment to snap her out of it. 'Well?' she says, offering herself for inspection. 'How do I look?'

'Well dirty, I'd say,' Rachel teases. The laugh does them both good. 'What's it like in the pamper salon? Is it just two of these pods stuck together?'

'You're not going to believe this, but it's actually pretty good,' Justine says. 'Really quite big, and lots of vanity areas with those big theatrical mirrors surrounded by lights. And not a man in sight, 'cos they're not allowed in.'

Rachel nods approvingly and grabs her vanity case. 'This I must see. Won't be long. Then the festivities can begin.'

She steps out into the alleyway and turns right towards the communal area but stops in her tracks within two paces. There, outside the two pods immediately next to theirs, are the Costa Four peering at the numbers on the side. Four pairs of eyes turn towards her.

It's Dave who speaks up first. 'Rachel! What are the odds of that?'

***

The Manc lads are back in the Stratford Bar barely thirty minutes after leaving it. They've not bothered getting changed and have merely thrown their bags under their bed bases. In fact, they could have been there and back more quickly if not for a confab over the pairings for the two pods. Basically, nobody wanted to share with Stoggy but couldn't say that directly, so a series of feeble excuses – snoring, farting and sleepwalking – were unconvincingly cited as factors to be taken into account. In the end, Dave declared he'd share with

JJ and that was that. At least Stoggy, who'd remained aloof throughout their bickering, was happy at the decision.

Once Dave has got the drinks in again, their conversation, kicked off by Ent, turns first to their new neighbours. 'She didn't look too pleased to see you, Dave. I don't think kipping next door to you would have been mentioned in the competition prize.'

The fall guy isn't having that. 'I think it was the sight of you three that gave her the heebie-jeebies, not me.'

'She didn't hang around though, did she?' Ent reminds him. 'Legged it without a word.'

Dave shrugs. 'It's hell of a coincidence though, isn't it?'

That gets JJ thinking. 'The probability of them being next to us is a thousand to one. But if you multiply that by the chance meeting on the boat, it's…'

Dave cuts him off. 'Can we please just give it a rest? I'm getting bored now.'

He's met with a mocking chorus of *Whoo* from JJ and Ent.

Stoggy has ignored their banter as he's been busy studying his phone. He waves frantically to capture their attention. 'Hang on. Sifter's just posted,' he announces.

They eagerly give him the floor – this is important. 'Go on then,' Ent urges. 'Tell us what he's saying.'

Stoggy squints at his screen – reading was never his strong point, but no need to worry because Dave has already located the latest blog page on his phone. 'Shall I read it out?' he asks. They all nod in agreement. Leave it to the pro.

He begins:

Sifter's blog:

Thursday, Hull, 1800.

He's immediately interrupted by Ent. 'He's only in Hull? Not here yet?'

Dave shakes his head. 'Are you going to let me read the bloody thing or not? OK, I'll proceed.'

> *Two days to countdown and the great migration begins. The prawn sandwich brigade is Holm-ward bound and will be checking into their luxury accommodation right around now while the true fans are overnighting here before we are allowed aboard the prison ships tomorrow.*

'"Prawn sandwich brigade." Not wrong there,' Stoggy sneers.

'Well, it didn't stop you from coming, did it?' JJ shoots back.

'Have you finished?' asks the exasperated narrator.

> *The corporate johnnies will be tucking into a 'themed' welcome dinner shortly followed by a cosy disco. They're fucking welcome to it at twelve and a half grand a chuck. Meanwhile, the real Oasis gang is heading for The Jolly Roger pub near the port for a night of utter madness – it's not too late to join us!*

'It might be for us to get back there,' Ent says over his half-empty glass.

'Do you want to read it yourself?' Dave offers. He carries on:

> *Had an interesting discussion with some fellow travellers this afternoon, talking about the time Liam and the others (but not Noel) were banged up in the hold for being drunk and disorderly on the ferry taking them to their first overseas gig in Amsterdam back in 1994. My new buddies said being in Hull, we would*

be following in their footsteps. But wrong, 'cos it was Harwich they sailed from.

'Bugger me. I always thought it was Hull. Fancy that.' Something Ent didn't know. 'Why would they go from Manchester to Harwich when they could have gone from Hull?'

'Well, I knew it was Harwich,' JJ crows.

'Bollocks. You're just saying that now,' Stoggy says.

Dave continues through gritted teeth.

Anyway, I digress. What you really want to know is what's happening with the boys. The inside track is the fragile peace is still holding at rehearsals. L and N have kept to separate camps so far and want to keep it that way. They've hardly spoken, but then they've not resorted to fisticuffs either. Still time, obviously, but it appears that the reported hundred million pounds they're receiving for one night is keeping minds on track (and who can blame them?).

The gang nod sagely at this observation.

No news on the setlist, but it's not going to take a genius to work it out. They've made no comment at all (besides a poxy press release) on the reunion, because they've signed an exclusive interview with Disney + for Sunday broadcast. Disney + of course have secured the film rights to the gig. But no media interviews also means they don't have to answer any of the criticism that's come their way for selling out in agreeing to this gig in the first place when so few fans can actually see them.

'Disney,' Stoggy sniffs. 'Says it all.'

'That's just sour grapes from people who aren't lucky enough to be here,' says a defensive JJ. 'They're going to watch the live simulcast, they're going to be able to listen to the live album, they're going to be able to see the movie when it comes out. Would they rather nobody got to see them because they can't?'

Dave can't resist joining in at this: 'You're forgetting that poll Sifter ran asking people would they prefer Oasis *not* to reform for this gig if they couldn't attend. Ninety-nine per cent said no. Let's face it, any Oasis is better than none. Anyway, let me finish it.'

> *More tomorrow when I arrive, but am I getting excited? You bloody bet.*

'I wonder who the one per cent were in that poll?' Ent queries. 'Your missus probably, Dave.'

'Ha, bloody, ha,' Dave groans. 'No, it's a serious point. Everybody wants to see the Oasis reunion, and everybody will through the various platforms and the like. We've no need to feel embarrassed just because we've been fortunate enough to attend.'

'Thanks to your generosity,' JJ reminds everyone.

Ent is philosophical about the situation. 'Yeah. And Sifter's making it to the gig too, so he can't really complain. Not that I think he's complaining. Is he?'

'He had to fight tooth and nail to get in,' Stoggy grumbles. 'The biggest Oasis blog in the world, and he has to beg. Mainstream media only. Only got a pass – a Supernova one – at the last minute through the inner circle.'

'Doesn't sound like hardship to me,' Dave huffs. 'He used his contacts. Very resourceful. The first rule of journalism: Don't bite the hand that feeds.'

JJ is dubious about that. 'Really? I've never heard that before. I thought it was never disclose your sources.'

Dave shrugs. 'Whatever. Anyway, sod 'em. Sod 'em all.'

They raise their glasses in a toast: 'Sod 'em. Sod 'em all.'

7

LITTLE BY LITTLE

Determined not to be ambushed again, Rachel and Justine are on full alert for the Manc lads as they make their way into the giant marquee. Luckily, the coast is clear as they wander over to the cocktail bar. The 'Whatever' market package has been designed to be as simple as possible, with punters receiving a series of vouchers to add to their festival app in exchange for meals, drinks and a specially branded memento. This premium package is mandatory for Supersonic ticket holders, on top of the admission ticket, and no refunds are available for unspent credit. Rachel hasn't paid for their Whatever packages as it's part of her prize; Dave, on the other hand, has kept very quiet over the extra six grand it's set him back on top of the price of admission. This is separate to the cash account each punter is encouraged to set up to pay for festival expenses on their RFID wristbands. Still, and you'd expect it at these prices, it's pretty upmarket: *An exclusive and luxurious sea and land culinary experience prepared in conjunction with Gordon Ramsey, including wine pairings, craft beers and cocktails inspired by the best of the British Isles.* (An earlier suggestion to theme the catering experience around Manchester and the north-west had fallen at the first hurdle.)

The first couple of vouchers go on two Shakermaker cocktails – Hibiscus-infused Blanc Vermouth, London dry gin, Campari, syrup, served frozen. 'I don't see too many dirty shirts,' Justine observes before knocking half her drink back in one. She winces. 'Jeez, that's just given me a brain freeze.'

Rachel takes a delicate sip of hers. 'Nice, though. Maybe use the straw.'

Justine picks up on her earlier point. 'Seriously, not many women in here are dressing down, are they? Just look at them. Net-a-Porter must be doing a bomb this month.'

Rachel has to admit that the dress code guidance has been widely interpreted by many women in the marquee and shrinks within her Mia Wallace white shirt. But there is consolation on hand. 'What about the blokes though, Jus. They look like they've just done a ramraid at Sports Direct.' She's not wrong. Stripes, diamond and swooshes are in plentiful abundance among the males, and while expanding waistlines have forced last-dash shopping trips on many there's more than a few crammed into 'vintage' Man City tops and Oasis T-shirts. It's not a good look. Rachel can't tell if they're being 'ironic', showing off, or suffering from genuine wardrobe-poverty. And if they're wearing this on the first night, what are they going to be wearing come Saturday night? (Answer: the same, probably.) A guy with tinted John Lennon shades pushes past wearing, despite the temperature, a full-length panelled training jacket bearing the Manchester City and Umbro logos. 'He must be hot in that,' she whispers to Justine as he makes his way to the bar. He's doing a funny walk as well, full swagger with knees and elbows pumping as if he's treading on treacle. As soon as he's spotted by other drinkers there's a spontaneous ripple – shouts of 'nice one' and thumbs raised aloft. Rachel and Justine are puzzled by this, until they overhear a man, bulging out of a Knebworth 1996 T-shirt, explaining to his similarly perplexed wife: 'Liam. Top of the Pops. "Some Might Say". 1995.' What was it Justine said earlier? *Like members of a religious cult.* She knew for a fact, having done his washing for years, Matthew had no Oasis tat lurking at the bottom of his bedroom drawers. Would he have gone off and bought some if he was coming here? *No – don't start that again*, she tells herself. He's not here.

Food stations are positioned down both sides of the marquee – pasta, BBQ, fish, desserts of every kind – and queues are starting to form. Seating is unreserved, and the quickest out of the blocks are already sitting down at the long trestle tables. These are decorated with place mats in the shape of Oasis 45 singles and table lamps with shades representing the band's albums, all of which turn out to be bolted into place to avoid them being nicked.

'Let's beat the rush,' Rachel suggests, and they head to the salad bar. Another voucher each down, they head for the nearest table (Standing on the Shoulder of Giants) and plonk themselves next to a smartly dressed couple with whom they exchange polite nods. Spotting the pair's bottle of organic Tempranillo, Rachel realises they've not queued for drinks to accompany their meal. Bugger. They're going to have to get in line again. They could be queuing all night at this rate.

'You think they'd have come up with a better system,' Justine moans, but at least she volunteers to go to the bar for some wine.

Rachel finds herself earwigging her neighbours' exchanges as she awaits Justine's return. They're plummy, self-assured and definitely not northern. Not wearing any Oasis clobber, new or old, either. Rachel then realises that the woman is holding forth on the 'types' on display in the marquee and being far from complimentary. OK, she and Jus have shared their own observations on some of the people in attendance at Be Here Now, but this jumped-up stick insect isn't holding back – she's taking the piss, much to the amusement of her floppy-haired gammon of a partner.

'You have to admit they do talk funny.' She attempts a comedy northern accent: '"Yeah, yer know. Result. Sorted. Mad for it."'

'Oh – Kevin and Perry,' he gleefully proclaims, spotting where she's lifted it from. He drops his voice a couple of octaves: '"Yer don't know nowt",' he guffaws, topped off with a signature *na-ha-ha-ha-ha.*

She continues. 'I don't think many have seen the inside of a gym recently. More muffin tops than a WI bake-off.'

'I think it's their diet,' he confides. 'Too reliant on pie, chips and beer. *Na-ha-ha-ha-ha.*'

'And their clothes. Really. They could at least wear garments that fit. I don't think some of those tatty old T-shirts have been washed since Dolly the Sheep was cloned. I can literally smell them.'

'That's because food banks don't provide detergents. *Na-ha-ha-ha-ha.*'

Rachel is bristling with indignation – how dare they? Why are they being so horrible and snooty? Why are they even here if it's such a big joke to them? They certainly don't look the type to enter competitions – could they have wangled a freebie from somewhere else? That wouldn't be fair. She might not be the biggest Oasis fan in the world, but at least she's glad to be here. It strikes her if the Manc lads were in earshot they'd make mincemeat of this pair of pricks and their condescending sniping. Should she say something? What would be the point? One thing she knows for sure – when they go up for a main course, they're not going to come back to this table. This stupid bloody system has that advantage at least.

The moment Justine reappears with two glasses of Pinot Grigio, the background music cuts and spots illuminate the stage at the far end of the marquee. Cleo and Jez bound on, to the opening bars of "Hello". (Clearly, this intro is to be the pattern for the weekend.)

'Who's having a good time?' Cleo enquires brightly. She's met with a muted response. Another pattern is irrevocably set for the weekend. 'I said, *who's having a good time?*' she repeats, thrusting the mic towards the crowd.

Jez beams maniacally, the lights refracting off his newly whitened teeth like a laser off a glitterball. 'Have we got a surprise for you tonight,' he cries. Cleo makes out like she doesn't know what it is for the next two minutes, until Jez offers to put her out of her misery. If only. 'Tonight, Supersonics, we're gonna get you in the mood. The weekend starts here, and we want you to have it large.' Cleo echoes his entreaty with a high pitched *Yeah. Have it large.* Jez finally gets to it. 'In conjunction with our sponsors, tonight's entertainment will be a spectacular BRITEPOP disco, with yours truly spinning the biggest and best nineties hits.' BRITEPOP. What else? Well, they don't want the punters peaking too early – there are two nights to go before Oasis.

Cleo then comes into her own, informing people that food will stop being served at nine, tables will be cleared by ten, with the curfew at two. She doesn't explain the brace position.

The hubbub in the marquee is getting louder. Their salads seen off, Rachel whispers in Justine's ear and they grab their glasses and head for the sushi line as that's now the shortest queue.

So far, no sign of Gordon Ramsey.

***

Having been denied the use of the helicopter pad, Amanda Teale is late arriving. Proving a point, no doubt. Not that she sailed all the way from England; she flew to the nearest rig and made the short crossing from there. The conversation in the green room quietens as she sweeps in. Amanda isn't known for her small talk – if she were a dog, she'd be a Jack Russell terrier; yaps a lot and demands a lot of attention. She proudly considers this a sign of being naturally assertive, vital in her job. Others don't see it quite that way. Most can't get past the barking and her propensity for digging holes.

The room has been set up with the most sumptuous buffet that nobody has yet dared to start. On being offered a plate by Martin, Amanda looks positively insulted to discover Gordon isn't present to personally serve her. She waves him off. 'Let's get up to date first.'

Salt is nowhere to be seen, but Eclipse is closing in rapidly. Martin is acutely aware he needs to manage this, and ushers them into the far corner of the room for some privacy. A waiter brings over drinks – Scotch for Amanda, Merlot for Eclipse and a sparkling water for him – and they're ready. He tries a soft-shoe intro-outro: 'I expect you've got lots to do, Minister, so I'll just summarise by saying we're fully on track.' He hopes that will get him swiftly excused and back to his office for a bit of peace and quiet. And his mini fridge.

But no such luck. 'Well, that sounds very vague,' Amanda says. 'I expect a full briefing. Detail matters. It's all about the details.'

Here we go, Martin thinks.

But before he can say anything further, it turns out Eclipse has rather a lot to get off her chest following her run-in with

Salt. 'There's little point in me pussyfooting around on this, Amanda. I'm afraid the green agenda is being watered down every time I turn my back.' She looks accusingly at Martin. 'The guarantees I received are falling apart one by one. I'm here under false pretences. Lipstick on a pig.'

Amanda blinks as she tries to work out if that's a direct criticism of her. No, that's not possible. She fixes on the hard-pressed head of marketing and has but one simple question: 'Is this true?'

Martin has a familiar feeling of being ambushed. It's his fault. Everything is his fault. In fact, it's the unwritten rule of his role: down to everybody else if all goes well; all down to him if it's a fuck-up. Success has many fathers, but failure is a bastard. He tries to remain composed. 'It's my view that the environmental messaging of this event is unparalleled. We're reaching a vast audience with some vital messages, thanks mainly to Eclipse,' he says as sincerely as he can. Remembering also that it's always a good idea to kick the can down the road he adds, 'And I think our tracking research will bear that out in due course.'

Eclipse shakes her head. *Nope.* 'Everywhere I turn, all I get is "It can't be done" or "That's not how we do things". I feel I'm in a constant fight, a losing fight. This is not what I was promised. Not what I signed up for.'

These are charges not to be taken lightly. Amanda fixes Martin with her basilisk stare, demanding he explain himself.

Martin reaches for the charm defence. 'I truly believe you've moved the dial on the environmental agenda here, Eclipse.' He beams at her in awe and admiration. 'Your initiatives for an event of this nature are a step forward and they'll be repeated in the future. I'd go as far as to say you've established a new green standard for the entertainment sector.'

Does this paean set Eclipse's mind at rest? She banks it and remains on the offensive: 'And what about the public? Where's our cut-through there?' And now we get to the heart of Eclipse's pain. 'I was basically ignored during my talks to your so-called Supersonic arrivals. I could feel their scorn.'

Amanda nods sympathetically. She's been there. But come on now. 'Doesn't that just tell you you're doing something right, Eclipse? I'm a warrior, too, fighting for a better country. The public are ingrates – always the last to recognise what we do for them – but we endure and strive to save them from themselves.'

'They don't deserve saving,' says Eclipse bluntly. Martin and Amanda are taken aback at her vehemence. 'One half of them look like Chelsea tractor owners, while the other half look like they tap their energy from the nearest lamppost.'

Martin laughs heartily at Eclipse's joke (it was a joke, wasn't it?). 'They were just giddy with excitement at arriving, that's all. We've bombarded them, we've bombarded the whole country, with environmental messaging for months. Material you've approved, Eclipse. You're getting through. We're getting through.'

The mention of BRITE's social media, advertising and direct mail campaigns reminds Amanda of a key undertaking Martin has yet to deliver. 'And where are we on the endorsement of these messages by Noel and Liam Gallagher? You promised they would personally feature on everything you put out.'

Martin's chest tightens. It's true that this idea had been mooted by Amanda in the dim and distant past, and he'd diplomatically said he'd get Salt to check it out. He had in fact broached it with the impresario who had erupted with mirth at the request. He'd moved to pleading with Salt to at least put it to Oasis' people so he could report back. Salt eventually confirmed the boys wouldn't do it even if their fee was doubled – not their bag. Martin, suspecting Salt never raised the question with them in the first place, duly informed the minister for CLEAN that there was 'a certain reluctance' from the superstar siblings to be too closely aligned with specific brands or causes.

Amanda, however, has conveniently forgotten this. 'I didn't put all this money in not to have their ugly mugs up front,' she asserts. 'We own them. And it's not too late to do a video with them backing Britain's move towards energy self-sufficiency. I want it to happen, Martin.'

Eclipse nods her approval. The great unwashed talking to the great unwashed. Yes, that would work.

Martin is grasping for the right words to inform Amanda that it's possible while being impossible (or maybe the other way around) when he espies, over the minister's shoulder, Salt's head peering around the door to the green room. Before Martin can beckon him over, the hard-pressed promoter takes in the triumvirate huddled in the corner and ducks out of sight. *Bastard*! 'I'll speak to Salt again,' is all he can muster.

'As if that will make any difference,' Eclipse sneers.

Amanda takes an altogether steelier approach. 'Just don't fuck it up. Have you got that?'

Martin has, of course, got this. It's his life. 'Understood,' he replies. Then, thinking he may as well take the piss, adds, 'And would you like me to arrange a press photograph with the two of you and the Gallagher brothers at the same time?'

Neither can help themselves, 'Ooh, yes,' they squeak in unison.

Now he has a means of escape. 'Let me go and find out where Salt is and get him on the case.' He leaves the two women to stick more pins in his effigy the moment he's out of the room, and heads straight back to the sanctuary of his office and a stiff, non-judgemental, forty per cent proof pick-me-up.

8

CIGARETTES AND ALCOHOL

Stoggy blows a perfect smoke ring heavenwards and passes the joint to his companion.

Ent takes a huge draw and holds it for as long as he can before loudly exhaling. 'So much for the drugs ban, eh?' he giggles. 'How did you get it in?'

'Yer don't wanna know,' is the laconic response.

The two are sitting on a pile of pallets behind the huge marquee where the muffled sounds of "She's A Star" by James can just about be made out.

'Pants in there, innit?' Ent ventures. 'Full of tossers.'

Stoggy reclaims the spliff. 'Yeah – they don't know what they're missing out here.'

Their reverie under the stars is disturbed a minute later as Dave and JJ stumble upon their position. 'We've been looking all over for you,' says Dave, a hint of irritation in his voice. 'We wondered where you'd gone.'

Stoggy simply shrugs and extends his hand. 'Smoke?'

Dave hesitates, then sits down alongside them and accepts the proffered J. 'I might have known. How did you get it in?' Stoggy flaps his hand dismissively. *Not now.* Dave makes himself comfortable, then readies himself. It's like he's about to attempt a world record ski jump. Stillness, focus, measured breathing – then he raises the joint to his lips and inhales. Two seconds later he erupts in a fit of coughing and urgently hands the joint back to Stoggy. 'Christ, that went down the wrong way,' he exclaims. Wiping his eyes, he adds. 'Must be a bit out of practice.'

A bemused Stoggy turns to the fourth member of the team. 'J, JJ?'

The man from the local authority solemnly shakes his head. 'I'll give it a miss, thanks.' He ruefully rubs his stomach. 'Got a bit of a gippy tummy. Think it's best to save myself for Saturday.'

'You got the shits again, JJ?' Ent joshes. 'Glad I'm not sharing with you.'

It's hard to tell in this light, but JJ is looking a little peaky. 'It could be something I ate,' he says weakly. This is unlikely as the four of them took one look at the queues for the food stalls in the marquee and immediately sacked it off in favour of going back to the bar. Dave, aware he'd paid a big wodge of cash for the food element of their package, tried to trade their vouchers in for booze, but with no success. Determined not to feel downhearted at this knockback, he reminded himself about opportunity cost and continued to flash his wristband as the drinks piled up.

'What's going on in there now?' Ent asks, jutting his chin towards the marquee. 'We gave up after five minutes.'

'It's not that bad,' Dave replies. 'People seem to be enjoying themselves. Food has stopped though.'

'Music's dodgy,' Stoggy pronounces. 'Got to be down to Jez, that.'

'Put in a request in that case,' Dave shoots back. He'd not thought the music bad at all.

'Good idea, that. Maybe I will,' says the quartermaster.

There's an awkward silence which is broken by JJ. 'Sorry, guys, but I'm going to turn in.' He points at his stomach. 'Want to be right for tomorrow.'

Dave, who has been espousing the idea of pacing themselves, especially on the first night, wonders if this is his cue too. Get some ZZZZZs, leave Ent and Stoggy to it. But before he can decide, two figures come tottering around the side of the marquee in their direction. Rachel and Justine, arm in arm, and clearly in a merrier mood than they'd been the last time the boys saw them.

'Hiya,' Ent shouts and beckons them to come over. Much to the men's surprise, they do.

'Is that pot?' squeals Rachel, sniffing the air. 'Naughty boys.'

Stoggy extends his arm once more with the offer of a smoke. 'Get stuck in.'

Justine recoils. She's never done drugs and isn't about to start now. Plus, she's had four drinks already, a month's ration normally. Rachel screws up her nose. She's had five drinks, plus it's a long time since she's been acquainted with Mary Jane. Then again, they're supposed to be at a rock gig for heaven's sake. 'I will,' she giggles.

Justine doesn't hide her disapproval. And if people think she's a wet blanket, then so be it, because one of them has to be sensible. She whispers urgently in her friend's ear, but not so quietly that everybody else can't hear it. 'I thought we were turning in for the night.'

Rachel is torn. She's up for it, even if Justine isn't. 'One little puff. Where's the harm? Then we'll go back.'

Who'll crack first?

It's JJ who rides to Rachel's assistance. 'Well, I'm heading back, Justine, if you want an escort. Perfectly safe, I assure you.'

This is exactly the sort of thing they've had drummed into them their entire lives: *Don't get separated. Don't trust strange men. (Don't trust any man for that matter).* They've come together and should stick together. Rachel knows this only too well. 'Is that OK with you, Jus? I'll only be five minutes.'

Justine, aware the code has been broken, huffily replies, 'Fine.' At least if this chinless wonder tries it on, she'll give him short shrift, not that he looks like he could knock the skin off a rice pudding.

As soon as JJ and Justine disappear towards the pod village, attention turns back to the matter in hand. Stoggy reaches into his top shirt pocket and produces a fresh joint. 'You can go first,' he says with uncommon chivalry. 'Lady's privilege.'

Rachel is unsure how to proceed. It's been so long. 'What do I do again?'

Stoggy is delighted to have a new student in the remedial class. 'Right. I'll light it, and you take a big pull. Swallow the smoke right down and hold it in your lungs for as long as you can. Then blow.' Dave and Ent are rapt with attention. She's game, they'll give her that. The beanpole fires the joint up and passes it deftly to Rachel. 'One big pull. Give it the biz.' She follows the instructions impeccably and feels the THC set to work on her senses.

Light-headed, she slumps back against the pallets and laughs. 'I feel all dizzy now. I'd better sit down.' The three men chuckle too and help her onto the stack. Dave gently prises the joint from her hand and takes a macho toke. This time without coughing (or inhaling). Rachel feels most relaxed; her head is spinning – no it's swooning – in the most pleasant way.

She can hear the heavy bassline of whatever nineties anthem Jez is playing inside the marquee, but can't make out the actual song, not that it matters. It's good to just sit. The three men are babbling away but she's not really taking much notice of them. Everything seems to have slowed down. She's aware of a lapping motion like waves. No – that is waves. She tells herself she'll just have five minutes and then get back. In fact, it would be nice to lie back and look at the stars, because that would be even more relaxing.

She awakens to find Dave is giving her shoulder a soft nudge. 'Are you alright?'

She pulls herself upright and composes herself. 'Just drifted off there for a second.'

'Well, it was more than a second, but as long as you're OK.'

Ent and Stoggy are nowhere to be seen, and she's aware the music has stopped. 'Where's everyone gone? What time is it?'

'It's late. As for those two, God knows what they're up to. They disappeared ten minutes ago. Up to no good I'd have thought.'

Rachel's head is starting to clear, and she feels a sense of relief combined with mortification over her unaccustomed behaviour. She only had the one drag, yet it had a kick like a mule. Not at all like the stuff she'd very occasionally shared with Matthew in the early days. 'What the hell was in that?'

Dave shrugs. 'I know what you mean – I had some too. It's skunk. Stoggy gets it from a mate who's got a hydroponics set-up in Rusholme. I think he deals in it if I'm being honest.'

She suddenly realises how exposed she's been. 'Well, thank you for not leaving me here,' she says.

Dave waves her gratitude away. 'As if. Anyway, I was a bit zonked myself there for a while.' They both laugh. He helps her down from the pallets. 'Allow me to walk you home?' he says playfully.

Before she can respond they hear loud whoops as two spotlights rapidly approach. They realise it's an electric platform truck, heading directly towards them. Just as they're about to jump out of the way, it swerves wildly, skids, and disappears out of sight behind the marquee. Dave shakes his head in despair. 'Now we know where Ent and Stoggy are.'

***

The music has also stopped for the night in The Jolly Roger in Hull, with drunken revellers heading for a short kip before the great embarkation (second class) to Holm in the morning. But in Room 9A, the three occupants are not yet ready for bed – Bryan, Bob and Cody have important plans to run though for a final time. In common with every Oasis fan, they are preoccupied with what time the band will hit the stage; unlike the rest of the attendees, they have zero interest in the music.

Bryan Yateman has spent the greater part of the past twenty years seething in resentment and anger at how the country has been run down by lefties and saboteurs. He proudly campaigned for Brexit back in the day and has vowed never to forgive the Remoaners who wrecked its successful implementation. He enthusiastically campaigned for Boris Johnson a decade back, only to quit the Conservative party in disgust after the best PM of his generation was unfairly ousted. After that, he briefly joined the now defunct Reform party. Finally, having despaired of mainstream politicians, Bryan started his 'Had it Up To Here' crusade in 2025 (he's particularly pleased with its strangulated acronym, HUTH, because it sounds like huff) and began small by trolling enemies of the state on social media via encrypted software. Invoking reaction to his vituperative comments brought him an enormous amount of joy, whether it was simply being blocked, or when a bleeding heart went crying to the media or withdrew their accounts altogether. At one point, there was speculation he was a Russian bot – he didn't know whether to be pleased or disappointed at not receiving his due recognition. It was easy, it was fun, and his anonymity was assured behind his multiple firewalls. And the authorities never once tried to investigate or interfere. When he was made redundant it gave him even more time to concentrate on his vital work, with the result that he was soon earning more money than ever through membership fees and ad revenue as the HUTH subscriber base grew. As he got older though, he realised one thing – if you really wanted to change things you had to take matters into your own hands. Direct action. Those lefty nutjobs had got one thing right; forget writing to your local MP – you got far more attention padlocking yourself to the goalpost in the middle of the Merseyside derby, chucking soup at the Mona Lisa, or pouring milk on supermarket floors. He decided to branch out. Daubing anti-Islam slogans on local mosques was remarkably effective – maximum payback for minimum effort. He got bolder after that, sending envelopes of white powder to five MPs he expressly disliked, causing panic in their offices over an anthrax scare. Bored of that, he stepped it up with a plan to fire-bomb a nearby migrant centre, only to narrowly avoid turning himself into a human torch when he misread the 'How to make your own Molotov' instructions he'd found online. He decided something smarter was required. And then it was announced Oasis would be playing their comeback gig on Holm Island.

Be Here Now offered multiple opportunities to a mind as complex as Bryan's. The whole world would be watching this weekend – what could he do to make his mark? Wind turbines were blighting the land and affecting house prices; they were impairing residents' quality of life while the nation was spaffing billions of pounds to convert to so-called green energy while we still had coal in the ground and oil in the North Sea. Bryan knew all of this to be the case, as he'd read it on the internet. There were personal consequences too, as industries linked to fossil fuel extraction and processing were phasing out thousands of jobs – including Bryan's – due to this mass deception. He would disrupt Be Here Now and warn the world this madness had gone far enough.

Recruiting Bob and Cody into his Holm Island plan was important for cover as much as helping him with the mission. He didn't want to stand out as a Billy-No-Mates at a festival, and he figured the two younger men wouldn't look that out of place at an Oasis gig. They could even at a pinch pass for his sons. Moreover, he trusts them as they have been on anti-migrant marches with him and, more importantly, they aren't going to challenge him.

Cody is attending to the video recording they're making. His mobile is resting within a ring light mounted on a tripod, and he's testing the sound level of the wireless microphone clipped to Bryan's shirt. Bob stands patiently behind Bryan with a carefully painted placard.

'All set,' confirms Cody. 'Remember, keep it short and snappy.'

Bryan clears his throat, ready to begin.

'Wait,' Bob shouts. 'The masks. We need to cover up.'

The two in shot pull up their Union Jack bandanas to just below their eyes. 'Can you still hear me OK?' asks Bryan. He gets a thumbs up from the cameraman. 'And you can't tell it's me? I've only got the bottom half of my face covered.'

Cody ponders this for a second. 'Hang on. We need to think about this. Don't we actually want people to know who you are this time?'

Bryan's eyes crease in puzzlement above the viscose. 'We do?'

The cameraman nods. The whole point of this mission is for the team to eschew anonymity and be seen to protest. They'll be arrested for their action, sure, but that's all part of the plan. They've seen it with those lefty disrupters – they get acres of coverage, a second media opportunity outside the court, followed by a slap on the wrist and a fine from the bench. Heroic status just for showing some *cojones*. 'Yeah. You want to be seen on this one. That's why we're doing the video now, so it can be posted immediately afterwards.'

Bryan holds up a hand in apology. 'Sorry. Forgot. Old habits and all that.' He pulls the bandana off before adding a concerned, 'Is my hair alright? I've not ruffled it, have I?'

'You too, Bob,' Cody instructs.

'I'd rather keep mine on,' comes the reluctant reply from the placard bearer.

Bryan, however, is with it now. 'No, Bob. Cody's right. We have to be seen on this one. Plucky fighters. Personal sacrifice. Martyrs for the cause. Come on, get the bugger off.'

Bob slowly removes his mask and turns to Cody. 'Maybe if I stand on a chair behind Bryan, you can see the sign better and my face won't be in the frame. Would that work?'

Cody hasn't shot an awful lot of propaganda videos but knows that would be ridiculous. 'That would look bloody daft. Come on, stay as we are and let's get on with it.'

Bob moodily turns to hit his mark again but has one small detail to clarify before the red light comes on. 'Remind me, will you, this is going out immediately afterwards?' His colleagues nod. 'But what if there's no WIFI?'

Bryan frowns. 'Listen. It's all in hand. Now, can we please shoot the bloody thing.'

Cody checks the composition of the shot on his mobile and prepares to count Bryan in. No – not yet. There's another problem. 'Bob, you're tilting that sign. Can you make sure it's directly facing the camera?'

After a few clumsy turns, they're ready. The voice of the people composes himself. 3-2-1...

They've not noticed, immediately behind Bryan and Bob, the sign on the wall reading 'Save Energy: Turn off the lights when you leave'. No matter, because Bob's poster is bigger and more colourful: 'Green Energy is Whistling in the Wind. Stop Climate Hoax Now.'

9

WHO FEELS LOVE?

Not being one to let things fester, Justine tears straight into Rachel the second her companion opens her eyes. 'How could you, Rach?' She doesn't expand on what exactly Rachel has or hasn't done. The four monosyllables speak volumes; in any case, her friend doesn't require the point elaborating any further as she struggles to wake up. Rachel's mouth is like the bottom of a bird cage, and her eyes feel swollen. Did she even brush her teeth last night? She searches for her water bottle and gulps half the contents down in one. Last night is a haze, but she is to be spared no quarter here – she's going to have to piece it together under the scrutiny of her disgruntled friend.

She starts with a weak, 'I was only a few minutes after you, Jus.'

'No, you weren't. I waited up for you I don't know how long. What were you doing?'

Rachel strains to remember – the marijuana, the stars, the sound of the waves lapping, the whoops of laughter from the platform truck as it cut across the back of the marquee. 'Talking, that's all.'

Justine can hardly mask her disdain. 'With those louts? In the middle of the night?' Rachel is stung. Are they louts? Has she shown poor judgement in staying out with them? OK – Stoggy is a lout, and Ent isn't far behind him, but surely Dave and JJ couldn't be placed in that category? But Justine is only warming up. 'And did you smoke that stuff with them? Did you?'

The last conversation of this nature Rachel recalls was the bollocking she administered to Tim when she discovered a vape in his school bag. Now she feels like the fourteen-year-old. 'I only had one puff. Hardly grounds for calling in the drug squad.'

Justine doesn't mask the disappointment she feels in her friend. 'I just think it was inappropriate, that's all. Anything could have happened to you.'

Inappropriate. The ultimate condemnation. The single word that sums up a thousand misdemeanours. She shrinks at the loaded accusation. But what did happen to her? She strains to recall. That joint knocked her right out. Ent and Stoggy disappeared. She was left with Dave. It's an impenetrable fog. But hang on, she's not going to be lectured by Mother Teresa of Kirklees. Hit the ball back. Deflect. 'If you were so worried about me, Jus, then why did you leave me?'

'Oh, it's my fault now, is it? I can tell when I'm not wanted, that's why.'

Rachel can't, in all honesty, answer that, so changes tack with a solicitous, 'And did you get back alright?'

Justine thaws for the first time that morning. 'With JJ? He couldn't wait to dash off to the toilet. I thought he was going to have an accident.'

They giggle. Rachel is relieved. She's got away with it. But got away with what? She can't remember a thing. Dave didn't try anything, did he? Oh my God, she didn't try anything did she?

Justine breaks her chain of thought. 'Come on, get up – let's get breakfast.'

Rachel drains the remnants of her water bottle and resolves to pull herself together. She consults the app. 'Ooh, look. We've got Reiki booked at eleven.'

***

'Did you shag her?' Dave is squirming under interrogation from Ent and Stoggy. 'At least cop a feel?' It's noticeable they don't put the same questions to JJ who is nursing a dry piece of toast as they horse into a full English on this bright, sunlit, festival morn.

Dave shakes off their crude enquiries. 'Jesus, are you twelve years old, or what?'

That's all the proof Ent needs. 'He did, I can tell.' Laughter all round.

'Can we change the subject, please,' Dave demands of his tormenters. 'Nothing happened. And you know nothing happened, so stop taking the piss.'

Stoggy isn't ready to leave off his hounding just yet. 'We saw you when we drove past. You had a right grip. Plus, she was practically comatose after the Joe Soap.'

'Yeah,' Ent echoes. 'Putty in your hands.'

Dave feels his colour rise. He most definitely did not have 'a right grip', or any grip at all, of the lady in question, but the memory is fresh. He'd thought about it. Momentarily at least. He found Rachel attractive; it was no lie. As she lay there last night, under the stars, she reminded him of a Pre-Raphaelite nymph, tempting and seductive. He'd reached out to touch her cheek – purely to check she was OK, of course – but had stayed his hand. No. He wasn't like that. And besides, the image of his wife suddenly appearing from behind the pallets had popped into his head. Ah, his wife. Suzanne. Dave didn't care to remind himself, but he and Suzanne hadn't had sex in three years. It wasn't that this need was being met elsewhere; more a case of the thrill had gone, submerged beneath a monotony of work, kids, routine and over-familiarity. Briefly last night, the sight of Rachel had awoken in him an old urge, until he remembered himself. It had perplexed him. He knew he had few grounds for complaint; life had been good to Dave. He'd done all right for himself financially, and there were worse marriages than his. Not that he could really argue he was in a bad marriage – just one lacking a spark. Maybe it was the dope, or the giddiness of being at a festival again, or the glimpse of opportunity that had put that predatory thought in his head before common sense intervened. Or rather, more to the point, some form of middle-aged crisis.

Still, he's determined not to rise to the bait again with Ent and Stoggy. He switches the play. 'What about you idiots then, stealing that platform truck? You could have got us kicked off the island.'

JJ snaps to attention at that. They did what?

Stoggy is unrepentant. 'Just took it for a spin, is all.'

Ent backs him up. 'Come on, it was only for five minutes. Nobody saw.'

'It was still a stupid thing to do.'

Ent shifts uncomfortably. 'We were test driving it. They told us to go electric, so we did. We even parked it back in the same place.'

Stoggy goes full circle for the second time that day. 'We'd have taken you with us,' he says, 'but you were busy.'

JJ isn't for being diverted though. This sounds serious. 'I don't think borrowing a site vehicle is going to endear us to the organisers, never mind the Health and Safety aspects,' he declaims. The accused shrug their shoulders and offer nothing in defence. 'I mean, Dave has put a lot of money up for us all to be here, so the least we can do is avoid being thrown out before Oasis even get to play.'

That again. *Dave. The 'loan'.* Even their host squirms at the reminder. 'Yeah, well, you know. Just don't get arrested and all that.' Ent and Stoggy stand on their privilege to remain mute in the witness box, forcing Dave to move the conversation on. 'So, any updates from Sifter?'

JJ is the quickest on the trigger and scrambles for his mobile. 'They're on their way. Just left Hull,' he reports. He scans the feed. 'Wild night in The Jolly Roger. Reckons they've left a few behind – can you imagine? – and a few sarky comments about some of the types on board.' He keeps reading for a few seconds before looking up. 'That's it. Bugger all, really. Nothing about what's going on with the lads.'

They consider this lack of news. 'I'd have thought he'd be better informed, wouldn't you?' Dave gripes. 'This is just social commentary, where what we really want to know is what's going down in the rehearsals, how are they getting on, what's being planned, that sort of thing.'

JJ agrees. 'Yeah, you'd have thought he'd have had better access.'

'Hang on,' Ent protests. 'Everything we know we get from Sifter. He only posted last night, so he's hardly going to be writing a shedload this morning. The main thing is the brothers haven't kicked the shit out of each other yet so it's all going to plan. Until we hear otherwise, and Sifter would be the first to know, then it's all good, isn't it?'

It's a fair point, echoed by Stoggy. 'Yeah, and Sifter is definitely a bit more informative than The Daily Telegraph on these matters, hey Dave?'

Ent draws a line under the matter in hand with: 'I'm going up for another sausage. Anyone else?' JJ turns green at the thought, while the rest of the table falls into silent contemplation. Yes, no news is definitely good news.

***

Salt feels a frisson of excitement as he takes in the sight of five hundred expectant figures milling around in front of the stage. This, the team who will make it all happen, from the stage crew to the security detail, from the medical team to the catering staff, from the presenters to the broadcast techs, from the stewards to the cleaners. And everybody in between. Events like Be Here Now aren't just thrown together; this crack team has been working for months to make it a reality. Now it's all very real indeed. D-Day minus one and time for Salt's pre-engagement address to the troops. A stirring of good-natured shouts and applause greets him as he takes to the microphone. The largely empty auditorium looms before him, while a forest of white turbines frames the horizon as far as the eye can see.

'What a beautiful sight,' he exclaims as he gestures, hands outspread, to the assembled crowd. That elicits a cheer. 'Who thought we'd never make it?' A few random shouts of 'me' are heard from the crowd, followed by laughter. Salt basks in the gentle banter. 'But here we are.' He's getting into his stride now. 'What's it like to be making history?' he continues, before launching into a list of landmarks: 'An event that will be spoken about for decades. On this unique location in the

North Sea. The comeback gig of all comeback gigs.' The crew punctuates each boast with a wry cheer.

'First it was never, then it was maybe, and now, thanks to you, it's a case of definitely.' Salt's cack-handed rhetoric draws a mixture of groans and ironic sniggers. 'OK, I asked for that,' he concedes, and moves swiftly on. 'I've just heard that tomorrow night's simulcast will have the largest pay-per-view audience ever.' A spontaneous round of applause ripples around the auditorium. 'It's official, and we still have thirty-six hours to sign up more households.' It's true – Salt has just had that figure confirmed, with sales to nearly one hundred countries, on every continent, from Japan to the USA, from Canada to Australia, from Brazil to China. The PPV revenue alone will largely underwrite the entire exercise as well as delivering the promoter an eye-watering commission.

'Tomorrow, we also have Be Here Now fanzones set up in forty key cities around the world, where friends and families will gather to watch the show.' Salt has been amazed at how the sales team has cranked the handle on this idea, given any Tom, Dick or Harry could have put a fanzone on. But the ex-FIFA consultant he hired told him not to be so silly: *Punters are mugs for anything with an 'official' stamp, and our lawyers will crush anybody daring to rip us off.*' He was right. Another few million in the bank.

'And there's more,' Salt teases. Really? This exercise in Mammon knows no bounds. 'We are taking augmented reality to a whole new level for this gig, with a fully immersive experience for people who can't physically be here on Holm Island. Our mobile-only AR package has been snapped up by over one million fans. We won't get to see the turbines turning here tomorrow night, but our AR audience will.'

You can almost hear the cash register ring. But never mind the money, feel the artistic legacy: 'Our headliners may represent the best in music of the past thirty-five years, but Be Here Now will set a new standard, globally, in the presentation and enjoyment of live music in the future.'

From the side of the stage, Amanda Teale, Eclipse, Martin and Ross look on. Each in turn is to give an address to the team and needs to pitch it right between logistics (Martin and Ross), fuzzy love (Eclipse) and hard-boiled politicking (no guesses…). They have to hand it to Salt though, he has the crew in the palm of his hand. And he's not finished yet.

'Tonight's spectacular will allow us to test every element of site organisation and planning with a capacity crowd in the arena for the first time. While this will form part of the eventual movie, tonight it's strictly local, our dry run if you will.' The evening show is a bespoke theatrical extravaganza, whose gestation has come about in the time-honoured fashion of 'Shit: what else can we do?' Salt initially wanted to put on a failsafe line-up of nineties bands who had been contemporary to Oasis, but their management had vetoed that idea out of hand, saying they wanted the focus to rest solely on their performance (not that they said it quite as politely as that). This was a blow, because it was vital to have the punters on the island for more than one night (otherwise it was hard to justify charging them as much). It was Martin who came up with the idea of 'something like the 2012 Olympic Games Opening Ceremony'. Brilliant! The idea took off. There was initial disappointment when Danny Boyle declined the invitation to direct, but game-changing theatrical disrupters Tipsy Pipistrelle had no such qualms. When they came up with the title of 'Cool Britannia' for the cross-cultural collaboration, Amanda Teale was so moved by its potential she stumped up even more cash to 'make it happen'. Salt has popped into a couple of rehearsals in the lead-up and is confident enough to share his expectations with the team: 'I can promise you; you'll have seen nothing like it.' He doesn't know that Amanda Teale's team have not only attended all the rehearsals, but they've also insisted on numerous 'improvements'. It's been fraught, but if Tipsy Pipistrelle pull it off tonight, they'll have earned stiff drinks all round.

The other speakers start to fidget as Salt carries on. He's only supposed to have ten minutes, but there's no doubt he's enjoying this. 'Anybody here got a bet on the Gallaghers not turning out this weekend?' he teases. It's apparent from the shouts that some have, and the wagers are still live. 'Well, sorry to disappoint, because nothing is going to stop us now.'

Stage left, Martin feels his guts contract. *No, no, no, no. Please don't tempt fate.*

Amanda isn't listening by this stage – *get him off, now.* Eclipse dutifully catches Salt's eye and draws a line across her neck.

Glancing at his watch, and surprising himself at the time (how it flies when you're having fun), Salt moves to wind up. 'I'll now hand you over to my colleagues for their words of wisdom and encouragement.' The four speakers yet to come heave a sigh of relief. 'But one final thing.' The minister for CLEAN looks set to combust as she hears him out. 'Look up there, ladies and gentlemen, into that blue, blue sky, and behold: Bright Phoebus, our very own yellow dwarf, the old currant bun. The sun has got its hat on and is smiling down on us. And so may it continue tomorrow. Thank you.'

This time it's Ross' guts that rumble in the deep. Did he really have to say that?

10

PART OF THE QUEUE

Sifter's Supernova ferry from Hull is on time, but there's a problem – the cabins aren't ready due to a problem with the check-in software. As a result, everywhere is rammed, with people sitting on floors, in gangways, wherever they can find a spot. Sifter trips over numerous rucksacks and wheelies as he tries to find somewhere to have some time to himself before reaching Holm. Reaching deck seven, he spots a door with a large sign announcing *Private: Freight Drivers Only*. Tutting, he continues down the corridor. Then the thought strikes him that there can't be any freight on board, so he loops back and enters. Bingo. Plenty of Oasis fans have twigged to the same idea, but there's a spare seat next to the window. He doesn't ask if it's free – he parks his bum and puts on his headphones to signal he's not really there. Looking around, he congratulates himself on his find. Comfy chair – check. Nice and quiet – check. There's even a toilet – double check. The serving area where they would normally have food and drink available is empty today, but no problem, no problem at all.

He sinks back and sets his thoughts in order. Last night was a blast. It got blurry around one in the morning, but he must have had a good time because his feet are killing him and his throat is red raw, tell- tale signs of mad dancing and singing at top volume. The DJ was smart. Some would have played Oasis every track, but over five hours that would have been overkill. Not that there wouldn't have been enough songs, but you can have too much of a good thing. It was an appetiser, not a pie eating competition, and the DJ had got it spot on. Made the tracks he did play all the more powerful. The thought reminds Sifter of a piece he'd once started writing and never finished, about the total running time of Oasis' recorded output. He had the idea when reading that the total running time of music recorded by The Beatles amounted to ten hours, twenty minutes and forty-three seconds. Oasis did more than that, but how much? He started building a monster playlist on Spotify, so he didn't have to do any adding up himself. Putting in the seven studio albums was easy enough, but then he had to identify and add all the singles that weren't on the original LPs. That was tricky enough, but what about all the B-sides, live albums, re-issues and bonus tracks? At that point he lost heart – let somebody else crunch it if they must (not that anybody has). Still, it would be a good quiz question.

The boat is making steady progress, and the rhythmic rocking of the waves is relaxing. He's bagged a good position here. The sea is a brilliant blue while the bright yellow sun hangs high in the cloudless sky like a David Hockney iPad painting. Sifter unconsciously crosses his fingers in the hope it will stay that way. Unsurprisingly, the weather has been at the core of endless discussion among Oasis fans ever since the gig was announced. Being the UK, there's no such thing as guaranteed weather. More festivals are washed out than bask in a heatwave; cases of trench foot outstrip sunstroke by ten to one. Weather expectations were generally low anyway –

battle-hardened festivalgoers would never travel without their cagoules and wellies. But holding a gig in the middle of the North Sea was a beast of a different stripe. If you're going to hold an event in a wind turbine field then, surely, it's going to be windy? The organisers have been quick to put minds at rest by pointing out that the turbines only require a gentle breeze to operate; it's not like they're planning to hold the event in a gale. In the middle of summer, in fact, the location would make for very pleasant conditions. What about rain? They say they've crunched the data for the 'optimal window', but then we've heard that before, haven't we? Bottom line – as anybody who's ever been to a festival knows – is you hope for the best and plan for the worst when it comes to packing. But there are definite advantages to this site. There's the composition of the island for one – the industrial construction is unlikely to turn into a quagmire following a downpour. Plus, no tents or camping means there's less to lug there and back. That suits Sifter whose needs are modest – he has everything he needs in his battered Adidas sports holdall, which is older than Liam's two front teeth.

A young woman, hand clasped over mouth, suddenly rushes past his seat in the direction of the toilet. Hungover? Drunk? Pregnant? Sifter smiles. Nope. Seasickness. (Now that's one thing you don't get at a normal festival.) Amazing, as it's like a duck pond out there. She must be in her late teens, bucking the trend amid the seriously middle-aged crowd. Most likely some lucky daughter, part of a rich family's Oasis outing ('let's do something different this year, darling').

That's another thing about this Be Here Now gig, and another thing that has engaged – and enraged – his followers online: genuine Oasis fans are being shat on with this jamboree. It's been hijacked by the corporate johnnies, the sort of superannuated skanks who brag about going from Glyndebourne to Glastonbury, from the Chelsea Flower Show to the Notting Hill Festival each year. At least that young girl looks old enough to tie her own shoelaces – no sign on this trip of the wet-wiped terror tots you tend to see at festivals these days. 'Little people' getting under everybody's feet at gigs is one of the worst ideas ever unleashed on a leisure-loving population. Fresh-out-of-nappies Jocastas and Caspers running amok, their Mummy and Daddy's mobile numbers (but not – 'for security' – the kids' names) perma-inked on their arms so they can be reunited with their negligent parents once they've ruined somebody else's day. (There's a thought: will mobiles work on Holm – they've not worked at any other festival Sifter has attended). He shifts his gaze around the room. Yes, a real oddball crowd. It's a mix of the rich and entitled, who have never seen Oasis before, and the sort of grey, grizzled and hollow-cheeked scallies you see knocking around the Northern Quarter. No point in asking how the latter can afford to be here – they just are. He knows who he prefers, anyway. He spots three characters staring into space near the servery hatch – now they don't fit the obvious bill. Stern and grim-faced, they're hardly exuding the same pre-gig party spirit as the rest of the crowd. One is quite old, even for this outing, while the other two look like off-duty squaddies. Are they even together? They're dressed similarly though: baseball caps pulled low, polo shirts, cargo pants. That's it – they *are* freight drivers, probably pissed off at seeing their private onboard space invaded. God knows where they're going, though – surely not to the gig?

A ping draws his wandering mind back to his mobile. When he sees who the message is from, he eagerly opens it. But his first reaction on reading it is one of disbelief. *WTF?* This can't be happening. He almost forgets to breathe as he absorbs the impact of these tidings. With an almighty effort he brings himself round: this news can't be dressed up or downplayed in any way whatsoever and he has a responsibility, a solemn duty, to report it to his followers. Without delay.

***

Rachel is walking on a cloud as she sips her matcha latte. 'I hadn't realised how stressed I was,' she confesses. Justine, who has a far better idea of where her friend stands on the uptight scale, nods tactfully.

The just concluded Reiki session has been an overwhelming success. The laying on of hands has given Rachel's life force and energy a pleasing boost, and she's feeling radiant and relaxed for the first time in months. Justine, less so. Still, it's been a great start to the day.

'Once we've had this, we need to get down to the Buy Here Now merchandise mart,' Rachel announces. 'Before the boats arrive and there's nothing left.' She can hardly go back empty-handed for Tim, can she? He'd be beyond disappointed. Another thought: what about Matthew? A T-shirt perhaps? Or would that send the wrong signal?

Justine has a better idea. 'You can get it all on the app and have it delivered home, you know. Far easier.'

'I know, but I like to look and see what I'm buying. Check the sizes. You can't do that on the app, can you? And I want to give Tim something I've actually bought here. Make it special for him.'

Justine sniffs. 'Why don't we have another drink and go through the app first to see what you want to buy? Then you'll be a lot quicker when you get there.' It's not a bad suggestion.

Rachel re-orders as Justine helpfully fires up 'Shop' on the Be Here Now app.

Within seconds, Rachel realises she shouldn't have entrusted the role of 'personal shopper' to her companion. 'Oh my God,' Justine exclaims, 'look at this.' She tilts the screen to share the image of a large dildo. She reads on: *Never be alone with your very own "She's Electric". An oasis of pleasure guaranteed. Available in five sizes.*

They giggle conspiratorially. 'I didn't know you could get different sizes,' Rachel admits. 'Just think of the stock they'd have to carry. What section are you looking at there?'

'Personal. You can also get "Waiting for the Rapture" branded condoms and lubricants…' she scrolls down, '… cock rings and love eggs.' She laughs. 'Or then again, maybe not.'

Rachel shrugs primly. 'I think I'm after a T-shirt mainly.'

'Bet you anything they're all made for fifty pence in a sweatshop somewhere.'

'Do you really think so?'

'Well, maybe a quid,' Justine allows. She swipes back to the menu, and cackles. 'Listen to this: *Cosmetics. Never get the brush off with our unisex "Eyeball Tickler" mascara.*' She hesitates. 'Is that rude as well? Tickler?' She doesn't wait for an answer as she's already on to the next section. 'I don't believe this,' she exclaims, and offers up the screen again. '*The "Gold and Silver and Sunshine" jewellery range. Select from our unique collection of pins, badges, bracelets and earrings.* Christ – there's a bracelet here costing ten thousand pounds.' Rachel has to check to make sure her friend hasn't misread it. Yup – ten grand.

Justine is in her element by now, reeling off a succession of imaginatively conceived, named and priced mementos to mark this historic weekend: A "Rocking Chair" – you've guessed it

– rocking chair, the "Pass Me Down the Wine" vino collection, an "I'm Outta Time" wristwatch (his and her models available), a "The Shock of the Lightning" light switch cover, and, inevitably, a Holm Island handheld fan (batteries supplied) shaped like a wind turbine. It's all rather overwhelming, not that it stops them looking for a good half hour until Justine finally clicks on 'Apparel'. Rachel takes command of the app and navigates swiftly through Hoodies, Jackets, Hats and Trainers to T-shirts, where she reckons the simple white one with black lettering reading 'Oasis, Holm Island 2029' will do just fine. 'It's got the logo on and everything.' And it's available in small, which she reckons will probably fit Tim best. As for a second T-shirt, she finds herself thinking aloud: 'I was wondering whether to get one for Matthew,' she says, 'but it might send the wrong message.'

Justine doesn't hang about with her follow-up. 'You think it's definitely over, then?'

Rachel could kick herself. Why did she have to mention Matthew? She's set Justine off now. She doesn't want to talk about it really – this weekend is supposed to be about getting away from that for a while. But the truth is, she can't think of anything else. Does being at something like this really help her to decide? Is she seriously taking time out to consider her – their – future, or simply kidding herself, running away and hiding? The more she ponders, the more confused she becomes. 'Oh, Jus, if only I knew.'

Justine fixes her in her sights. 'So, what did happen last night?'

Rachel is shocked – how has her friend brought it round to that again? She springs, once more, to her own defence. 'I told you, Jus. Nothing. It wasn't anything like that.' Justine's lack of a reply forces her to elaborate further. 'We were just talking, that's all.' A thunderbolt memory from the early hours suddenly strikes her. 'God, I've just remembered, I think he was having some difficulties in his marriage too.'

Justine scoffs. 'Oh, how tragic. And convenient. Kindred spirits, abroad in the world.'

Rachel strains to recall the early morning hours when she was alone – and let's be honest, zonked out of her gourd – in Dave's company. No, nothing *like that* happened, but he did talk about his wife, how they'd drifted apart, how he had misgivings about the future. That had resonated. As she recollects, he had seemed quite sad – a mirror of her own preoccupations. The memory jolts her – had he been saying that in a false show of empathy, in a bid to lower her defences? Lower her knickers? Could he really have been that devious? No – nothing had happened, she was sure of that. 'I think you're putting two and two together, Jus, and coming up with five. It was all very innocuous, really.'

Justine's response takes her by surprise. 'I'm not judging you, Rach. You're a grown woman. One night of fun – if you had one – isn't the issue. What you need to decide is the bigger picture: what you're going to do with the rest of your life.'

Where on earth did that come from? Was she being told off? Ticked off over her prevarication? But it was a fair enough question: What was she going to do with the rest of her life?

At least her friend spares her further interrogation and changes the subject: 'Come on. Let's get down to Buy Here Now and see what they've got left. I've got my eye on some "Turn Up the Sun" tan lotion.'

Rachel drains her cup and gathers her bag. Would it really send the wrong signal to buy Matthew a T-shirt, or was she just being mean?

11

GAS PANIC!

JJ is still feeling green around the gills as the first order of the day is made at the bar. 'It's definitely something I ate,' he speculates.

'Stop moaning, will you,' Ent chides as he passes him a beer. 'Here. That'll sort you out.'

JJ bristles. 'I'm not just thinking of myself here. These temporary kitchens have all sorts of implications for food storage, prep and hygiene. Some of the best restaurants in Manchester have been served one-star ratings because…'

Stoggy cuts him off in brutal manner: 'For Christ's sake, we're not interested. Right? It's your arse that's the problem here, not the kitchen, and we're sick of hearing about it.'

That stuns the group into silence until an abashed JJ offers a weak, 'I was only saying.'

Ent feels the need to lift the mood. 'Now, now, girls. No fighting.' He emits a loud burp before adding, 'I think I must have eaten whatever's done for you, JJ. Know the name of any good lawyers?"

As if on cue, Dave – who has been calling the office – arrives to join them. 'You'll never guess who I've just seen,' he says excitedly.

After random guesses at Pep Guardiola, Lord Lucan and 'that bird with the big tits that used to be on Countdown', he puts them out of their misery. 'Amanda Teale.'

'Who the fuck's that?' Ent and Stoggy want to know. JJ does recognise the name but, standing on his dignity after being humiliated, leaves it to Dave to explain.

'The government minister for… building on green belt land or something like that,' Dave elucidates. 'You know, face like a bag of spanners. Always on the telly.' That doesn't help, so he continues, 'Was the first to be booted out of *Celebrity Big Brother* that time and was the MP with the highest expenses claim last year.'

'Oh, I know who you mean,' Ent says. 'Queen Bitch. Scary.'

JJ finally feels compelled to inject some accuracy into the description. 'I think you'll find that Amanda Teale is the minister for CLEAN. That's Climate, Life, Ecology and Nature. She's in charge of the country's green energy programme, and a prime mover behind this event, which is presumably why she's here.'

'So just another festival freeloader,' Stoggy says. 'They're bloody everywhere.'

JJ can't resist the opening. 'Exactly. I suspect she's probably paid the same as you to be here.' As Stoggy's face turns murderous JJ adds a crisp, 'I'm only saying.'

That conversation arc clearly exhausted, they all reach for their beers to signal a time-out. Dave is the first to break new ground. 'I was looking at the festival terms and conditions on the app this morning,' he chuckles, 'and I reckon we're already bang to rights on a few areas.'

'Like stealing electric platform trucks?' says JJ.

'Jesus, JJ, what's got into you this morning?' Ent says. 'Wind your bloody neck in, will you.'

Dave ignores the two of them and presses on. 'There are hundreds of rules on what you can and can't bring in. I think we've already failed on the drugs front. I just wanted to check you've not packed a gun, Stoggy?'

'Very funny.'

Dave pulls out his phone. 'Let's see what else. No flares or fireworks. Sensible. We'd have the RNLI out if there was, I suppose. No flags either.'

'I've got a flag,' Ent pipes up. 'You didn't say anything about that.' It's true – he's brought along an old 'MCFC: Definitely Manchester' banner together with interlocking flag poles to raise it aloft. 'Well, sod that. I'm taking it in.'

'They might confiscate it,' says the lawyer as he studies the small print.

'I'd like to see them try,' Ent says darkly.

'Balloons and kites are on the *verboten* list too. We don't have any of those, do we?'

'Well, you can see why,' JJ concurs. 'We're in the middle of one of the largest wind turbine fields in the world.'

Ent is sceptical. 'Yeah, but a bloody balloon isn't going to jam up the works on one of those buggers, is it? It's just health and safety gone mad.'

Dave scans the list further. 'No rugs or folding chairs inside the arena. Well, I'm all for that.'

Stoggy stirs. 'Twats who think they're on the beach instead of at a gig – does my head in, that.' It's not often he finds himself on the side of the rule makers, but he's onside with this: 'Shouldn't be allowed.' Nobody disagrees.

Dave has found the Q and A now. 'Oh, it's not all bad news. You'll like this one, Ent. Breast pump stations are available at any of the medical tents. Privacy is assured – just don't forget to take your own breast pump.' His chubby companion shoots him two fingers in reply.

'One for you, JJ. Medical prescriptions are allowed, as long as they're clearly labelled with your name and match your ID.' His hypochondriac chum shakes his head at the lameness of the jibe.

Dave's getting into this now. 'This can't be right: Where is the nearest bus stop? That's a good one. Anybody seen it?'

Stoggy is getting bored with this. 'Forget that bollocks. Check if Sifter has posted anything.'

Dave obediently obliges and waits for the page to load. They watch as his eyes widen, his jaw drops and the blood drains from his face – not exactly the portent of glad tidings. 'Sweet Jesus,' he finally exclaims. 'You're not going to believe this.' They dumbly await the bombshell, in the knowledge that Dave is incapable of a skilful wind-up. 'It's Liam. Liam's throat,' he reports. He begins to read aloud to his stunned companions:

> *Sifter's blog:*
>
> *I don't quite know how to break this, so I'll go straight in: Saturday's Oasis reunion gig at Holm Island is under threat due to unconfirmed reports Liam has a bad case of laryngitis. The band and organisers have apparently been trying to keep the news under wraps but figures close to rehearsals have reported Liam hasn't been spotted for two days.'*

Ent is immediately in denial. 'No. No, no, no, no, no. I'm not having that. No,' before being told to shush.

> *This wouldn't be the first time Liam has experienced inflammation of the voice box, or the first time he's*

pulled out of gigs because of it. In fact, he has quite a track record in this area.

JJ doesn't need reminding. 'Including the V Festival, 2009, the beginning of the end,' he says gloomily.

Of course, there could be more sinister factors at work here. Is Liam ill, or have the Gallaghers found it impossible, despite the deal on the table, to be in the same room at the same time after a twenty-year break?

Dave ponders this last point. 'You know what, I reckon that's a more likely explanation. Your nodules don't just pack up. In the middle of a tour, maybe, but not before a one-off.'

Stoggy is stirred to a challenge at this. 'So, you're a doctor now, are you? How would you know?'

Dave ignores him and continues the post:

Looking on the bright side, doctors recommend complete vocal rest for laryngitis, so depending on when Liam is supposed to have started this problem there's still time for him to make a full recovery ahead of Saturday.

JJ joins his hands together in prayer as the others also begin to wish this interpretation to be true. 'He used to swear by tea and apple cider vinegar with honey for his voice. He'll be on that for sure.'

'Yeah, and brandy if I recall,' adds Ent.

JJ corrects him. 'No, he knocked drinking before a show on the head years back.'

Dave holds his hand up. 'Please? Let me finish.'

Hopefully, there's nothing to panic about and there's a perfectly sensible explanation for the rumour. Please don't let us down, lads.

'Nothing to panic about?' Ent shrills. 'He's the one spreading the bloody panic. It's a rumour. He says it's a rumour. Why tell us at all? What the fuck?'

'There is no way on God's earth this gig isn't going ahead,' JJ states gravely. 'No way at all.'

Dave agrees. 'Totally. The stakes are far too high to cancel it, or even move it. There would be massive financial repercussions, not to mention reputational ones. No. I just can't see it.'

Stoggy, though, remains silent and strangely conflicted. He gets that it's a rumour, and he doesn't want it to be true, but he's always depended on Sifter for Oasis news. Would he really get it wrong?

***

Fresh from her address to the crew ('do you think it went down well?'), Amanda Teale convenes an impromptu meeting in the green room. Salt, Ross, Martin and Eclipse trudge in, scarcely believing they are being diverted from essential jobs at such a critical time. Their irritation only mounts when Amanda announces she's called them together 'to ensure everything is on track'. At the same time, they understand the quickest way to get back to their duties is to play along.

The minister eyes Martin first. 'Where are we on the endorsement messages from the Gallagher brothers saying they're fully behind Britain's move towards energy self-sufficiency?' She only doubled-downed on this unrealistic demand less than twenty-four hours ago, but in her view that's a perfectly acceptable timescale for results.

Martin doesn't miss a beat in response. 'All in hand,' he declares. 'We've agreed to schedule a half-hour shoot with them backstage tomorrow afternoon. Scripts – one liners – are being worked up as we speak.'

Amanda is impressed although she doesn't show it – this is nothing more than was required. 'Good. About time.'

Salt suppresses a smirk. He knows full well Martin hasn't arranged anything as he'd have had to go through him. But he's got the menace off his back for now and will inevitably inform her tomorrow that a longer than anticipated rehearsal precluded the recording session taking place (*but don't worry, we're re-scheduling for next week*). Neatly played.

Teale turns her attention to Ross. 'And you can guarantee that absolutely nothing will go wrong on the staging?' The head of production hesitates. *Guarantee?* 'I'm happy enough with the arrangements, yes.'

This doesn't sound like the cast-iron pledge Amanda is looking for. 'I'm afraid *happy enough* doesn't cut it in my world. I want to hear that everything has been tested, nothing will malfunction, and you have back-ups for all contingencies.'

Ross has been doing this job, what, nearly forty years, and doesn't appreciate his technical competence being challenged by a woman who has her assistant change the batteries in her TV remote. 'You can take it from me,' he says tersely, 'apart from an act of God, we're good to go.'

The minister sniffs. 'Well, I suppose we'll have to rely on Him in that case.'

Ross tenses. He should let it go, let the interrogation move on, but no. 'Can I just say, it wasn't my stupid bloody idea to stage a gig on an island in the middle of the North Sea, but it is me who's having to make it work. And I will, despite the obstacles.' They all stare at him. Where's that come from?

He's normally so composed. But he's not finished. 'Back-ups for all contingencies? Let's see. What about being told to use only green energy from source? Well, sod that. If I'd listened to you lot, we'd have no fallback at all, so of course I've got a back-up.'

Salt discovers a cobweb on the ceiling to study: what on earth did Ross disclose that for? The others look to Eclipse, who this outburst is clearly directed at. She appears to be absorbing this latest information more slowly than the others. Then it lands. 'You mean generators? Here, on the island?'

Ross deals with the enquiry in short order. 'Of course I bloody well do.'

The eco-warrior turns pale. 'But the whole point of having Be Here Now on Holm Island is...'

Ross cuts her off. 'Yada, yada, yada... Yes, we know, but it's stupid, risky and unnecessary to hang our arses out the window without a fall back. So, I took an executive decision. And you'll be glad I did if we hit any problems.'

Eclipse is stunned. *The whole point...* She turns to the Minister for CLEAN with a weak appeal: 'Amanda?'

If Amanda Teale required any justification for convening this impromptu meeting, this proves the point. The uncovering of any issue only she can resolve. She resents Ross' tone but has to concede, as nice as being entirely reliant on green energy would be, it's probably a good thing they have a proven failsafe in place. 'Let's be practical, shall we? The event *is* one hundred per cent green, and will remain so, but it provides a comfort to know the generators are there. Plus, no one need ever know about them. Agreed?'

Ross, Salt and Martin can hardly believe their ears. Good. Some common sense at last. Eclipse, on the other hand, bursts into tears and dashes from the room, almost knocking over one of Amanda's aides as he comes through the door.

Salt, next in line, braces himself for whatever nonsense Teale is going to throw his way, but the minister is deep in conversation with the stony-faced gorilla who's just entered. The promoter watches as first the minister's throat, then her face, flushes a deep vermillion. This doesn't presage good news. And it's not.

'I'm afraid we may have a security situation unfolding,' she reveals as her aide slips out of the room. 'The counter terrorism monitoring unit has picked up a viable threat during Oasis' performance.'

Martin's stomach lurches. This is his department along with everything else. 'What sort of threat? Who's behind it?'

'We don't know much more at this stage. It could be anybody.'

There's an awkward silence as they project the consequences of this intel to the *nth* degree – evacuation and cancellation, embarrassment, and a stonking financial loss. Salt is quick to calculate how much this could impact on his own pocket. 'The last thing we want to do is over-react. I've been in these situations many times, and they normally turn out to be a hoax. Probably a Blur fan or something.' Nobody laughs. 'Look, we couldn't be better protected out here on our own little island. We've swept the site three times, and everybody has to go through airport style screening on arriving. Martin has a massive security team in place, and we've even got the Royal Navy to call upon. We need to keep our cool.'

It's true that – a regrettable sign of the times – security has dominated a large part of the pre-planning stages for the event. Amanda assumes control. 'We must treat this as a credible threat, but I don't want to cause unnecessary panic until we know more. News of this cannot leak out.'

Martin spots the contradiction. 'If it's credible, then don't we need to be putting everybody on a substantial threat footing?'

Amanda shakes her head. 'No. That's most likely the goal of whoever is behind this – to cause chaos and disruption. How they'd like that. Well, we're not going to oblige them until we have harder evidence. We cannot be seen to bow to terrorism, to crumble at the first hint of peril.'

'Business as usual,' is Salt's ringing endorsement of this declaration of defiance. 'Quite right.'

Ross, who's seen and heard all this before, considers he's wasted enough time already and excuses himself.

Martin's thoughts automatically leap into reaction mode: how would they justify ignoring a warning if they were hit in some way? No – for once Teale is right. No need to panic yet. In fact, he was only thinking the other day how little criticism BRITE comes in for despite being a major energy provider. It *was* good to be green. They'd been on the end of relatively few threats since he started, and most were clearly from cranks. In fact, he'd binned one without referring it upstairs only last week, but surely the Conserve Aquatic Reserves Partnership weren't the sort of protest group to resort to extreme action.

12

ALL AROUND THE WORLD

The animals may have gone in two by two, but the Supernovas remain in strict single file as they disembark on Holm Island. Waiting at the bottom of the gangplank are Jez and Cleo, ready to shrink-wrap this exciting moment live for an international audience – and for the poor unfortunates who couldn't afford a ticket.

'How does it feel to *be here now*?' Cleo trills as she thrusts a mic in the face of the first passenger off the boat, a smart-looking woman of around fifty.

The interviewee ponders this searching question for a few seconds before admitting: 'I didn't want to come, really. It was my husband's idea.'

Cleo's mouth gapes at this – not a good look on camera – leaving Jez to pick up. 'What a hero,' he declares. 'What more can a man do to demonstrate his undying love for his partner than score two tickets for Oasis? Where is he so we can have a word?'

She shifts awkwardly. 'He couldn't come.'

Jez and Cleo respond with well-practised forced laughter. 'Don't tell me,' Cleo says as she scrambles for a line, 'he has a dentist's appointment.'

'Or he had to put the bins out,' is Jez's follow up.

The woman appears to weigh up what to tell them, then: 'No. The cheating bastard ran off with my sister last week.' She looks directly at the camera: 'So if you're watching this you pair of shits, I hope you both rot in hell.' With that, she grabs the hand of the bewildered teenager standing behind her and walks on.

Flustered, Jez pulls himself together, 'We'll cut that later,' he guffaws.

'No, we won't,' Cleo corrects him, savvier than her co-presenter as to the social media gold they've just struck.

A grim-faced man, sporting a baseball cap, polo shirt and cargo pants, is the next punter to be accosted by Jez at the bottom of the gangplank. 'In three words – how excited are *you* to be seeing Oasis?'

The new arrival promptly covers his face with his bag and rushes past, as if he's arriving at The Old Bailey to face a murder charge.

Cleo is mock amused for the benefit of the viewers. 'Now there's someone who hasn't told his boss where he is this weekend.'

'Or maybe he's just overawed at meeting you, Cleo.'

'I'm beginning to think it's you, Jez. You did wash this morning, didn't you?'

Two more camera-shy arrivals take a sharp right to avoid the interview party, leaving the showbiz duo on the point of embarrassment. Surely, someone wants to share with the world how this unique moment in their life is 'magic' or 'top'.

Jez grabs the arm of the next passenger, a grizzled geezer who looks like he lives in a cardboard box behind Deansgate Locks, and ploughs straight in: 'Let me guess. This isn't your first time seeing Oasis, is it?'

The tracksuit-clad gadgey tips his Kangol bucket hat towards the presenters. 'You'd be right there. Number forty this weekend.'

'Forty times?' exclaims Cleo. 'That's amazing. You're not related to the band, are you?'

'Nah,' he grins, delighted at this opportunity to cement his superfan status. 'From Manchester. Grew up on 'em. First time at the Academy 1994 – the smaller gig in the summer as well as the Christmas show.' He makes a show of counting his fingers. 'Glasto '95, Maine Road both nights. Knebworth both nights. You name it, I was there.'

'Incredible,' says Jez. 'I don't think we're going to beat that this weekend.' He turns to face the camera, 'Or are we? Oasis fans are known for their dedication. Who's been to more than forty gigs? We want to know!'

Punters are pouring off the boat behind him, but the producer's instruction is loud and clear in their earpieces: *Keep going with this one. Get his name.*

Cleo obliges. 'This is fascinating. We must ask your name.'

The interviewee, needing no further invitation, gently lowers his bag to the ground. In for the long haul. 'Sifter,' he swaggers.

Cleo doesn't have a clue, but the name chimes a distant bell in the back parlour of Jez's memory. 'Oh, like in the song?' he strains. 'What was it again?'

Sifter pulls a face. *They don't know?* He turns directly to the camera lens and sneers: 'Extra homework for them tonight.' Cleo and Jez, professionals to the bone, grin inanely while doing their best to mask how they'd like to give this overweening Manc a good kicking. The producer delivers his next cue – *one more and get rid of him* – but before they can come up with a final question, Sifter carries on. 'I do the

Sifter blog, don't I? Best Oasis blog on the planet.' He leers at the camera lens once more and points at the unseen audience. 'They know.'

You can almost smell the burning rubber as the producer performs a U-turn and screeches in the presenters' ears: *No. Stick with him.*

Jez doesn't miss a beat. 'Ladies and gentlemen, we have genuine Oasis rock 'n' roll royalty in the house. We are honoured.' He doesn't even sound sarcastic. 'So, you must have met the boys. Tell us what it's like in the inner circle.'

That knocks the wind out of Sifter's sails. The inner circle? If access to the band was a dart board, his best arrow would be a double. He shrugs his shoulders as nonchalantly as he can. 'Yeah. Great lads. Everybody knows that. Salt of the earth.'

Jez, his bullshit detector alerted, suppresses a smirk as he follows up. 'Come on, Sifter. You're the man on the inside – share something with us about this weekend that the viewers won't know.'

The cogs in Sifter's brain grind like tectonic plates at being challenged to prove himself live on air. Jez – he remembers the old fossil from back in the day – is trying to hang him out to dry here. Then again, he's got the inside dope on a hot story. But it's one thing putting it on his blog and quite another broadcasting it to the world. What did he say on his urgent update not five minutes ago: *Hopefully, there's nothing to panic about and there's a perfectly sensible explanation for the rumour.* It *is* only a rumour. He has no hard evidence. He wasn't supposed to know anyway. Plus, his source is hardly inner circle – more of a treble man – so what if he's got it wrong? But he's already blogged it, so it's attributable to him anyway. And what if it *is* true – he'd have a world exclusive. He hedges, 'Well, I don't want to worry anyone, and I'm sure there's no cause for concern, but the latest intel I've received is…' he pauses, '…I'm not sure I should be telling you this.'

Cleo squeals, 'Oh, you've got to now! Don't be such a tease.'

Jez is loving this. *He's got nothing.* 'Just pretend it's the two of us here, Sifter,' he coaxes. 'Keep it between mates.'

That does it for Sifter. Bollocks to it, and bollocks to this patronising old fart – he'd show them how bloody connected he was. Like a doctor delivering a teaspoon of hope to wash down a bathtub of bad news, he solemnly discloses: 'Well, the latest is that Liam has a sore throat. Laryngitis. Could be touch and go for Saturday.'

Cleo and Jez stare at Sifter in disbelief as the producer barks at them: *Details. How bad? Recovery? Source?* As soon as they start to press him, however, the blogger becomes evasive, confidence in his own revelation crumbling quicker than a Manchester tart in the rain. He attempts a weak qualification. 'I'm sure there's nothing to it. You know how these rumours start.'

An old saying crosses his mind as he mitigates his own testimony: A lie is halfway round the world before the truth has got its boots on. No. He's had it on good – goodish – authority it's not a lie. He's stressed it was a rumour. He's only passing on what he's heard, which is his job as a blogger. He's not, like, signed it in blood, has he? He shrugs, reaches for his bag, and sidles off with a backward wave and a cheery 'See yer'.

Jez is left to wrap: 'You've got to hand it to Oasis fans; they love a good wind-up. We'll obviously dig deeper into that but I'm sure there's no need to panic just yet.' His psychotic smile, like a dog fitted with a set of human dentures, conveys anything but reassurance.

***

The social hierarchy at an event of this nature is delicate. Do the Supersonics feel uplifted by the arrival of the Supernovas at this other Eden, demi-paradise? Not a bit of it. Now they have to queue for everything as the different worlds collide. The VIP marquee remains off limits to the new arrivals, but it's packed to overflowing now all the elite ticket holders have retreated there to avoid the *hoi polloi*.

The Manc Lads, possibly the best hope of bridging the invisible divide, escape the crush to see if they can spot any familiar faces among the Johnny-come-latelies. They stroll down Burnage Boulevard (surely an oxymoron?) lined with every manner of food concession from pizza to paella, curry to crepes, fish and chips to fajitas, breathing in the comingled aromas before resting their bones on one of the gaily painted picnic tables opposite the Fu King Chinese takeaway. Much to their amusement, they immediately pick up on a heated exchange unfolding at the counter.

'How fu king much? £30 for a hot and sour? You're taking the piss.' The complainant, a flinty-looking man sporting a baseball cap and cargo pants, doesn't look the type to back down gracefully, but it appears he's met his match in the proprietor.

'Do you know how much this pitch costs, smartarse? I probably won't turn a profit until the last hour of the weekend, and you're moaning about the prices?'

'Yeah, well, that's your problem, not mine. You should have stayed at home or done a school fete in that case. It's a bloody rip off is what it is.'

Less than happy at being accused of profiteering, the vendor snatches the biodegradable oyster pail from the counter. 'Give it here then and fuck off.'

The punter makes to grab the container back and there's a brief tug of war, much to the alarm and disgust of the people further down the line. 'I didn't say I didn't want it, did I?' gasps the complainant, having recovered his meal. 'Just making a valid point, that's all.' He tosses three £10 notes in the direction of the stallholder. 'Still daylight robbery though.'

'We're cashless,' protests the stallholder, but wearily pockets the notes to spare further bickering. 'Try that at the jerk chicken stall and see what you get,' is his parting shot.

Having struck a blow for consumer rights, Mr Hot and Sour retreats to the nearest picnic bench to eat his overpriced repast while it's still warm. The two customers behind, who appear to be with him, are politeness itself as they place their order.

'How much did they rush you for that, mate?' Stoggy enquires of their table guest, knowing full well the score.

Through a mouthful of glass noodles the exasperated diner relates the damage, then lowers his eyes as he digests. Bryan could kick himself. He's briefed Bob and Cody not to draw attention to themselves, and here he is, squabbling with a stallholder and being embroiled in general chitchat with people he doesn't know.

'Never mind the prices,' says the fat one. 'It always makes me laugh how they call it fast food. I mean, just look at those queues.'

'You could die of starvation, just waiting,' adds the beardy one.

They all nod sagely. Having considered this, a further member of the group holds forth. 'Rule number one when it comes to festival food,' he declares. 'Always, always, go to the stall with the shortest queue. Whatever it's selling.'

This festival tip is met with ridicule. 'I'm not having that, Dave,' says his well-fed friend. 'That'd mean...' he squints down the line of concessions '...instead of eating burger and chips or something nourishing, you'd be noshing an acai super bowl or some such vegan bollocks. You can forget that.'

Dave defends his stratagem. 'You're just too stuck in your ways, Ent. It's good to try new things. There's nothing wrong with vegan food – we have it at home from time to time.'

The thin one sniggers at this confession: *surprise, surprise.*

But it looks like Dave has a fellow food adventurist to back him up. 'As for nourishment, Ent, an acai bowl is far better for you than burger and chips. Seriously.'

'You're only saying that 'cos you've got a beard.'

Throughout this exchange the only person on the picnic table to be eating bolts his grub down in double-quick time, nods gruffly, and shoots off to intercept his two colleagues before they can make their way over. 'Charming,' is Dave's assessment. 'Should have charged him more,' is Ent's.

No sooner is the space on the bench vacated then JJ spots Rachel and Justine taking the air. He waves wildly in their direction, and they're drawn in like iron filings. 'Fancy seeing you here,' he jokes as they make room for them. That's another rule of festivals. You always seem to be stuck for the duration, whether you like it or not, with the people you first bump into. These six certainly seem to have accepted that law by now.

'Are you eating here?' Rachel asks, surprised they'd be shelling out for food when it was included with their passes.

Dave explains they're people watching and will grab something in the marquee later. 'Join us if you like.' The two women exchange glances and remain non-commital.

Ent produces two plastic glasses and pours a Pimms for each of them from the jug on the table. They gratefully accept. 'What do you reckon to the news, then?' he asks.

It's clear from the confused look on their faces that whatever tiding he's alluding to hasn't yet reached them. 'Liam,' he clarifies. 'Laryngitis. It might all be off.' As an afterthought he adds, 'Allegedly.'

Justine shrieks. 'Really? That would be hilarious. Imagine!'

Seeing the shock on the men's faces, Rachel rows back on her friend's reaction. 'Well, not hilarious, obviously. That would be terrible. Are you sure?'

Dave recounts the intel they have been party to, while trying to play down its authenticity. 'No big gig is complete without a rumour of this sort,' he intones, as if he was the veteran of a thousand festivals.

Justine won't let it lie. 'All these people, here for one thing, and then "Sorry, can you come back next week". You'd have to laugh, really.'

Stoggy is anything but amused. 'Ha, fucking ha,' he scowls, causing both women to tense.

JJ gallantly rides to Justine's defence. 'I think Justine means it would be unlucky rather than comic, and she does have a point: I mean, we can enjoy the weekend and the company regardless, can't we?'

Ent clearly disagrees. 'No, JJ. I'm not having that. No Oasis, no party. We've not come all this way, waited all these years, and paid all this money to be kicked in the teeth.' (The reference to the cost is uttered without any sense of irony.)

'Seriously, what would happen if he can't perform?' Rachel ponders, concerned how it might impact on her BRITE prize package. Surely, they wouldn't pay to send her here twice.

Dave, in his lawyerly way, has taken the time to read the small print. 'Sunday's been nominated as a reserve day in the event of any unforeseen circumstances or acts of God. So, I guess that would apply if Liam had a sore throat. Assuming he was OK by then, allowing the extra day to recover.'

'And we'd have another day on the island,' Ent reckons. 'That wouldn't be so bad.'

JJ isn't so sure about that. 'The logistics of an extra day would be quite problematical. Not so much the accommodation, or even the live broadcast, but the food and beverage stocks. Surely, they won't have a full day's supplies knocking around *just in case.*'

Stoggy dismisses this consideration out of hand. 'Who gives a toss? We're here to see Oasis, not wine and dine. Well, I am, at least.'

Rachel has a further thought: 'I'm supposed to be back at work on Monday, as well.'

They each contemplate the enormity of the disaster Liam's inflamed voice box could betoken, up there with climate change, a worldwide recession or another global pandemic, and pray it isn't true. It's up to Dave to break them out of their reverie. 'Look, we're probably worrying about nothing. Come on. More Pimms and a bit more positivity, please.'

Stoggy sullenly tells them to count him out as he's going to have a look around, at which point Ent says he'll tag along with him. JJ does the honours replenishing the empty jug and finds the three of them studying the app on his return.

'Look at this, JJ,' Dave reads as his friend tops up their glasses. 'They've just put up more detail about tonight's extravaganza. *Cool Britannia. Tipsy Pipistrelle recreate the sights, the sounds, and the excitement of the nineties.* What do you reckon?'

JJ nods approvingly. 'It sounds very cultural, doesn't it? I'm definitely up for that.'

Dave, Rachel and Justine clunk their plastic glasses against JJ's in a toast. So are they.

13

HEADSHRINKER

Salt, Ross and Martin are sitting on the back row of the arena stand, taking a break from the Cool Britannia rehearsal. It's not going well. Martin, The Genie of What If, twists the top of his flask and takes a long pull on the contents. He immediately feels better. Beyond pretending at this point, he hands it to Salt and the impresario follows suit. Ross, the busiest man on the island, sensibly declines.

Salt is the first to pass comment. 'I thought this was supposed to be a celebration of the nineties, not a rerun of a Nuremberg Rally.'

Martin takes another swig. 'It's not what I had in mind when I suggested something like the 2012 Olympic Games opening ceremony. The blessed Amanda has seen to that with her *patriotic flourishes*.'

Ross is more focused on the staging rather than the content. 'I couldn't give a shit about any of that. As long as we get through it without falling over.'

Salt extends his hand to Martin for the flask again. 'I'm just glad it's got nothing to do with me.'

Ross shrugs him off. 'It's a rehearsal. That's why you have rehearsals; to iron out any wrinkles. It'll be fine.'

Salt takes another slug. 'I told you we should have just stuck a couple of bands on. It didn't need to be Blur or Pulp. We could have reformed Swing Out Sister or The Fall for the night – they'd have been bloody grateful, and the Gallaghers wouldn't have had to worry about being upstaged.'

Ross points out a small problem with this idea. 'I suspect Mark E Smith might have had a problem with that, seeing he's been dead for over ten years.'

Salt shrugs. 'Nobody would have noticed. You get my point – anything but the Last Night of the Proms is what I'm saying.'

Martin retrieves the flask. 'Do you know,' he says, 'I couldn't give a toss. Really. I've done my bit, and it's out of my hands now.'

Ross is unimpressed at this devil-may-care nonchalance, given much of the responsibility has now been placed in his hands. 'Must be nice for you, Martin. You just take it easy, why not?'

Martin smirks in agreement and raises the flask to his lips, only to find it's empty. Not a problem. He rummages inside his man bag and produces a sleek pewter hipflask. His back-up. Holding it aloft, he offers a toast to the heavens: 'Fuck 'em all. Fuck Teale. Fuck Eclipse and most of all, fuck BRITE.'

Salt and Ross are used to backers and sponsors losing their shit as curtain-up approaches and recognise a man on the edge. Salt tries to calm him. 'Listen, Martin. We've got this. Why don't you have a kip and get yourself right for tonight. It's all in hand.'

The head of marketing lets out a hysterical squeal. 'All in hand? Have you told Liam Gallagher's doctor that? Do you know what's going to happen when we announce…'

He gets no further as the impresario cuts him off. 'That's enough, Martin. That's not going to happen. Now, take my advice and get your head down. Lie low for a bit, and we'll see you later.'

Taking the hint, even in his confused and agitated state, Martin totters to his feet and almost falls down the steep gradient. They watch as he slowly descends to the floor of the arena, grabbing the end of each row for support.

'What a mess,' Ross says, almost sympathetically.

Salt is less charitable. 'A fucking wreck. He'd be doing us all a favour if he passed out for the next forty-eight hours.'

'I guess dealing with Teale and Eclipse would do anybody's head in.'

'Granted, but you've got to keep your eye on the prize, not wallow in self-pity and vodka.' Ross is about to remind him he's been drinking too, but Salt beats him to it. 'One or two medicinal bracers is one thing; losing your shit in the bottle like that is another.'

The two look out to sea from their vantage point until Ross breaks the silence. 'This rumour about Liam Gallagher having laryngitis – it is just that, isn't it? A rumour.'

Salt lets out a pained groan. 'Not you as well, Ross. How many times have we heard mad speculation like that? Punters in a panic because the singer's lost his voice, the guitarist has fallen out of a palm tree, the drummer has cut his hand making a ham sandwich.'

'Well, all of those things have happened in the past.'

Salt nods. 'Yeah, but not to us, Ross. Not to us.'

'So, you've spoken to Liam, and established there's no truth in it?'

The impresario wavers momentarily as he finds the right words. 'Yes, of course,' he says. 'Obviously, I've not spoken to Liam himself…' He breaks off to mime an imaginary phone call: *Liam? Hi. Salt here. Just checking. Yes. Your voice.*

What's that? Can you speak up a bit? 'There's nothing to worry about. It's a load of bollocks. Forget about it.'

'In that case, are you going to put out a statement reassuring everyone, to stop all the anxiety that's flying around?'

Salt ponders this for a moment, then shakes his head. 'Nah. A statement only gives it wings. We'd be giving the rumour credibility, not scotching it.'

Ross rolls his eyes. 'I'm not going to be here on Sunday night, then? You can at least promise me that?'

Salt grins. 'No way. I'll even bet you on it. Hundred quid?'

The head of production ignores the offer, but he's not finished with the questions. 'Say – what if – the gig had to be put back twenty-four hours or canned altogether. You're insured up to the hilt, right?'

Salt emits a high-pitched cackle. 'What do you take me for, Ross? Copper-bottomed, me.'

'And against the weather too?'

Salt spreads his arms to embrace the blue sky and warm sunshine. 'Weather? I don't think we need to worry about that, do you? Couldn't have planned it better myself. It's like Marbella here.'

'Well, even Marbella gets bad weather sometimes.'

'It's good of you to worry on my behalf, Ross. Now, if you really want something to fret about, why don't you get down there and persuade the bat people to lose that "teeming womb of royal kings" scene. That would be doing us all a favour.'

Salt watches as Ross makes the long descent to the arena, albeit far more steadily than Martin did, and lights another cigar. What was it Rudyard Kipling said? *If you can keep your head when all about you/Are losing theirs and blaming it on you, /If you can trust yourself when all men doubt you...* Well, he knows who to trust – yours truly, the man who's done it a thousand and one times. This is no time to buckle. Keep calm and carry on. After this weekend he can call it a day and fully enjoy the fruits of his long and lucrative career. He's earned it. Hasn't he mounted some of the biggest grossing tours of all time? Given millions of ticket buyers pleasure? It took talent to achieve that, dealing with narcissistic stars, bumptious managers, over-anxious underlings, technical hitches, fussy authorities, health and safety zealots, hoax calls, bomb scares and… you name it, he's been there. Granted, he's taken a few risks along the way, cut a few corners, but who doesn't in his position? It's all part of this wonderful, rewarding, who-dares-wins game. And nobody plays the game better than him. He feels the sun on his face and leans back to enjoy the sheer perfection of the afternoon. Yes, it's a good job someone is keeping it all together. Old Rudyard would approve.

In no hurry to be anywhere – leave them to it – he quietly draws on his cigar, savouring the full-bodied taste and scent of the smoke as he rolls it around his mouth. Serene in the moment, he idly picks up his mobile and automatically taps the weather app. He expects to see a solid bright yellow circle with eight radials, the same as he's seen a hundred times in the past week. Instead, what he sees causes him to choke and splutter. What else was it Rudyard said in that poem? *If you can meet with Triumph and Disaster/And treat those two imposters just the same.* He tosses the cigar aside and almost falls down the stairs in his rush to the bottom.

***

Amanda Teale has a crisis of her own to deal with, having just discovered she's left her outfit for tomorrow night at home. Landmark achievements such as winning her parliamentary seat and being promoted to cabinet office pale into insignificance when weighed against Amanda's proudest moment to date – being voted the best dressed MP in Westminster by Women on Top magazine. Amanda is only too aware of the importance of looking the part at the biggest music event these offshores have ever mounted; it's vital she transitions from sophisticated – and stylish – representative of the people to 'rock chick' for the occasion, especially as she has a personal photographer along to record her 'look'. The missing outfit isn't anything outrageous, of course – she has her position to think of – but *en pointe*: skinny jeans, three buckle platform boots, her 'classic' denim jacket (still fits her from its Glastonbury debut in 2010; oh, the joy when Kylie joined The Scissor Sisters on stage) and tasteful statement jewellery. But in the rush, she's forgotten to pick up the bag from the spare bedroom. She can't possibly wear the same outfit twice, not least because tonight's red, white and blue creation has been assembled to echo Cool Britannia, not Mad Ferrit. She gives this predicament all of five minutes before coming up with a solution. All she has to do now is let Eclipse in on the change of plan.

The eco-warrior is wary as she's summoned to meet the minister at short notice. What now? She guesses it won't be good news, which is why she's surprised to be met with the sort of smile Amanda reserves for attendees at her constituency surgeries (whatever the size of the pothole or the irregularity of the bin collection, the MP understands, empathises, and will leave no stone unturned as she tells her aide to make a note). Even more worryingly, Amanda goes straight for the personal touch. 'Ah, Charlotte. Thank goodness you're here.'

Eclipse shudders. Charlotte is not a name she recognises. It's an identity, a shackle redolent of old-school thinking and societal brainwashing, that she has proudly cast off. Is Amanda playing some type of mind game here, or simply being stupid?

'I don't use that name anymore,' she says.

Amanda (yes, she was just being stupid) pulls a face. 'Sorry. My bad.' Not the start she'd been planning. 'Look, Eclipse, we have a major problem, and I'm going to have to seek your indulgence somewhat.' Eclipse is puzzled. It's not in her gift to allow the minister anything, and it's certainly not her experience to be consulted. She waits. 'Some halfwit in the department has failed to forward my red boxes. I'm sure you can imagine how serious that is.' Eclipse's shrug shouts *what's that got to do with me?* so Amanda ploughs on. 'I'm afraid the only way they'll be able to get them to me is by helicopter.'

Eclipse immediately understands why she is being soft-soaped. No. Her response is instant and unequivocal: 'Over my dead body.'

The smile slides from Amanda's face like a caterpillar slaloming down a wet lettuce leaf. 'I beg your pardon?'

Eclipse is defiant. First the generators, now this. 'No helicopters. Not even for Oasis. This is supposed to be a green event – just one exception will make a mockery of everything we are trying to achieve here.'

Amanda bristles. So much for trying to be nice. 'Are you suggesting that the interests of the nation are secondary to your – and let's call it out for what it is – environmental cosplay?'

Eclipse flinches in the face of such an insult but doesn't buckle. 'It's interesting you should call it that, Amanda. Very revealing. I personally think the state of the environment is of far more interest to the nation than what's in one of your red boxes. Sandwiches and your bedtime read probably.' Amanda is stung at the insinuation (if only the eco-warrior knew how snugly her rock chick attire fitted into one of those dispatch boxes). But the crusader isn't finished yet. 'Remind me again about your title, Amanda. Minister for Climate, Life, Ecology and Nature – CLEAN. Don't you think it's about time you lived up to it?'

Amanda's face and neck flush a deep red. Where is the respect for her office? Who does this nepo baby think she is talking to her in this way? Forget the real reason she needs a helicopter so badly, this is insubordination, pure and simple. No, it's worse than that – it's treason. 'Listen here, Char-lotte,' she hisses (no mistake this time), 'I don't need your permission for anything. And you'd do well to remember on who's say-so you've been allowed to run around pretending you're relevant. What would your father say if he could hear you now?'

The petty insult bounces off the eco-warrior. 'Ah – the patriarchy. I wondered when that would come up. Well, you just knock yourself out, Amanda. But I'm warning you, if any helicopter lands on Holm this weekend, you'll be the first to regret it.'

The minister can hardly believe her ears. This is what happens when you extend a kindness – it gets shoved back in your face by ingrates; zealots who think their views trump all others. 'Well, I'll tell you what I regret, young lady, is bringing you on board in the first place.' To compound sounding like a disappointed schoolmarm she adds a magisterial, 'You are dismissed.' The naughty child obliges without another word, angrily slamming the door on her way out.

Amanda slumps into a chair and tries to recover her composure. But it's no good. This is the thanks she gets for being progressive – however much she tries to make a difference there's always somebody ready to carp and complain. People might think being an MP, a minister, was its own reward – prestige and power and the rest. But the reality was somewhat different. Did people know how hard she had to fight to fund this weekend? No. Without her, nobody would be here at all – now, then, or ever. Would people appreciate how she had been forced to step in and sort out tonight's pageant to save it from ridicule? Of course not – the credit will go to others. How about the stress of having to deal with terrorist threats? That will never be made public. It was her failing really, and a curse, how she made everything appear so easy. If only they knew. As for that little shit, Eclipse – Miss Charlotte Cholmondeley if you please – welcome to the real world. She was only here as a bit of window dressing and because her father was a generous party donor. Amanda has received no such leg-up on her personal journey to this position of responsibility. Bloody hard work and sheer determination, that's what she's depended on, not wheels within wheels. The little upstart should know her place. No helicopters? We'll see about that. The world may well be burning, but if it does Amanda will be sporting her classic denim look as the flames lap, and no cut-price Cassandra is going to tell her otherwise.

Meanwhile, the maligned prophetess, destined never to be believed, is looking out to sea with vengeful intent in her eyes.

14

FADE IN-OUT

Rachel – Tim via Metuyu Messaging

Hi Tim. Hope you're being good for Dad. I'm sure you are.

Did you have toad-in-the-hole for tea? Remember to help with the washing up if you did (the kitchen is bound to be a mess). What takeaway have you decided on for tomorrow? Pizza or Chinese?

All smooth getting here. You'd love the little cubicles we're sleeping in – very snug! We're being looked after like royalty – the food and drink is very nice, and we've not had to spend any money – it's all included! Well, that's not true because I might have been down to the merchandise stalls to buy a certain someone something special... Guess who? The weather is incredible – is it the same at home? I don't think they could have picked a better weekend. It's strange being in the middle of the North Sea though – we're underneath thousands of wind turbines, but they're not turning while we're here for some reason. Plenty of seagulls too. I'm just waiting to get pooped on! (it's supposed to be lucky – did you know?). Me and Jus went for Reiki earlier – it's a mad Japanese massage. Don't think you'd have liked it, but it was very relaxing. We're getting ready to go to the big show they're putting on tonight. I think it's supposed to be like a West End musical or Abba Voyage. But all anyone can talk about is Oasis, Oasis, Oasis.

Oh. Did you hear the rumour? That Liam has a sore throat? People we've spoken to here – and they seem to know what they're talking about – reckon it's a load of rubbish, and a way of whipping up more interest. Can you imagine if they weren't on tomorrow night after all this? Maybe they'd have to get Blur at short notice? (ask your dad). Right – got to go. Having our tea in the VIP marquee – very posh – before the show thingy. Will send pics! Love you lots. XXX

Justine – CatsWhiskers via Metuyu Messaging:

Hi. Only me, checking to make sure everything is alright with Luna and Coco. Hope they're not missing me too much. I was going to set up one of those camera thingies so I could speak to them while I was away, but I was worried that might make them miss me even more (and vice versa). What do you think for next time? Do you know anybody else who has one?

Anyway, I know I've told you this, but just in case... Luna has the Felix with jelly (grey bowl) and Coco the Sheba with gravy (black bowl). Treats morning and night (make sure Luna doesn't steal Coco's) and change their water morning and evening. Oh – and could you pooper scoop the litter tray on each visit? I should have asked before. There are some sandwich bags you can use in the top drawer next to the oven. (I changed the litter yesterday morning so it should be OK until I get back unless... well, you decide!). I'll stop fussing now! It's the first time I've left my little ladies with a cat sitter so I'm sure you understand. Thank you. And give the girls a big hug from me. Justine.

Dave – Suzanne via WhatsApp:

Hope all is good back at home. Bit of a culture shock here this afternoon when the boat people invaded the island! We settlers had to withdraw to our compound to protect our supplies! Seriously, it's like Lord of The Flies or something. We had it all to ourselves yesterday, but it's rammed now. Shame. Luckily, our package has its own bars and restaurants to keep the hordes from the door. Survival of the fittest (and the richest).

The Supersonics (that's us) are an odd mixture. Plenty of professional looking types, but also a few who look like benefit claimants. I don't know how they can afford it – probably pulled a few Cash for Crash claims (so I can't really complain, can I?)! Not spotted any celebs yet – not real ones at any rate. You're better at knowing who's who, but I'd have thought this was THE event to be seen at. Maybe they're only coming in on Saturday? (Let me know if anybody big is reported though).

Me and the lads have been sensible (so far!). Pacing ourselves for tomorrow night. Don't want to come all this way and ruin it. The sleep pods are hilarious. They barely fit two midgets – I'm sure they're modelled on Strangeways prison cells, cos everything else is themed (like the pods – Bed Here Now. How naff). I'm sharing with JJ. (He's had the runs again, but you don't want to know that.) Ent and Stoggy are next door. I know you don't like them (much/at all) but they're on their best behaviour, joining in and adding to the fun. There's a daft rumour going round about Liam having laryngitis – have you picked up on that? People were panicking earlier, but I put their minds at rest. As if. I bet Oasis put that rumour out themselves to up the ante even more. Well, tell someone who's gullible. I'm used to people telling porkies and can spot it a mile off. Anyway, time for the cultural highpoint of the weekend soon – Cool Britannia – some mash-up of Trooping the Colour and The Brit Awards by the sound of it. At least if it's crap we can retreat to our VIP bar – it will be easier to get served when it's on.

I know it's a lads trip, but I think you'd have really enjoyed it if just you and me had made a weekend of it like I suggested. Now I feel guilty for coming as you've not lined up anything spesh while I'm away. I'll make it up to you! Back Sunday (allowing for Liam's tonsils). Missing you. X

JJ – Mum via WhatsApp:

Hi Mum. Just checking in! Weather is lovely and everybody is having a good time. Had a bit of a gippy tummy overnight – thank goodness for Imodium! Looking forward to Oasis. Call you when I'm back!

Ent – Her Indoors via WhatsApp:

Hi Doll. All good here. Had a few messages from that moaning old cow Mrs McCrum in Alty. Going on about 'a serious leak' or something. Can you message her and tell her I'll send one of the lads around first thing Monday? Ta. PS – if it is serious, tell her to turn the stopcock off.

Stoggy – Sifter – via WhatsApp:

Hiya mate. Saw you'd arrived. You up for a pint? Cheers. PS – is Liam really crook, or just messin?

Eclipse – action@campaignhq by direct message:

You reached out to me last week in my role of eco-warrior on Holm Island. Apologies for not having got back to you sooner. I take the aims of the Conserve Aquatic Reserves Partnership very seriously and would be happy to assist in any way I can.

Rachel – Matthew via Metuyu Messaging:

Only me. Don't forget Tim has cricket practice Sunday at 11. I washed his whites. I should be back at teatime to pick him up. Will let you know if it's going to be any later. R

Amanda Teale to Chief of Staff by encrypted email:

I am very concerned at the state of preparedness on Holm Island. Frankly, it's a mess, not helped by all the rumours in circulation about terrorist threats and even the state of the singer's tonsils. I'm beginning to wonder what we've let ourselves in for.

Everybody gives the impression of being relaxed and in control but then become evasive the second I challenge them on detail. This 'it will be alright on the night' attitude is not how I like to operate. I may be jumping the gun, but I want you to go through, line by line, our written agreement with BRITE and supply me with a one-page checklist of exactly what they are contracted to deliver. Please let me have this by first thing Sunday morning. I am not prepared to waste taxpayers' money on any areas they fall short on.

Luckily, with me being on the ground, we'll get through it, and it will be a triumph.

Why is it these days one must do everything oneself?

AT

PS: You had better tell the media team their weekends are cancelled – just in case we need to manage any unanticipated fallouts here.

***

Space is at such a premium on Holm Island that Bryan, Bob, and Cody have trouble finding a quiet spot to take stock of their operation. They eventually find a small clearing behind the main toilet block, oblivious to (or perhaps unimpressed by) the low water consumption vacuum conveniences now working overtime.

Bryan is keen to remind his accomplices of the importance of maintaining a low profile now they've arrived. 'We need to keep our heads down,' he stresses. 'That TV ambush at the bottom of the gangplank could have been very dodgy but I think we got away with it.'

Cody isn't so sure. 'Don't you think you drew more suspicion to us by covering your face and running away like that? Act normal, you said.'

Bryan is stung by the idea he's not leading from the front. 'I was taken by surprise. Lots of people are shy of cameras – it's nothing out of the ordinary. Nobody will have thought anything about it.'

'Well, what about you kicking off over the prices at that Chinky?' Bob says. 'That wasn't exactly lying low, was it?'

Bryan remains on the defensive. 'I was acting the part of a concerned consumer. It would have been more conspicuous to just cough up at those prices. Other people there agreed with me.' Bob and Cody remain unconvinced. 'Look. Fit in is all I'm saying. Can we move on? Run through tonight? That's far more important.'

They re-focus. 'Reconnaissance,' Bob submits.

'Surveillance,' Cody affirms.

Bryan nods. 'Correct. We split up and check out the backstage area for access. Half hour intervals, one at a time, as soon as the theatrical thingy starts. Anything that looks like a way in, make a mental note. If you can slip in, go for it, and explore further. No mobiles – if anyone gets collared just say you're supposed to be meeting a mate who's got a spare Supersonic pass, and you're lost.'

'Can I go first?' asks Bob.

'No,' Bryan counters. 'I'm going first, then you, then Cody. Why do you want to change what we've agreed?'

'I'd quite like to see the show, that's all. It sounds interesting.'

Bryan is dismissive. 'You're here for business, mate, not on your holidays.'

Cody, at least, is more considerate. 'You can swap with me if you want, Bob. Then you'll get the first hour. You might even get the end as well.'

Bryan puts his foot down. 'Bollocks to that. This is a military operation, and you'll follow orders.'

He can read them like a book. Now they're on the island and it's suddenly real, they're bricking it. He can smell their edginess: how the plans outlined to them by their intrepid leader suddenly don't seem as easy to achieve as they did in the pub back home; that it's beyond them to disrupt the concert and get their message across; what if Bryan's plan is doomed to failure from the off?

He softens his tone. 'Do you think, lads, we might be better off standing down and simply watching the gig?'

Bob is the first to break. 'I reckon you're right. We could be being over-ambitious here – sometimes a tactical retreat is a sensible option.'

Cody contemplates this before adding. 'Maybe we don't have to go all the way and *actually* invade the stage. We can still post our video and alert the world.'

Bryan gives the impression of carefully considering these comments before scolding them. 'Real warriors you two are,' he sneers. 'That's your commitment to the cause, is it? "Oh, let's forget about it and enjoy the show." Bloody pussies.'

Suitably chastised, Bob and Cody are about to reassert their undying opposition to the great climate hoax when Bryan's phone buzzes. They welcome the break as he reads the message he's received.

'Well, well, well,' he smiles. 'A tug on the line.' He holds the phone in front of them. 'That, gentlemen, is the power of black ops at work.' They look suitably impressed. 'We have made contact with the other side, but the other side doesn't yet know it.'

They wait. The 'other side' is a sizeable category – he needs to narrow it down a bit. Bryan studies the message again, weighing each character as if he's deciphering the Rosetta Stone. His brows furrow as he digests the words. Finally, he delivers his assessment: 'This could be the game changer we've been looking for.'

15

(GET OFF YOUR) HIGH HORSE LADY

Even though Cool Britannia still has an hour to run, the Supersonic bar is already filling up with punters who've seen enough. Unsurprisingly, the Mancs are in that number.

'Fuck me with a knotted prop,' Ent laments. 'What a load of crap that was.'

JJ, who had mildly objected when it was suggested they leave early, isn't quite so quick to condemn. 'I can see what they were trying to achieve, but it possibly fell a little short in the execution.'

Ent isn't having that. 'The only execution needed there is for whoever came up with that rubbish in the first place. We're at a festival, right? Why didn't they just put a couple of bands on instead? Christ, I'd have preferred two hours of Simply Red over that.'

'No, you wouldn't,' Dave reminds him. 'You once said Mick Hucknall should be locked in a hospitality box at Old Trafford with "Holding Back the Years" blasted out on repeat until he apologised for his crimes against music.'

Ent considers this for a second. 'Exactly my point.'

Dave realises they're one light. 'Where's Stoggy? Don't tell me he's waiting until the end?'

'You're joking. He bunked off after five minutes in there,' Ent informs him. 'Good judge if you ask me. He won't be far.'

JJ is keen to return to their critical forum. 'What did you think of it, Dave? Really.'

What did Dave think of it? He'd not really been concentrating if the truth be told, his thoughts having been elsewhere, but he'd at least read the programme notes. 'A valiant effort. I liked the patriotism,' he admits. 'I think, as a nation, we should fly the flag more often.'

Ent throws up a mock salute. 'Hark at Winston Churchill. If you liked it so much, why aren't you still in there? Oh – I know. Hoping to bump into a certain someone by any chance?'

Dave pretends not to have heard the accusation, but as if on cue, the 'certain someone', plus companion, chooses this moment to enter the marquee. Ent can hardly contain his glee as he waves Rachel and Justine over.

There's nothing like a festival for proving there's no such thing as a stranger, only a friend you haven't met yet. Their initial resistance eroded via over-exposure (and the absence of alternatives) the two women fall in without protest.

'No surprise to find you in here,' Rachel says as they take a seat.

'One of those going begging?' Justine asks, pointing at the drinks on the table.

Dave eagerly pushes two beers in their direction. 'Has it finished? What did you think?'

The pair giggle like schoolgirls and seem unable to answer this question at all, suggesting these aren't the first two drinks they've seen all night.

It's Rachel who finally stops snickering long enough to reply. 'They're still at it. I'm not sure hiring Nigel Farage to direct was such a good idea. It was all a bit too red, white and blue for my liking.'

Dave considers this. 'Interesting,' he says. 'We were just commenting on the jingoistic thrust of the show.'

Justine chips in. 'I'm a bit upset they didn't have a maypole, though. It was the only thing missing. Have you ever done it?' She stands up and unsteadily steps to the right – *one, two, one, two* – before knocking into a chair. JJ, thankfully, is on hand to catch her.

Ent beams – this is so much better than Cool Britannia.

'You left before us,' Rachel observes, 'so on the scale of things, that makes us more patriotic than you.'

Dave is conflicted. 'Oh, it wasn't that,' he says. 'We just wanted to bag a good spot for the Hacienda night later on.'

'Hassy-what?' Justine says. 'Is that like a Mexican barbecue?'

Dave, JJ and Ent are taken aback. Is she pulling their legs? Her confused expression suggests not. Rachel, however, has heard of it. 'It's a club, isn't it?' she says uncertainly. They stare at her.

'Yes and no,' JJ states. 'It was a club, but a bit more than a place of entertainment, *per se*. In possession of more cultural capital than bricks and mortar alone.'

Dave agrees. 'It's an iconic Manchester institution. Tony Wilson's greatest achievement.'

'Who's Tony Wilson?' the women query in unison.

Ent can't take any more of this. He half-closes his eyes and reels off a quick recap: 'The Hacienda is the most famous nightclub in the world. Opened by TV presenter and visionary, Tony Wilson, and associates in 1982. Synonymous with Factory Records, New Order, “Blue Monday”, performances by The Smiths and, I hate to say it, Madonna. The birthplace of acid house. Notorious for its drug-culture and gangsters, and celebrated for its iconic design and rave nights, it finally closed in 1997 due to constant persecution by the authorities and, it must be said, the owners’ appalling business sense. Central to the renaissance of post-industrial Manchester, for which it has never received due credit.’

Dave and JJ are impressed at their mate’s mastery of the topic. Justine has another take. ‘Did you just look that up on Wikipedia?’

Rachel squirms on Ent’s behalf. ‘Fascinating. You’re very knowledgeable.’

Justine does some mental arithmetic. ‘I wasn’t even born when that place opened,’ she says. ‘Did any of you ever go? You must have been in short pants if you did.’

Ent is the first to admit that this opportunity had, in fact, eluded them. ‘We would have done, but it closed at the wrong time. It doesn’t make it any less significant though, does it? We never went to the Hanging Gardens of Babylon either.’

‘Is that another club?’ Justine teases, before Rachel slaps her playfully on the hand to stop.

JJ moves to spare Ent’s feelings. ‘It really does have a very special place in the heart of Mancunians of a certain age, Justine. And tonight is a celebration of that, in the music. You’ll see. You’re going to love it, I promise you.’

Dave concurs. ‘Honestly, forget Cool Britannia, this is what’s going to get you in the mood for tomorrow night.’

‘Well, after all that, we’ll have to go now, won’t we Rach?’

Ent solemnly raises his glass. 'The Hacienda must be re-built,' he recites.

His two friends echo the toast. 'The Hacienda must be re-built.'

'Well, when it is, give us a shout,' Jus giggles.

Dave flips the record. 'Now, who's up for another drink?'

Four hands shoot up into the air. That would be all of them then.

***

A braided velvet rope strung across a series of brass stanchions marks the VVIP section of the Supersonic marquee. As in many clubs with a designated area for those of a stellar status, the space is tiny and offers a poor view of the dancefloor. Despite that, nobody gaining entry would willingly forgo the prestige that access bestows. In the centre is a large circular table that bears a sign reading 'Reserved for Ms Amanda Teale' – VVVIP territory no less. Salt, Ross, Martin and Eclipse are already in position and deep in two separate conversations.

Salt, concern etched on his face, is showing Ross something on his phone screen. 'Surely that can't be right?'

The indefatigable head of production glances at the image of a grey cloud with a white bolt emerging from it and shrugs. 'I wondered when you'd discover that, after what you were saying earlier. Yeah, I know. We've just got to hope it misses us.'

'But nobody predicted this. The weather is amazing, has been amazing – how can it just change like that?'

'It's weather. That's what it does.'

'But the forecasts, the meteorologists, all said this was the week, this was the bloody day.'

'Honestly, Salt, what's got into you? We've handled bad weather before and will again if we have to. We're prepared.'

'We've handled rain, Ross. Monsoons even. Gales, hail, even snow, but the only thing that can really knock us out is a storm. Lightning. A threat to life.' He points at the weather icon again. 'Like this bloody thing.'

Ross, the war-torn veteran of many a festival battlefield, is almost enjoying the impresario's panic. 'Look, you can't judge what the weather will be like from a phone. I've got the hour-by-hour shipping forecast, and I reckon we'll be done and dusted by the time it hits. If it hits.'

Salt snatches at these crumbs. 'You really think so? It will miss us?'

'We'll know better in the morning, but the thing is, we'll get through the show if it's just rain and wind. Then it's a site safety issue. Won't be much fun for the punters or the band, but we carry on. As always.'

Salt distractedly pulls a cigar from his pocket before realising he's not allowed to smoke in here. He stuffs it away again. 'Yeah. OK, Ross. We carry on. It will miss us. Good, good.'

Ross smiles. He's never seen Salt as shaken as this. Admittedly, it's a big event, but the promoter has been this way many times before. Maybe he's so nervous because it's his swansong? Who knows? He gives him one final word of encouragement. 'And if the worst really came to the worst, you've still got the insurance policy of the extra day to fall back on.'

Salt grimaces and reaches for his cigar again. Please, God, let it be tomorrow.

Alongside them, there is a conversation of a completely different nature taking place. Martin – barely bothering to disguise his over-relaxed state – and Eclipse have found a common cause around which to unite: Cool Britannia. Tears are rolling down their cheeks as they re-run their highlights.

'Did you see her face when the cannons wouldn't fire?' Eclipse squeals.

'Or when the dancers bumped into each other?'

'And what about the crowd booing her when she appeared on the screen?'

'Well, the half that hadn't left by then.'

'And what was she wearing? A Union Jack maxi dress by the looks of it – she looked like a hot air balloon.'

'All she was missing was a trident. What a fuck-up. An utter debacle.'

It feels good to bitch, until Eclipse finally raises a serious point. 'She's going to blame you for it, Martin, you know that?'

The Genie of What If is unconcerned. 'Of course she is, but I couldn't give a toss. Screw her. And screw BRITE.'

Eclipse laughs gleefully. 'I'll drink to that,' she says.

She much prefers this version of Martin, sozzled as he is. It's obvious he has been under an enormous strain in delivering an event of this nature, made one hundred times harder by having to deal with the interfering, patronising, up-her-own-arse politician that is Amanda Teale. Martin has made Eclipse's life difficult at times, sure, but she recognises just how many plates he's had to keep spinning, the myriad demands placed on him from different quarters. It's no wonder (the worst kept secret on the island) he's a raving pisspot as a result. Dealing with all that would turn anybody to drink. She's been used and abused too. Salt called her endeavours 'greenwashing guff' while the minister accused her of environmental cosplay. That's all her role was to them, a gaily coloured sticking plaster over a particularly nasty sore.

Martin dutifully tops up her glass. 'So, you've had enough of 'em too?'

Where does she start? Never mind Salt and Amanda Teale, just look at the state of the crowd: plastic people doing what plastic does – choking the planet. 'You know what gets me, Martin? This is going to be a big bloody success. Everything is set up, the audience is in place, and all anyone will talk about for years afterwards is the day Oasis played Holm Island.'

Matin doesn't agree entirely: 'They might not forget how bad Cool Britannia was, though.'

Eclipse sighs. 'They will, though. And all the work we did to make it happen. But most of all they'll forget the environmental messages behind why this event was staged here in the first place. Nobody will give a toss. It makes my blood boil.'

'Well, sod it. We've done our bit now, and I reckon I'm going to be out on my ear by Monday, so we may as well enjoy the party.'

They stand on the brink of history – it's up to others to deliver now. Does it feel good to have played their parts, to have contributed so much to the impending triumph? The kindred spirits think not.

'I've a toast,' Eclipse announces, raising her glass. 'Fuck Amanda Teale.'

Martin seconds that, then adds one of his own. 'And fuck Oasis too.'

They chortle conspiratorially. *Yeah, fuck 'em all.*

This cosy *tete-a-tete* is suddenly interrupted by the mistress of wind herself, the minister for CLEAN, blowing in like a giant red, white and blue carrier bag flapping in the breeze. 'I'm glad some people are having fun,' she snipes, rather suggesting she isn't.

Salt jumps to his feet. 'Amanda,' he exclaims. 'Can I just say, Cool Britannia – one word: Jubilant.'

Amanda scowls. She manages a terse 'thank you' in reply.

Eclipse is not to be left out. 'Exuberant,' she gushes, adding a warm smile for effect.

Martin theatrically mimes a chef's kiss to signal his awe at what he has just witnessed. It's as if Amanda has just won the final of Dancing on Ice and the judges are trying to outdo each other.

However, Amanda isn't here to listen to all this hollow praise. She calls the table to order. 'Yes, well, we've got more important matters to attend to at this juncture. In three words: Liam, weather, security.' That kills the Hacienda party vibe, in their corner of the tent at least.

Ross decides this is a good time to exit – leave Salt to handle things, which he manfully attempts. 'I can address the first two points, Amanda. As far as Liam is concerned – no problem. Just a rumour. All present and correct for tomorrow. The weather – yes, it looks like there could be a *bit* of a mini-squall heading our way, but nothing that would interfere with our plans.'

Martin and Eclipse exchange glances. He's almost plausible. Should they be worried?

Amanda isn't letting him get away so easily though. 'You've checked all of this, personally? And you can absolutely guarantee I have nothing to worry about?'

Salt sweeps his hand to his heart and solemnly declares, 'On my dear, dead mother's grave. We will be sitting here this time tomorrow celebrating a new high-water mark in the field of live entertainment.' That small matter dealt with, he deflects. 'What was it you wanted to say about security, Amanda?'

She is in two minds whether to get him to sign his promises in blood, but in a rare example of magnanimity, moves on. 'Very well. No developments since yesterday, which is good news. The usual cranks, it appears, but nothing to raise undue concerns. One new name has popped up, however, a group calling themselves the Conserve Aquatic Reserves Partnership. I've instructed further checks on them so they can be eliminated.'

Eclipse and Martin shift in their seats, the sound of a distant bell tinkling in their ears.

'See, I told you,' Salt scoffs, 'these threats always turn out to be hoaxes.'

Amanda tuts aloud at such casual bravado – all very well for him to say, but if she left things to chance what state would the country be in? 'As a precaution, I have deployed a team of undercover SAS to mingle with front of house and backstage security. Nobody, but nobody, is getting anything into the arena or anywhere near that stage tomorrow night.'

16

FUCKING IN THE BUSHES

Ent finds Stoggy by the pallets again, smoking a giant joint with a guy wearing a Kangol bucket hat. Ent has always taken his friend's claims about who he knows with a pinch of salt, but there's no doubt who his new acquaintance is: 'Sifter,' he exclaims, before remembering himself and acting like it's no biggie. 'Any of that going spare?'

Stoggy gives Ent an out of character hug and introduces him to the blogger. 'The Ent. The only bloke around here worth knowing.' The two of them are clearly well on in their evening's enjoyment, and so wired it's obvious the ganja is merely to take the edge off things for the moment.

Ent jerks his thumb towards the marquee. 'Thought we'd lost you. Didn't know you were meeting Sifter.'

'Yeah – hooked up earlier,' comes the wasted reply, as if this engagement had been advertised in the Manchester Evening News for weeks.

'Had to get out of there and leave the lovebirds to it.'

Neither Stoggy nor Sifter seem to hear or compute this.

Ent indicates the marquee again. 'Hacienda night. Music should be better than yesterday at least.'

The mention of the legendary club dislodges a book deep inside the library of Sifter's brain and it falls to the floor with a thud: 'Oasis, The Hacienda, fifth of September 1994.'

Ent is confused. 'But Oasis never played The Hacienda,' he objects, forgetting in whose erudite presence he finds himself.

He's soon corrected. 'Yeah, they did. Definitely Maybe launch. Seven pounds a ticket. Started with "Columbia", finished with "Walrus".'

Stoggy disguises his ignorance of this fact with a dismissive, 'You div,' in his friend's direction.

Ent, recalling Justine's comment about short pants, tries to recover his position with an enthusiastic, 'Were you there?'

Sifter allows a long plume of smoke to pass through his pursed lips before answering. 'What do you think?' he counters, to general gasps of awe and wonder. (In fact, on the night in question his mother had locked him in his bedroom to punish him for being expelled from school. He'd never forgiven her, and she'd been dead for twenty years). Reputation intact, he has a suggestion. 'C'mon. Let's check out the action.'

The New Fast Automatic Daffodils are playing over the PA as they enter the marquee – not that they recognise the band or the track. For all they've heard about the famous Hacienda, they have little time for the sort of rhythmic, hypnotic and repetitive dance vibe that made the club's name, their personal tastes being firmly rooted in anything with a prominent guitar riff, volume, and a 1-2-3-4 intro. 'Sounds like they've hired Dave Haslam for the night,' Sifter observes, never lost for an opportunity to impress.

Ent beckons them to the corner of the marquee, as far away as possible from Dave and JJ, only to be stopped at a flimsy rope barrier by a gorilla in a suit. 'VIP section only,' he grunts.

'We are VIPs,' Ent protests. Pointing at Sifter, he adds, 'Don't you know who this is?'

It cuts little ice. 'You need a special pass to come in here. I'm going to have to ask you to leave.'

A time-honoured stand-off unfolds, repeated at club nights up and down the land for decades, as the trio strive to convince the bouncer they're legitimate, sober, and know the owner. However, before the bouncer loses patience and gives them a last chance to leave in one piece, their entreaties are interrupted by the arrival of a guest festooned in a huge Union Jack, a one-woman Jubilee float. The bouncer jumps to attention, shoves the three scallies out of the way, and allows her to pass with a dip of the head and a respectful 'Minister'. The withering look she casts upon the three miscreants as she sails by would deforest an entire county faster than a gang of illegal Amazon loggers.

Her disdain for them does not go unnoticed. 'Stuck-up bitch,' Ent shouts after her.

She halts, hesitates for a moment, then has a quick word with her escort. Seconds later the three Mancs are ejected from the marquee.

***

Dave and JJ are so engrossed in conversation with Rachel and Justine they don't notice the commotion taking place at the far end of the marquee. The music – whoever it is at the turntables – is currently circling in a seductive holding pattern, the deep bass sound from the subwoofers chipping away inhibitions like Michelangelo freeing David from a block of marble. Many of the Supersonics are now on the dancefloor, swaying awkwardly, boats bobbing on the current.

Music, alcohol and chitchat dull the new acquaintances' senses as the night moves on. Have the four of them been there minutes, or hours? It doesn't matter. When JJ says he'll walk Justine back, Dave and Rachel hardly look up. They're not planning on going anywhere.

Alone now, Dave circles back to the previous evening. 'Do you think you'll go back to your husband?' he asks suddenly. Now there's a fork in the road, where he's careered down Serious Shit Street instead of staying on Harmless Avenue. Only seconds earlier she'd been telling him about her favourite Instagram accounts (cat_as_trophic and dog-tan-ion), while he'd been explaining the legal definition of a pothole (generally only repaired if the depth exceeds 40mm).

She freezes. As she suspected, she'd clearly let on more than she thought while under the influence last night. How much *had* she told him? He'd said something about his situation too – how far had the disclosures gone? Obviously further than she thought. Now he's picking up the thread again, does she try to dodge this direct inquiry? Is she resentful of such an intrusion into her personal affairs? No. She blindly plunges down the lane after him. 'Now there's a question.' Tears well and her voice cracks. 'It's been so difficult. I don't know whether I'm coming or going.'

The crowd, music and marquee fade into the background. 'I wish I had your courage,' Dave says softly.

'You mean…'

He nods. 'Me and the wife have been leading separate lives for years. And I don't know what to do about it. Am I a coward?'

Despite being stoned last night, she had remembered correctly – he *had* mentioned difficulties in his marriage. But was it her position to probe, to poke at a raw wound? She opts for the straight jab. 'In what way?'

Dave doesn't hold back. Out pours the self-pity and the resentment, measured against his sense of duty and responsibility, contrasted with his belief there might be a brighter future if he could only find the balls to act. *Could he/should he?*

Their exchange for the next quarter of an hour follows a well-established inebriated pattern, where each is trying so hard to unpack and articulate their inner thoughts neither really listens to the other.

Fortunately, the intensity of their collective angst is relieved as the tempo of the music takes a sudden upturn, the familiar strains of "Love Will Tear Us Apart" signalling that Hacienda Night is about to step on it and take off. Dave snaps to attention: 'I love this one,' he declares. 'Fancy a dance?'

Rachel hasn't danced in years. She'd prefer not to. She's drunk. It might send the wrong signal to Dave. Can she even remember how to dance? 'Go on, then,' she says.

They join the rush to the dance floor. Dave, although he's certainly not alone in the marquee in this, is channelling a sixth form disco vibe in a bid to impress. Rachel, demurely bopping from one foot to the other, takes in the sight of his puppet on a string impression, too fast for the music, and lets out a loud laugh. Does he mean it, or is he doing it to amuse her? It's funny either way, and it reminds her to put a bit more effort into her own moves.

As the song fades – who knew three and half minutes could last so long? – she turns and heads back to the table, Dave trailing in her wake like a faithful sheepdog. He looks unsure as to the situation. 'Worn out already?' he ventures.

She, too, is uncertain. Drinking and dancing past midnight with a man she's just met. Such abandon. But why not? She's not breaking the law. She's allowed a bit of fun – it's all very innocent after all – and that was fun. But it's late. She's had too much to drink. She can't abandon Justine two nights running. 'I'd think I'd better head back,' is her reply.

Outside the marquee, their route takes them past the pallets where they'd smoked dope the night before. It's deserted. Dave tentatively reaches for her hand – she's not sure if the contact is intentional or accidental at first, until he softly pulls her to a halt. *Oh, heck.* They gaze at each other under the moonlight. He's not going to kiss her, is he? Now she's the teenager again, an unexpected shudder of excitement passing over her body. He leans in, and she doesn't resist. Tongues! Totally unexpected – what's the etiquette on that? She doesn't know. But it's not unpleasant, just… she's not sure … like it's happening to somebody else. Not that she's resisting, which Dave takes as a cue to slide his hand around her waist like an anaconda locking on to a capybara. She should be alarmed, but instead, finds herself curious as to where this might lead next. She doesn't have long to find out, as Dave adjusts his stance to place his leg in between hers, as if he's about to throw her to the canvas in a surprise wrestling move. His entire body is almost fused to hers now, and Rachel breaks off the soggy snogging to giggle at the implausibility of the situation. Dave laughs too, but then comes back for more. It's then she hears it – a familiar jingle jangle emanating from inside the marquee. Muffled, yet distinctive, and instantly recognisable in its twelve-string glory: "Stop Me If You Think You've Heard This One Before". Matthew had once gone to an eighties party dressed as Morrissey, complete with hearing aid, sticking plaster on his forehead, and a bunch of gladioli tucked into the back of his jeans. He'd learned every word of this song and hadn't left off singing it all night. She pulls away from Dave. No. She must go.

No words are exchanged on the short walk back. A perplexed Dave trails one pace behind her trying to work out if he's misread the signals, overstepped the mark. Arriving at her pod, she turns to bid him a subdued goodnight. She throws the door open as a sign she's not hanging around, only for them to be met with an alarming and unexpected sight: Justine on all fours, with JJ pumping vigorously away from behind. In the background, the strains of "Ever Fallen in Love (With Someone You Shouldn't've)" can be heard over the stunned silence.

***

Back inside the marquee, the mood has lightened in the VVIP enclosure. Considering they have such a big day ahead of them, the team might be expected to be taking it easy tonight, but no – the drinks keep on arriving. Martin has given up any pretence and is lining up the double vodkas. They're knocking it back like soldiers about to go into combat (it won't help them perform any better, but at least they'll be less concerned about possible outcomes). The only abstainer is the minister, whose second Kombucha sits untouched on the table. Surprisingly, she doesn't appear peeved at the escalating revelry. Has she, satisfied all operational matters are in hand, decided to kick back and relax? It's not something she's known for, but here she is, lost in a world of her own, as if enjoying some form of introspective meditation exercise. Maybe this is a coping technique they teach them down in Westminster. In any event, the others are happy to leave her to it.

As the alcohol intake mounts, so too does Martin and Eclipse's *esprit de corps*. When Salt slips out for a smoke, Martin checks to see if Amanda is still occupied with her thoughts before launching into a low-pitched whinge about her earlier briefing. 'The SAS? I mean, the frigging SAS? At a concert? It's the final nail in the coffin of live music.'

Eclipse largely agrees. 'I get we need security, but calling in the army? It's sounds like East Germany before the wall fell.'

'I know. And they only had the Leipzig Industrial Union Oompah Band to protect there.'

'You'd have needed the army to make people go to that.'

'I think that was the general idea.'

'You never know. Oasis might appreciate some military protection.'

Martin shakes his head. 'I don't think so. They once made the Ministry of Defence withdraw two army recruitment ads that used "Wonderwall" and "Hello". Silly buggers never asked permission and had to junk the campaign at great cost to the public purse.'

'So, we can safely assume the Gallagher brothers won't be receiving knighthoods any day soon?'

'Like they'd care. All they want from the government is a hundred mill. Nice work if you can get it.'

They both look to the principal underwriter of the Gallaghers' windfall. Curiously, she seems to be dozing, tired out no doubt by the weight of responsibility in delivering for the people.

They return to their whispered conversation. 'Do you really think there's a credible threat tomorrow?' Eclipse asks.

Martin scoffs. 'What? From those watery whatever-they're-called Johnnies? You must be joking. It's probably a sixteen-year-old kid with a VPN and an overactive imagination.'

Eclipse is intrigued. 'Do you think so? What are they supposed to be objecting to anyway?'

'Oh, you'd be surprised. The impact of offshore wind islands on ecosystems, marine life habitats, fishing stocks and organisms for a start. Come on,' he reasons, 'it's not like something like Holm Island is thrown up without taking all of that into consideration.'

Eclipse has been so focused on low water consumption vacuum toilets and helicopter bans she's not really thought about the plight of what lies beneath the waves. It strikes her – not for the first time lately – that artificial energy islands might not be as green as has been made out. 'You seem well up on the whelks,' she quips.

He leans in. 'I didn't want to say anything earlier, but I had a message from those aquatic *whatchamacallits* a few weeks back. Save the fish or something. Binned it with the rest,' he grins, before gesturing to the waiter to recharge their glasses.

Eclipse's eyes widen at the intel.

Martin expands on this theme. 'The thing is, what could a protester do, even if they wanted to? I mean, look at it: airport level security for everyone on entry to the island and the arena; a no-fly zone; a full sniffer dog sweep of the island earlier this week; a security cordon and now the bloody SAS. Surely the first rule of terrorism – activism – is to pick an easy target, not go after an impossible one.'

Like 9/11? Eclipse thinks. But she's curious. 'A protestor doesn't always need to shoot for the moon. There have been some very simple and effective stunts in the past that have drawn attention to causes.'

Martin is sceptical. 'What, like a stage invasion? I'm telling you now, no one is getting on that stage tomorrow who shouldn't be there. Never mind what the Gallaghers would do to them – it's just not going to happen.'

It's remarkable to Eclipse how, despite the weight of vodka he's consumed, BRITE's marketing guru is still managing to sound relatively coherent. Must be all the practice. 'Well, I'm glad to hear that.'

He nods. 'Yeah. There's only one weak spot in the entire set-up that I can see. And that's…' he shakes his head '… nah, unlikely.'

She pulls her chair closer. 'Really? Now you're just teasing.'

Five minutes later, their cosy chat is interrupted as a shrill, echoing vocal rings out over the sound system. *Higher,* the hellcat supplicant demands, before giving way to the steady thud, thud, thud of a distorted bass drum. A chorus of Gregorian monks join the fray, appearing to call the faithful heavenwards. Amanda jerks upright as if she's been plugged into the mains. The track builds, snarling and menacing in its intensity, demanding dancefloor action, and that's exactly what Amanda now proceeds to give it, grabbing a stunned Martin by the hand on the way. It would certainly shock her constituents to see her like this, euphorically weaving and swaying to the beat like a swing voter with a short memory. Martin, scarcely believing what he's witnessing, gamely throws himself into it, mirroring her actions, laughing aloud, delighted to have this ringside view as Shaun William Ryder administers a good spanking. Eclipse watches on in astonishment (or is it horror?) as the minister presents her white paper, calling for a third summer of love, to the house. "Hallelujah" (the club mix), indeed. After six minutes – which seems like six hours – of this, Amanda bearhugs Martin and Eclipse, says she loves them, and dashes from the marquee into the night. The two stand open-mouthed in amazement. *What the absolute fuck was that?*

17

A QUICK PEEP

As the Oasis faithful on land and at sea wearily settle down for the night – one more sleep – the hush of the early morning hours is disturbed by the crackle of walkie talkies: the minister has gone missing. Protection Command is incandescent with anger at the poor police officer who failed to see her leaving the marquee – 'she must have slipped out of another exit' not cutting much ice as an excuse within the highly-trained unit. All the waiting staff at the VVIP Suite can offer is *she was there one minute and gone the next.* Not very helpful.

Salt and Ross are awakened from their slumbers, informed, and escorted to the green room but there is no response from either Martin or Eclipse – could they be with her? The impresario is less than impressed at this turn of events. 'Christ, she can't just disappear – you can check the whole island in half an hour.'

Ross shakes his head in dismay. As if he didn't already have enough on his plate. 'She won't be far. Can I go back to bed now? I do have rather a busy day tomorrow.'

The head of security, perhaps worrying he may not have that title for much longer, is in no mood to play this down.

'Nobody is going to bed until the minister is located. Do I need to remind you how serious this is?'

Ross groans. That bloody woman is the cause of so much trouble. 'Is she "missing" missing,' he asks, 'or just not answering your calls?'

Salt takes this up. 'Her phone battery might be dead. Or she might have gone for a moonlit stroll, not knowing you're looking for her. Or maybe she's taken a sleeping pill and hasn't heard you knocking.'

These suggestions are rejected out of hand by Mr Crewcut. 'The minister knows better than that – she would never go incommunicado without notifying us. We must work on the basis that this is a serious breach.'

Salt doesn't like the sound of that. 'When you say serious breach, what exactly are you getting at?'

The (current) head of security doesn't need to resort to the training manual for an answer. 'It means that we will have to close down the entire site, evacuate all civilians, and conduct an inch-by-inch sweep of the island.'

Ross frowns. 'You mean after the performance?'

Crewcut looks at him as if he's mad. 'Tonight? No. We couldn't allow that. We need to act now. This morning.'

Salt is horrified. 'What? Cancel the gig, send ten thousand pissed-off punters home without seeing Oasis, and disappoint millions worldwide, just because Teale forgot her phone charger? There's no fucking way…'

Security is unmoved and somewhat dismissive of their protestations. 'If the minister is in danger, that takes precedence over a mere concert. Surely, you understand that?'

Apparently not. 'But you don't know she's in danger,' reasons Ross. 'You're only guessing.'

Salt – momentarily stunned at the description *a mere concert* – decides it's time to be assertive. 'You are not cancelling this event. Whatever is or isn't happening. Do you read me?'

No. He isn't being read. 'Please don't patronise me, Mr Salt. I have full authority here and I will do what needs to be done.'

'Well, go out and find her is my advice, and then we can all forget about cancelling anything.'

Ross shakes his head at Salt. *You're just antagonising him.* 'C'mon, Salt. Let's go find Martin and Eclipse. I bet you she's with them somehow.'

Crewcut hasn't finished yet though. 'This is very likely a terrorist incident, most likely an abduction. No ransom note or demands yet, but that is the basis we're working on.'

Salt's reaction to this unwelcome news is uncharacteristic. He slumps to his knees, grabs his head with both hands, and screams *no, no, no,* like a hysterical toddler denied an ice cream.

Ross has never seen the impresario lose it like this and gently eases him back to his feet. He has one last question before leading him away. 'What terrorist group, exactly?'

This is classified information, obviously, but Crewcut shares it anyway. 'All the indications point to an outfit called the Conserve Aquatic Reserves Partnership.'

***

The reason nobody can find Martin and Eclipse is because they've gone underground, quite literally, to the processing plant deep within the heart of the island. The eco-warrior has never been down here, and Martin has kindly offered to act as unofficial guide. Is this sensible, permitted or safe? No, but vodka does have a habit of rendering those three adjectives redundant. There is a definite air of anarchy and rebellion afoot.

The minister for CLEAN is most decidedly not with them on this drunken jaunt and wouldn't have been invited anyway. Since they last saw her, disappearing into the night two hours earlier, they've hardly been able to stop laughing at her antics.

'Maybe she's trying to appeal to the youth vote,' Martin jokes as he punches in the security code for a heavy steel door.

'Get off your tits with Amanda. Legalise drugs now.'

'She was off her head all right, but you can normally tell a user – I wouldn't have put her in that category. Most MPs I've come across draw the line at a bit of Charlie, but that? Very odd.'

'Maybe she's having a nervous breakdown, what with all the pressure?

Martin is sceptical. 'I'm not having that. Pressure? She's the one who creates the pressure. She should try having my job.'

Or mine, Eclipse thinks. She can't resist a dig. 'But you already have your coping mechanisms sorted, don't you, Martin?'

'Damn right I do,' he laughs and reaches inside his jacket pocket for the flask. He takes a nip as he keys in the code for the next steel door. Eclipse notices it's the same code as for the previous door, 1-9-6-6-4-2. 'The next time she's a cow to us, just remember that dance,' he says. He jerks his limbs wildly in crude imitation. 'She holds no fear for us now.'

Eclipse throws in a few exaggerated mad twitches of her own. 'It will be like she's wearing no clothes.'

Martin recoils in mock horror. 'Enough! Don't go there, please.'

Eclipse suddenly remembers she's supposed to be compassionate and woke in these matters. 'Seriously, though, do you think we should have gone after her? Made sure she was OK?'

Martin scoffs. 'Nah. Fuck her. She'll be in bed sleeping it off right now, and tomorrow she'll pretend it never happened. But we know, right?'

Eclipse shrugs. 'I guess. Right, forget about her – on with the tour.'

Her guide nods and taps in the digits for the next door. '*Et voila*,' he announces, 'welcome to the Underworld.'

They enter a massive chamber where a network of different coloured pipes leads to a giant sphere in the middle. Eclipse stands back in wonder. 'It's like a set from a James Bond movie,' she exclaims.

Martin beams. 'State of the art,' he says proudly. It's like he built the place himself.

'It's so quiet,' she observes. 'Eerie.'

'It obviously noisier when it's working. The turbine generator hall is quieter.'

'Oh, this isn't where the turbines, you know, do their thing?'

Martin corrects her. 'No, this is the bioenergy plant, where all the shit is processed. Poo power. Just think, if we connected it directly to the House of Commons, we could increase output one hundred per cent overnight.' He goes into full guide mode. 'The different pipes carry the shit and piss – raw wastewater – from the mainland. It's separated in the centrifuge – that's the big round thing in the middle – then shot up to the surface where it eventually comes out as biomass fuel and clean water. Simple as that.' He indicates the small bank of control panels blinking silently along the right-hand wall: 'And it only needs a team of three to oversee the entire process. Energy efficient in every sense.'

Eclipse has read up on this, of course she has, but it's different seeing it up close. 'And it doesn't even smell,' she notes.

'No. It's just the politicians who pretend they're meeting the country's net-zero commitments who stink,' he gripes. 'Liars, the lot of them. They're going to miss that by years.'

Eclipse doesn't comment. It's something she's come to learn only too well for herself in recent months. 'Come on,' she says, 'show me the turbine bit.'

They pass through another door and enter a similar size hall, but with a different layout entirely where banks of generators line the floor. 'It's like the Marie Celeste down here,' she observes.

'Because of the shutdown for the weekend,' Martin replies. 'I'd never have got you in here otherwise.'

'Do they only have three men in here as well?

'Yes.' He points at a control panel in the corner: 'One to turn it on, over there.' He swings his finger to a second unit, 'And one to turn it off, over there.'

'What does the third one do?'

He pauses for effect. 'Oh, he makes the tea.' *Ba Dum Tish.*

She takes it all in. 'I can't believe that this little island could produce green energy for five million households. It's incredible.'

He laughs. 'Make that two million. Amanda's been inflating the figures to justify the cost. Still, I agree. The technology is impressive. And so simple, like a child's windmill, multiplied a gazillion times.'

'I'm sure it's more sophisticated than that.'

'Well, yes,' he concedes, and then starts into a well-practised spiel about wind speed and direction, lift and drag, drivetrains, nacelles, yaw and pitch systems until she urges him to stop.

'Christ, Martin, I get it. You're losing me now – have another drink.'

He takes her advice. 'Sorry,' he says sheepishly. 'I know all of that off by heart, 'cos I wrote the script for the corporate video.'

'It sounds like it.'

'Well, it's the last time I'm ever going to be saying it, so you should be pleased.'

She pauses. 'Are you really going to leave your job after this?'

He strokes his chin as if contemplating a tough decision: *Let me see now.* 'I don't think I'll have much say in the matter. Let's just say I know which way the wind is blowing.'

'Is that supposed to be a pun?'

'Eh?' he says, before realising what she means. 'Oh, right. OK. No. It's a case of shall I jump before I'm pushed.'

You and me both, thinks Eclipse.

He looks at his watch. 'Shit. It's nearly four o'clock. Better skedaddle before anyone knows we're down here.'

18

MORNING GLORY

A silver thread snips the sea from the sky as Dave, in need of clearing his head, stumbles from his pod. He has been unable to sleep given the events of a few hours ago; it's not only the shock of seeing Justine and JJ going at it like dogs on heat that's disturbed his rest, but thoughts of Rachel too. What went wrong? They'd shared a deep conversation, she'd been open to his clumsy advances, and then she couldn't get away from him quickly enough. Had he misread the situation? Was it something he had said? A sense of embarrassment – or is it shame? – envelops him.

He had come to Holm Island for the experience of a lifetime, and it was all going wrong. Oasis, the gig of all gigs, his fiftieth with his best mates – it doesn't get much better than that. But who was he kidding? Unhappy at home; unhappy here. What did he really have in common with his companions on this trip? Nothing. He'd gone to school with them, that's all. They'd not achieved like him in life and couldn't possibly know the sacrifices he'd had to make. You'd expect, given he had invited them and paid for all of this, they'd at least show him some kindness, admiration perhaps, or at least some respect. But they took the piss mainly. Ent had looked up to him in their younger days, but he'd given up on that it seemed. It was especially galling after he'd overcharged him for his kitchen and then fucked it up. And he'd not said a word to Ent about it, because he didn't want to upset him. What an idiot he'd been. In fairness, Stoggy had always treated him irreverently, but he now realised what he'd chosen to interpret as bants was in fact contempt; a deep, resentful, mocking sarcasm fuelled by Dave's pathetic willingness to suck it up. As for JJ, he'd been the one he felt most able to relate to, but that disgusting episode with Justine – he didn't want to think about it in detail – was nothing short of a betrayal. JJ dumped him, without a second thought, in favour of his dick. His 'friend' hadn't said a word when they got back to their pod last night, and was in there now, spark out, enjoying the sleep of the lust.

What had he done to deserve this? He didn't want to be here. Heaven knows, he's miserable now.

He's alerted to the sound of laughter coming from the adjacent pod – what are those twats Ent and Stoggy doing up so early? He listens for a minute – there's another voice in there, a man's voice. What are they up to? Mischief, probably. He should leave them to it but finds he's inching closer, his curiosity outstripping his fear of more humiliation. The door is ajar, and he espies them huddled around a mobile phone as if they're watching an important football match or a juicy porno.

Ent sees him first, and ushers him in with a cheery 'Dave', moving down the bed to allow him to sit. Stoggy is no less welcoming, warmly introducing him to the newcomer: 'Dave, Sifter; Sifter, Dave'.

They nod to each other. It would be uncool to ask straight out, but what's the famous Sifter doing in here? And why are his mates being so nice to him? Dave is perplexed, but in a good way. He immediately feels a tinge of guilt for thinking so badly of them just two minutes earlier. 'You're up early.'

That causes much merriment. 'Not been to bed yet,' Stoggy drawls.

'What are *you* doing up at this time?' Ent parrots but doesn't wait for an answer. Instead, he turns the phone screen towards him, like a proud dad showing off photos of his newborn. 'Here, cop this.'

Dave takes the phone and hits play on the video that's loaded. There's a middle-aged woman dancing, wrapped in what looks like a Union Jack. She's twisting, jerking and fist-pumping as if the entire megawattage of Holm Island is being channelled through her like she's an enormous earth. The camera zooms closer. Hang on, that looks like… *Queen Bitch. Scary.* Bloody hell, it is Amanda Teale. Wait a minute – he recognises the track she's dancing to, the Happy Mondays – this is clearly from the Supersonic marquee a few hours ago. Ent nudges him. *Keep watching.* Having grounded everything she's got, she succumbs to a state of ecstatic frenzy, eyes closed, quivering, a sacrificial offering waiting for a knife. It's dumbfounding. Finally, after two minutes, she grandly throws her hands in the air and propels herself towards the marquee exit, skirts streaming behind her like the vapour trails in a Red Arrows display. Ent, Stoggy and Sifter erupt in glee, despite it being the tenth time they've watched it.

All Dave can muster is, 'How the fuck…. Where did you get this?'

Ent performs a mock bow.

'She's off her head,' Dave says, in a statement of the obvious. He lets this sink in. He'd never had the minister for CLEAN down as a habitual substance abuser, but the evidence here is all too clear. He turns to Ent. 'You actually took this?'

'I cannot tell a lie.' Cue more laughter.

Dave's lawyer brain cranks into action. 'Ent. I strongly suggest you delete it. You don't want to let anybody else see this. It's a potential defamation of character. Or something. I don't know, but I get a bad feeling about it.'

The other three go quiet. It's Sifter who eventually breaks the silence. 'Bit late for that,' he says, and high fives Ent and Stoggy in turn.

Dave turns white and grabs his own mobile. He finds Sifter's latest blog and reads.

Sifter's blog:

Spotted this morning in the Supersonic Marquee: The Minister for CLEAN, Amanda Teale, getting down and dirty. We're all excited for tonight, of course, but one can only guess at what's helping to boost Amanda's mood. She might need a little time to wake up, wake up after this.

Bad form not to be out of it to an Oasis tune, Amanda, but I'm sure this clip will come in handy for the next election – it's a definite vote winner.

'Oh, God,' Dave gasps. 'They'll crucify you for putting this up.'

'Who will?' Sifter counters, wondering who this pathetic wuss is. 'Public domain, innit? It's my civic duty to report.'

'It's also a possible intrusion of privacy.' Dave is guessing now.

'What are you so worried about?' Stoggy snipes, the early morning good vibes wearing off. 'She deserved everything she got.'

Dave is immediately suspicious. 'How do you mean, *deserved everything she got*?'

There's silence, until Ent can't resist spilling the beans. 'Gave her a little bit of help, didn't we, lads?' They fist bump each other. 'She should be grateful – we gave her the full festival experience. That's what most people come for. Free an' all.'

The lawyer requires no more evidence. 'You spiked her? You bloody well spiked an eminent female politician, then recorded it and put it online? Are you fucking nuts?'

'Jesus, man, pack the good citizen crap in, will you.' says Stoggy disdainfully.

Sifter has a bone to pick too. 'What difference does it make it being a woman politician? Would it be different if it was a man?'

'It's a criminal offence, whichever way, as you well know,' Dave snaps back. 'What were you thinking?'

Ent takes it upon himself to explain. 'She dissed us, Dave. Had us thrown out of the marquee, so we got our own back.'

The logic of this is beyond Dave. Tit repaid with a thousand tats. A brainless rationale akin to setting fire to a pub because it doesn't sell roasted peanuts. Boneheads. The motive having been established, what about the means? 'How did you even get near her?'

Stoggy fixes him with a cold stare; it's beneath him to play interview room games like this. He's a strict 'no comment' man. Sifter is similarly reticent. Ent, however, is warming to his role of narrator. 'Easy. We went round the back, where the staff take their smoke breaks, to see if we could get back in. Sifter spotted a guy he knew waiting on, and let's just say some discussions took place.'

'I wouldn't be telling him anything, Ent.' It's Stoggy, in the role of counsellor for once. 'He'll grass.'

But Ent isn't going to be denied. 'Nah, Stoggy. We're mates. He wouldn't.' He turns to Dave. 'Would you?' He doesn't wait for an answer, and enthusiastically ploughs on. 'Stoggy gives him two mollies, one to slip in her drink, and one for him for later. Ten minutes later, it's done. And we sneak back in and wait for it to take effect. Simple as.'

Dave groans and buries his head in his hands. How many laws have they broken? Are they really that retarded? Could he even be implicated? Finally, 'I wish you hadn't told me any of this.'

Stoggy takes exception to that. 'Nobody asked you to stick your oar in, so do one if you don't like it. Thought you were having a weekend off the law?'

Ent, intent on being the peacemaker, intercedes. 'Come on, Dave. It was just a bit of a laugh. She'll get over it.'

A laugh. Ha, ha, ha, Dave thinks. What else has this weekend got in store?

***

Amanda comes to in a state of discomfort and confusion. It's dark. Where is she? Why does it feel like the world has ended without her receiving the memo. She tentatively stretches out a hand to establish some bearings but loses sight of the appendage in the gloom. She's sitting down, that much she deduces. She wills herself to stand, only to discover her limbs are unresponsive to the brain's unavailing commands. It's as if she were on the ocean floor, being slowly crushed by an unrelenting pressure. She slumps forward, head in hands. Think. She should process this, work out her options, come up with a solution, but this is beyond her in the moment. She cannot think. She does not want to think. Embrace the limbo and go back to sleep. Deal with this later. Yes. Later. She closes her eyes and drifts off again. Don't fight it. It's good not to fret. Sleep.

Seconds later she's abruptly roused from her stupor as a blinding shaft of light hits her, forcing her to shield her eyes. She makes out the silhouette of a woman, framed in bright sunlight, close enough to touch. Amanda adjusts her focus to note that the newcomer is wearing a dressing gown and has a roll of toilet paper tucked under her arm. 'Oh, sorry,' the woman says, 'I didn't know it was taken.' She politely pushes the door to in a bid to spare the squatter's modesty. Amanda, plunged back into darkness and with sweat breaking on her brow, gingerly stretches forward to push the door open two inches. Through the small slit she can make out a fistful of giant wind turbines glinting in the morning sun. Holm Island. She looks down. Oh, Christ – she's in one of the festival bogs. It doesn't matter that it's one of Eclipse's low water consumption vacuum toilets or that it's remarkably clean, it's a shitter, a dunny, and not where she – a minister of the land – should find herself waking. She sharply pulls the door to – she needs to assimilate, work out what's going on. But it's all fragments, and her ability to recollect is impeded by the nausea and fatigue sweeping over her in waves. How did she get here? Why can't she remember? Has anybody spotted her absence? How come her security detail is missing? More importantly, how is she to return to her room without being spotted? Maybe there she can piece it altogether. Taking a deep breath, she shakily exits the smart blue and white convenience. A couple of early risers are already afoot but take no notice of her. Good. She locates the main admin block and unsteadily makes her way towards it. Sanctuary. Get back and recalibrate. But barely has she gone fifty yards than a green blur appears out of nowhere and hurls her to the ground. The assailant lies heavily on top of her, squashing the very air out of her lungs, rendering her immobile. 'Don't move, Minister. SAS. You're safe now.'

***

They allow Amanda half an hour and plenty of water and black coffee before the inquest starts in the green room. Salt, Martin and Eclipse have been pulled from their beds as the last people to have seen her. Ross has better things to do. The minister is still in a considerable state of confusion but there is an overall sense of relief she has been found and no obvious terrorist activity appears to have been in play.

The head of security reports. 'You were last seen at one in the morning, Minister, when you left the marquee. Fearing you'd been kidnapped, we put out an all-points search, happily locating you this morning. At this juncture we don't suspect foul play; we're just relieved to have a happy outcome.'

There is a general buzz of relief the situation has been resolved. *Can we go back to bed now?* However, this precis of events is quite unsatisfactory as far as Amanda is concerned. 'Wait a minute. Where was my security when I left the marquee? How did I end up…' she doesn't want to say it '… where I ended up? And how did I become so…' again she searches for the right word '…incapacitated?'

Mr Crewcut deftly deflects. 'Martin and Eclipse were the last two people you were with, Minister.' He looks expectantly towards them.

The two in question have had barely an hour of sleep and are not far behind Amanda when it comes to their state of befuddlement. That doesn't stop Martin, professional as ever, breezing into a reply while still trying to work out what he wants to say. 'Yes, that's right. I recall, and I'm sure Eclipse will back me up on this, the minister didn't quite seem herself towards the end of the evening.'

'In what way?' Amanda snaps.

'Well,' Martin continues, 'you were your normal self to start with, but then you became quite… animated. We thought maybe you were letting off steam. Understandable given the pressures of the job.'

He looks to Eclipse to back him up. Both have jolted awake quickly under interrogation and are already three questions ahead as to why they didn't do anything about it, follow her, or report it. They have no wish to fuel this; reporting their suspicion Amanda had been chemically assisted would only lead to trouble. The eco-warrior coos sympathetically, 'Yes. Tiredness manifests itself in so many ways. Just think how hard you've been working these past few months, Amanda.'

Martin pivots. 'What's the last thing *you* remember, Amanda?'

The minister, still dressed in her crumpled red, white and blue get-up, strains. 'In a word, nothing. I was in the marquee checking messages on my phone. Then it all goes blank.'

There's silence. There's a lot that doesn't add up here; there's also an understanding that the longer this investigation goes on, somebody other than Amanda will have to take the blame. The head of security goes for a wrap before the spotlight turns back on him. 'If I may, Minister, I propose you get some sleep, and we reconvene later. This appears to me an isolated, extraordinary incident. Luckily, we've managed to contain the situation, no one is the wiser, so no harm done.'

There is a murmur of agreement, even from the minister, at that. But before anyone can move, Salt, who has been preoccupied with his phone while most of this conversation has been taking place, raises his finger for attention. 'I think, as far as containing the situation is concerned, we may have to review that position.' He allows an elegant pause, before holding his mobile up for all to see. He hits play and they watch in astonishment as Amanda Teale recreates Hacienda Night in her own unique style.

Twenty seconds in, she screams 'Turn it off.' She glowers in incomprehension and embarrassment. 'Whatever that is, I want it taking down,' she screams. 'Now. Before anybody sees it.'

Salt peers closely at the screen. 'It's already been seen twenty thousand times.' He adds, helpfully, 'There are a lot of Oasis fans in the USA.'

Amanda, not for the first time that morning, makes a speedy exit from a room, leaving the stunned group behind. All but the security man suppressing the twist of a smile.

19

STOP CRYING YOUR HEART OUT

Not being one to let things fester, Rachel tears straight into Justine the second her companion opens her eyes. 'How could you, Jus?' It's a reversal of yesterday morning's scolding.

There is an awkward silence as Justine contemplates the question. After the night she's had it's no wonder she's feeling a little rough. Does she really want this conversation now, or ever? May as well get it over with. 'How old are you, Rachel? Forty-two. Two years older than me.' She sits up. 'I'm a grown woman with no attachments. If I choose to have sex with a guy, then I will.'

Rachel isn't expecting that. 'But yesterday, you had a go at me when you thought I'd been, you know…'

'Only because you'd been smoking drugs. And had only just met Dave, so couldn't really know what he was like. You were vulnerable. And, if I'm being honest, because I think Dave is a bit of a creep. That's why.'

'You've changed your tune. You said JJ was a creep too.'

'No, I didn't. I said he was harmless. And he is. And I quite like him. And I fancied a shag, so where's the problem?'

Is Rachel such a prude she thinks casual sex is some sort of crime against humanity? It's not a turn in the moral maze she's had to negotiate for years. She was married. Is married. It's not crossed her mind – well, not until recently. 'You could have at least warned me,' is all she can muster in reply.

Justine smirks. 'Yeah. I suppose it must have been a bit of a shock. At least you had the decency to leave and let him finish me off.' The two break into laughter, the ice broken, friends again. 'Honestly, Rach, it was no big deal. What happens at Be Here Now stays at Be Here Now and all that.'

Rachel nods uncertainly.

'And you came back with Mr Big Time, didn't you,' Justine reminds her. Were you…'

Rachel doesn't let her finish the question. 'No!' she protests. 'Nothing like that.'

Justine looks her up and down. 'He tried it on, didn't he,' she wryly probes.

Rachel blushes. 'Not really.'

'N*ot really*? Should you be thanking me for rescuing you, or should I be apologising for spoiling your night?'

It's a good question; one Rachel doesn't know how to answer. 'I… he… we had a dance, and he walked me back.'

'And...?'

'That's all. Well, yes, we did have a bit of a… snog, I suppose you'd call it.'

'I knew it! Looks like I did put you off.'

Rachel is about to object to the insinuation she was about to have wild sex with Dave, but circles back. 'We had a kiss, that's all. It was harmless.'

Justine considers this for a second, then: 'But did you want to… go further? Nobody would have known, after all.'

Rachel recalls the shock of Dave's tongue sliding into her unsuspecting mouth, and his vice-like grip. She also recalls how it felt tempting and inviting. That is, until Morrissey intervened. She reaches for the whitewash. 'He spent most of the time telling me about his marriage again. He's definitely having similar … *doubts…* as me.'

'Oh, is he now? Talk about a stuck record. You're not going to fall for that, are you?'

Rachel is stung. She's been out of the dating game for a while, but Dave's disclosures appear quite genuine to her. Surely, he wouldn't stoop so low as to dupe her. She pulls herself together. 'I'm not falling for anything, Jus. Nothing happened. Can we move on now, please?

Justine shakes her head in mild exasperation. 'OK, fine. But don't let a bloody man spoil your weekend. They're not worth it.' She doesn't say which man she means.

Rachel feels the tears rising again. 'Sorry. It's just … I feel so uncertain. I don't know what to do for the best.'

Justine puts her arm around her and gives her a squeeze. She understands exactly what her friend means. 'You'll make the right decision, I'm sure. It's like I said yesterday, you need to think about what you want to do with the rest of your life; stop sweating the small stuff.' She hands her friend a fresh tissue. 'Come on, we've a big day ahead of us. We're seeing Oasis tonight,' she says brightly, before adding, 'and we'll steer clear of that lot if you like.'

It sounds like a plan. Yes, and yes. Stop wallowing and seize the day – time to get moving. Rachel blows her nose and nods. 'You get yourself ready while I go and get us some coffee.'

Minutes later, in the rather long queue for caffeine, she's deep in thought. She twiddles the band around her wrist – she must ask what balance remains when she gets served.

Don't forget Justine takes sugar in hers. Should she get some croissants too, or wait and go for a full breakfast? But most of all, she thinks about what she's doing here. Not here on Holm Island, but at this critical point in her life. Let's face it, it wasn't Matthew who asked for a timeout on their marriage. He's happy being married to her. That would be more than enough for most women. Or would it? Review the reasons again: Matthew is set in his ways. *Boring, not the man she'd married.* But who was she to judge? She wasn't exactly some Hollywood A-lister. What was she searching for? A different, brighter future? Or was she really yearning for her past, when youth and the possibilities it offered were endless? What had she realistically expected from this voluntary break? Finding what she was 'missing'? Some excitement and passion and – admit it – an idle fantasy of being swept off her feet by someone. Not someone like Dave, though. Last night had been… what? Harmless or pathetic? Or the ultimate taboo: *inappropriate.* But she'd felt a stirring, she couldn't deny it. And she'd not run away (well, not immediately). And what if she hadn't run away, and it had led to, you know. What then? Turn her back on everything and sail off into the sunset? Who was she fooling? It would have been a dalliance, pure and simple. Justine clearly had no problem with casual sex. A surprise package right there, and far more emancipated than her, Miss Goody Two-Shoes. Had the interminable routine of being an earner, a mother, a wife simply ground her down? Middle age? Couldn't she have more excitement, passion – and passionate sex – with Matthew if they put their minds to it? How was it Matthew had explained it to Tim? *I can't work your mum out at all. It's a phase she's going through.* Was he right? Had she gone crackers suddenly, thinking the grass was greener? And what about poor Tim? What must he be going through as she worked through this problem of her own making? Uncertainty, loss, confusion – having the rug whipped from beneath his feet at such an impressionable age. She'd read how kids get seriously damaged in family break-ups and never recover, but it hadn't stopped her calling a timeout, had it? But what if she returned to her old life and nothing changed? Would she feel an even bigger failure then? Why was this all so hard?

Her reverie is interrupted by a less than gentle nudge in the back – 'Your turn,' hisses a hungover punter as he points at the barista.

***

JJ is snoring contentedly as Dave hovers. *Wake up, you bastard.* Distracted, he consults his phone for the umpteenth time that morning, pulling up short at a new post. It's none other than Liam Gallagher:

> *MOONING. Lovely day for it. It's gonna be biblical.*

It doesn't sound like a man who has been deprived of the biggest day (and pay day) of his entire career. It also confirms Dave's suspicion that Sifter is an unprincipled rabble-rouser in his quest for clicks. Inside information, my arse. He can't wait any longer and gives JJ a shove.

'Get up, you dirty sod.'

JJ stirs and groans, before rolling over again. 'Leave me alone.'

Dave ignores this entreaty. 'I thought you might like to know that while you were shagging yourself senseless, Ent and Stoggy have been breaking every law known to man and beast and will probably get us kicked off the island before lunchtime. Oh – and their mate Sifter is full of shit.'

This is clearly too much information for JJ to absorb in one chunk. Not only that, but he also feels a hell of a hangover kicking in. 'What??' is all he can come up with.

'You heard,' says Dave gravely. But in case he hasn't, he spends ten minutes spelling out every detail.

JJ pulls on his clothes as the charges are read out. He's finding it wearisome if the truth be told. Finally: 'Well, strictly speaking, the video was taken in a public area, so isn't an invasion of privacy. You're a lawyer; you should know that.'

Dave is taken aback at this slight on his professionalism. 'And what does the lawyer in you say about spiking someone's drink with mind-altering drugs?' he shoots back. 'Not just "someone", of course, but a government minister.'

This isn't getting very far. 'Look,' says JJ, 'let me get my head together here, I've only just woken up. And I can't help but notice that you seem very pissed off with me as well.'

'Yeah, well, it's not every day you come across your mate hanging out the back of a librarian,' Dave huffs.

'Oh, so that's what this is about,' JJ sighs. 'Well, one, Jus is a primary school teacher, not a librarian. Secondly, are you saying it's OK for you to get your end away, but not me? Double standards or what?'

Dave harumphs. 'Rachel and I were just having a polite conversation, that's all. Nothing less, nothing more.' He realises that's a defence that may not stand up to scrutiny, so circles back to his earlier comment. 'And seeing you at it was a shock, as I'm sure you can imagine.'

JJ smiles. He gets the picture. 'She turned you down, didn't she?'

They both start sniggering. It's a fair cop. But they still have the bigger problem to deal with. 'What are we going to do about Ent and Stoggy?' Dave asks.

JJ pulls on his trainers, contemplates the situation, and shrugs. 'Nothing,' he says. Anticipating his friend's objections, he lays it out. 'You're not their mother, Dave. They're big boys now. First, they'd have to be caught, and evidence produced that they'd spiked her. They'd deny it anyway. And it's nothing to do with us if they did get collared.'

Dave is astounded at his friend's lack of concern. Normally, JJ would be the one wringing his hands and offering to type up the confession. 'So, we just… forget it?'

'Exactly. To be honest, they're getting on my tits. You have this rosy notion that we're the fab four somehow, brothers-in-arms, but we're not. We're relatively normal, while those two were delivered by Harold Shipman. They're trouble, and you encourage it.'

It's a strong condemnation, but he has a point. All lads together hasn't really worked, and half the party is taking the piss. In indulging them, he's endorsed their antics, fuelled their disdain. Dave can't deny it. 'I know. I just thought this would be special for us.'

'And I appreciate that, but face facts: they're users, aren't they? The more you give them, the more liberties they take.' It's a blunt summary, but one that's hard to contradict.

Dave is crestfallen. All this effort – all this money – and it's going to rat shit. 'This was supposed to be the best day out in years but I'm beginning to think I shouldn't have bothered.'

JJ isn't having that. 'It will be the best day out in years. Lighten up.'

'But what about Ent and Stoggy?'

'What about them? We don't have to do everything together, and they're always bunking off anyway. Stop worrying about them. We're here for one thing. Oasis. Go let it out and all that.'

'What, like you did last night?'

JJ is far from coy in his response. 'Well, I have to say, I do feel a certain spring in my step this morning. I've not had an adventure like that since the last time I saw Oasis, probably.'

'Smug bastard,' Dave concedes, but he's right. They're here for one thing. Oasis. It's tonight. It's on. Nothing must get in the way of that. *Get a grip.* Ent and Stoggy can look after themselves, and if they can't, they can get another bloody lawyer to represent them as he's buggered if he's going to be offering his services. As for Rachel… it's no biggie. He just had a case of the beer goggles, that's all. Lucky escape, really. Forget about her. 'You should get shagged more often, JJ. I've never seen you so cheerful.'

'Very funny. What were you saying about Sifter, anyway?'

Dave has had so much to recount, he's almost forgotten. 'You know all that stuff about Liam's sore throat – gig in jeopardy, doctor has ordered rest and all of that? Turns out to be complete bollocks. Sifter's as reliable a source as a Siberian troll factory.'

'Liam's alright, then?'

'Right as rain, apparently.' He grabs his mobile. 'And so are we. Only one item on the agenda today. Let's have it.'

JJ laughs. 'At least let me get a shower and a coffee first.'

'OK. As long as I get the full blow-by-blow of last night's action. It's only fair.'

JJ grabs his towel. 'A gentleman never tells,' he says primly. 'Don't you know that?'

'You're no gentleman, JJ.'

20

CAST NO SHADOW

Salt mops the sweat from his forehead as he climbs the stairs of the auditorium. Why does Ross always have to sit at the bloody top? The impresario knows there is more than his age and physical condition weighing on him this morning; on the biggest day in his entire career these are the crucial hours. He has every right to feel stressed, even if he's determined not to show it.

Ross greets him with a wry smile. 'How's the blessed Amanda? Has she come down yet?'

Salt grimaces. 'That fucking woman. I can't say I'll be sorry to see the back of her after today.'

'So, what happened?'

'She was spiked. The doctor did a blood test. Ecstasy. They should have given her a double dose in my opinion.'

'Awkward. How are they going to explain that away?'

In the hours since the video of the minister for CLEAN's maniacal dancing went viral, Amanda – in between an urgent call from the PM – has been dusting down the crisis communications manual. 'By denying it, of course,' Salt informs him. 'Or rather, not saying anything either way. They've gone for a jokey unofficial briefing line that *she likes to dance, and she's come to the right place for it this weekend* instead. It worked for Micheal Gove in the past, so it's standard issue now.'

'But who spiked her?'

'Christ – there must be at least ten thousand suspects. It wasn't me at least, although Martin and Eclipse were with her last night and they're both acting bloody odd if you ask me.'

'You seriously think it was them?'

Salt shrugs. 'I dunno. They had access, that's for sure. And they must hate her guts given the shit she's put them through. Plus, they're both surplus to requirements after this weekend, so maybe they're getting their retaliation in first.'

Ross ponders this. It sounds highly improbable to him. 'But they'd never work again. They wouldn't risk that, surely?'

'Well, whether they would or not, it doesn't really matter, because it will never get out she was spiked as that would be too embarrassing. *Ergo*, nobody can be accused of doing it. End of.'

Ross nods. He gets it. Sometimes an investigation only inflates a scandal. Far better to pretend it never happened. As for the jokey 'non-denial denial', it will probably bestow unlikely street cred on Amanda further down the line. You couldn't make it up.

'Anyway, enough of her,' Salt insists. 'To business. Are we all set?'

Ross raises both thumbs to signal all is in hand. Every detail, contingency, planning matrix and action list has been checked and checked again. They're good to go as far as the areas Ross has control over. 'All on track. Assuming the band turn up.' He looks expectantly towards the promoter.

Despite the rumour circulating over Liam's sore throat, which Salt knew to be rubbish, he has spent innumerable hours imagining the Gallagher brothers un-burying the hatchet and cancelling the gig. But he has remained in constant touch with them, and he's confident they're not going to piss on their own chips at this late stage. 'They'll be here at two o'clock. Never fear.' He has more news to impart too. 'By helicopter.'

Ross lets out a laugh. 'Does Eclipse know?'

'Whether she does or not who gives a toss? We don't need to worry about her anymore. The boys heard Amanda had a chopper flying stuff in, so what's sauce for the goose and all that. They want to do the Knebworth helicopter thing again. Good idea.'

'I take it Liam and Noel will be in different choppers this time though?'

'As long as they both touch down on that big bloody H, I don't give a shit. Then it's over to you for the soundcheck.'

Ross feels an involuntary tightening in his stomach. The soundcheck. *The Duchess of York, Leeds, September 1993: It should have been louder, man! Slide the fuckers up!* Of course, Oasis are not going to play Be Here Now without a soundcheck, but the venue does have its limitations. The audience on the small island is basically inside the arena even when they're not, and the band insists on some privacy. Granted, with digital technology, most of the work has already been done but there is still a need for line checks and monitor mixes. Ross is happy to leave most of that to the Oasis techs. All he has to do – and by God, he has – is ensure it's going to be louder than war. *Salt, they're going to be able to hear it in bloody Bergen.*

Which leaves… the weather. Salt looks up into the azure sky and shields his eyes against the bright sunshine. He points skywards. 'What's it saying now?'

Ross was wondering when he'd get round to this. He opens his iPad to show him the latest shipping pages. 'The forecast is looking better than last night – that's a plus.'

Salt could kiss him. 'It is? Really? That's fantastic news.'

'Steady on. By "better", I mean not as bad. It doesn't look like we're going to get lightning, so that's an improvement, but we are in for strong winds and rain unfortunately.'

Salt weighs it up. No lightning. No potential threat to life. That's good. Yes, he'll take that. A bit of rain and wind? *Poof.* Festival conditions. Adds to the atmosphere. They can ride that out. Crucially, no need to implement the extra day. 'And even that will probably miss us, you said.'

'Well, I didn't say that exactly. I said we might be done and dusted by the time it hits, but looking at the updated forecast, it looks like it might hit earlier now.'

This is all too inexact for the promoter's promoter. 'For Christ's sake, Ross. That's not "looking better", is it? I'd prefer it to hit after they've finished, not before.'

Ross holds his hands up in the air. 'What do you want me to do about it, Salt? Have a word with Him upstairs? It is what it is. We'll manage, like we always do. And if the worst comes to the worst, we'll do it tomorrow. But I'm sure it won't come to that.'

The blood drains from the impresario's pasty face at the prospect. 'I don't believe it, Ross, I just don't bloody believe it. How can this…' he thrusts his finger heavenwards again '… suddenly turn into Glastonbury 2007 at the flick of a switch? Where's the justice?'

Where's the justice? The doughty, 'seen it all', head of production regards Salt with a quizzical eye. He's losing it. Just as well he's retiring. He decides a few words of comfort are in order: 'You never know, we may just get lucky. Let's not worry about what we can't control. Let's just concentrate on what we can.'

***

Bryan, Bob and Cody have spent the morning debriefing last night's reconnaissance. It didn't go well, as all they discovered with any certainty was getting anywhere near the backstage area was impossible. Bryan, the master of stealth, was so conspicuous in his snooping he was threatened with ejection from the island if he was spotted out of bounds again. He doesn't mention this to his colleagues as they discuss their options. Instead, he posits: 'What if we just rush the stage from the front?'

Bob is dubious. 'It will be even harder from the front. There will be barriers, security men and God knows what.'

'There will,' Bryan concedes, 'but if we mount a synchronised triple assault from left, right and centre, we might confuse them. And even if we don't, we'll cause a disruption, and that's headline worthy.'

Nobody looks convinced at this masterplan.

'Won't Oasis fans be trying that anyway?' questions Bob. 'They'll just think we're crashing the stage.'

'But we'll have our banners out, won't we,' Bryan reasons. 'We'll stand out.'

'When people pitch invade or streak at a football match, the cameras cut away,' Cody says. 'They go out of their way not to show it. An attack like that would be futile.'

Futile? Bryan can't believe how cowardly his handpicked squad is turning out to be. 'You two need to rediscover your balls. We've not come here for a picnic. And this has cost me a fortune so far.'

Cody has a suggestion. 'What about that message last night? *The game changer*?'

Bryan hasn't forgotten his excitement at receiving a reply to one of his 'black op' dispatches, but now he's established contact 'with the other side' he's at a loss as to what to do with it. He scratches his head. 'Yeah, there's that, of course. The thing is, we need to be careful how we use it.'

Bob is confused. 'I don't get it, Bryan. How does pretending to be *wokerati* help us?'

Cody nods in agreement. 'I don't understand what you're driving at either.'

Bryan bristles. It's obvious, isn't it? 'Once more, for those at the back of the class. I set up a couple of bogus green accounts and reached out to prominent PC brigaders asking them to support our cause.'

'What – Stop Climate Hoax Now?"

'No, Bob, you plank. The green cause. Stay with me, here. So, if they agree with our aims – the green aims – then they might be disposed to help us here on the island.'

Bob weighs this up for a second before giving up. 'Like how? I still don't get it.'

It's apparent Bryan doesn't either. 'I don't bloody know, do I? We infiltrate, we find a friendly dupe. As Sun Tzu says in The Art of War: *To know your enemy, you must become your enemy*. It could be anything, but ideally a backstage pass. These people are well connected, aren't they?'

His colleagues stare at him. That's the idea? Really? It appears their options have narrowed to a full-frontal stage assault again.

Cody tactfully sums it up, for his own benefit as well as Bob's. 'I get it, Bryan, I do,' he says softly, 'but don't you think it's a bit of a long shot? Especially as we're just hours away from the band being on stage. And you've not actually established contact as much as had an acknowledgement of your message.'

These are minor quibbles to Bryan – he'd never expected to get a reply at all. He scrolls through his phone. 'Look, read what it says there. *Happy to assist.* Let's get in touch now and ask to meet up. Nothing ventured and all that. It's got to be worth a punt because, one thing for sure, we know we're not going round the back tonight.'

Bob has no objections. There's no chance of it working, so fire away. Then they can try to talk Bryan out of the full-frontal assault. (He wonders what advice Sun Tzu might have to impart regarding that stratagem.)

Cody, however, has some practical considerations he'd like to raise. 'Hang on. Who are we supposed to be – I mean what's our cause? We need to gen up. Who are we supposed to be talking to? We'd need background. Then how the hell are we going to get whoever it is to help – just say: *Hi, my name's Bryan. Pleased to meet you. I'm greener and woker than you, so any chance of a backstage pass?*'

These are trivial deliberations as far as Bryan is concerned. 'That's detail. We'll work all of that out if – when – we get a meet. As Sun Tzu also says: *Opportunities multiply as they are seized.*' At that, he starts to type a message on his mobile before flamboyantly pressing send. He holds it up for the others to read:

> *Great to get your reply and fantastic we can count on your support. Would love to meet up if you're free. On the island now. You about?*

'There,' he says contentedly. 'Done.'

They continue to stare at the screen as if it's a hypnotist's pocket watch.

Fifteen seconds later, the screen buzzes with an incoming message:

> *Am about. 4pm at Bubble and Speak, Burnage Boulevard?*

Mouths agape, they continue to stare at the screen in dumb stupefaction.

21

WAITING FOR THE RAPTURE

The sun beats down on the tiny anvil of Holm Island, forcing the circumspect to their Factor 50 while the more reckless sizzle like a pan of Danish rashers on full heat. The blessed few are only a few hours away from Oasis, and the sense of anticipation (and self-congratulation to have made it here) couldn't be higher.

Ent and Stoggy have slept through the entire morning and are somewhat puzzled that JJ and Dave are nowhere to be found. 'They can't just vanish,' Ent observes as they check inside the Stratford Bar for the third time. 'I mean, there's nowhere to go.'

'We must keep missing them,' Stoggy deduces. 'Best park up here. They'll come round eventually.'

Given they've spent most of the past two days in their own little bubble, it's curious to now feel at a loss separated from their companions.

'Do you think I should ring them?' Ent says.

This suggestion meets with a swift knockback. 'Nah. All in good time, eh? Have a beer and chill.'

Ent picks distractedly at the foil on the neck of his bottle. 'You don't think we've upset them somehow? I mean, Dave was pretty wound up this morning.'

'Dave's always wound up.'

'Yeah, but, you know. Like angry.'

'No excuse losing it over that cow. She got what she deserved. Anyhow, it was Sifter who posted the vid, not us.'

'Yeah, but you supplied the mollies.'

Stoggy suppresses a smirk. 'I didn't put one in her drink, though. Not guilty.'

Now he's sober, Ent isn't feeling quite as carefree and invincible as he was earlier. What if their antics were to catch up with them? 'You don't think Dave would dob us in, do you?'

'I wasn't being serious. He's not that big a wanker.'

Ent continues to fret. 'But what if somebody saw? Or the waiter gets collared? We could be in the shit.'

'Will you put a sock in it?' Stoggy snaps. But is Ent's mithering starting to cause him concern too? 'Go on – check your phone. See what it says now.'

He does so. 'Fucking hell – over a million hits on the Amanda Teale video now,' he reports. Scrolling down, 'Oh, man, you should see the comments.' Alarmed at the reach of their handiwork, he switches to BBC News. It takes him some seconds to find what he's looking for. 'There's just a little bit on her in the entertainment section. *'Amanda is mad for Oasis.'* He reads on. 'It makes out she's just having a good time in anticipation of the show. That's all. Like she's really cool or something.'

'Told you,' Stoggy crows. 'Nothing to worry about. A million sussed people know she's off her tits on E, but all the straights are pretending *it's just high spirits.* Suits us, though. Can't be pinched for a crime that didn't take place.'

Ent absorbs this pearl of wisdom. It makes sense and puts them in the clear. He won't be the only one to take comfort from this assessment. 'Dave will be pleased once he knows as well,' he says. Then, softening his voice, 'Do you think we've been a bit hard on him? I mean, he didn't have to bring us here, did he?'

Stoggy shifts in his seat as he considers this thesis. 'Mebbes,' he finally concedes.

It's remarkable how, in the absence of the butt of their jokes, the joke is now on them. Are their friends simply out and about, or could it be they've found somewhere better to be? Somewhere without Ent and Stoggy? The fear of missing out is suddenly as real as their growing self-reproach.

They sit in silence, Ent returning to his mobile, until he sits up bolt upright. 'No way, that can't be right' he bawls. 'It says here there's going to be a storm tonight. Right when Oasis are playing.'

Stoggy isn't falling for that one. 'Yeah, course there is.'

Ent thrusts the mobile in front of his face. 'It's on the BBC, smartarse. Look – wind, rain.' He reads it aloud: *In the event of the show having to be postponed tonight, the reserve day will be invoked tomorrow, although organisers are confident that this will not be necessary.*

Stoggy remains sceptical. 'Bollocks. You could fry an egg on the pavement out there. You can't believe anything the BBC says these days – there's no fucking way it's going to piss it down tonight.'

Ent hopes he's right. But what if he's not? He couldn't stand it if, for some reason, he didn't get to see Oasis today. He knows it's pathetic, but this reunion gig is the best thing that's happened to him in years. The band he grew up with, the sound that has locked his musical compass on magnetic north since he was a lad. Forget world peace, long life and a happy marriage – if he had found a magic lamp and been granted one wish, he'd have asked for an Oasis reunion. And lo, it was so. But if it took one wish to make it happen, another was required to be able to attend, and that was down to his old mucker, Dave. Ent wishes his missing friends were here so they could have a proper discussion about any fallback plans. It was normally Dave and JJ who worked stuff like that out and decided anyway – they'd have a far better idea about the weather and what might be happening. 'Do you think we should go have another look for them?' he asks.

'Mebbes,' comes the echo of an answer.

They push out of the marquee and into the blinding sunlight. 'Storm, my arse,' scoffs Stoggy as they shield their eyes against the glare.

They decide to check the pods again but barely cover twenty metres before they are halted in their tracks as a steady *chup-chup-chup* cuts the air. The wind turbines? No – a helicopter. As the sound gets louder, they see it approaching from the west. So does everybody else, and a spontaneous cheer goes up as the elongated shadow of the craft sweeps the ground. The chopper makes two circuits of the island before dropping out of sight behind the stage area. Scores of people rush wildly in the direction of the arena in the hope of seeing, well, they don't quite know what, but something, anything. *They're here, they're here.*

Ent and Stoggy are rooted to the spot. What should they do now?

***

Chup-chup-chup. Eclipse doesn't need to look skywards to know what's going on. So much for Amanda's red boxes being an exception, an emergency. Of course, Oasis have insisted on one too. Why wouldn't they, the fuckers? Why not give them one each? In fact, why stop there? Why not make a few extra quid and offer punters helicopter flights over the island? You can get airborne trips over the Grand Canyon and Christ the Redeemer, so why not here? Who gives a toss about carbon emissions and noise pollution when you can indulge in a bit of tourism terrorism – *it's the only way to see it and I offset the carbon.* Why bother about the impact on the local flora and fauna when the ultimate Insta shot is at stake? She watches the chopper do two gratuitous circuits of the island. In your face, triumphant showboating. They may as well be blasting out "Ride of The Valkyries" from speakers slung over the side. Apocalypse. Now. Fuck that, she'd give them apocalypse if she could. She has been well and truly suckered. Greenwashing guff – bang to rights. As she walks down to Burnage Boulevard for her four o'clock, she passes a column of punters rushing in the other direction towards the arena. Fools. What do they think is going to happen there? Liam and Noel doing an impromptu meet and greet? An invitation to the sound check, an autograph, a selfie? No – a snatched video clip of a human scrum – *they're in there somewhere…* Since when did people become so pathetic, so empty-headed, that their lives could only be validated though a tenuous brush with celebrity? Let's forget that the planet is burning, because some old farts are going to be knocking out a tune from yesteryear. This entire weekend is a sham, an obscenity, and she's played a bigger role than anybody in pretending otherwise.

She arrives at Bubble and Speak seething with resentment, whereupon a young man stands to greet her. 'Eclipse, hi. Tony from the Conserve Aquatic Reserves Partnership.' Pleasantries are exchanged. 'I recognised you from your photo,' he says, blinking wildly as she sits down. Eclipse, used to people being in awe of her presence, takes his nervousness for granted.

He's not what she was expecting. She's very much against stereotyping – of course she is – but had somehow assumed she'd be meeting someone sporting a combination of piercings, tattoos and brightly-dyed hair. But this guy looks like he's army or something. She chides herself for being so presumptive.

They settle down with drinks – she opts for a Mango Boba Tea, her new acquaintance taking a breakfast tea with milk and sugar – while he tells her how grateful he is for her sparing the time to meet him. *If only he knew*, she thinks, *I've got more time than anybody now the island has been declared emission central.*

But to business: 'I'm not really familiar with the aims of the Conserve Aquatic Reserves Partnership,' she says, 'but I'm happy to help if I can. We environmentalists should stick together, after all.'

Tony – or more accurately, Cody – nods enthusiastically. Sent into battle by Bryan – *there's more chance of her thinking you're legit 'cos of your age* – he's had an hour and a half to bone up on a backstory. He takes a deep breath and unrolls: 'We call it CARP for short,' he informs her. 'People don't realise how wind farms like this affect marine life. Increased levels of noise affect the behaviour of fish, whales and other species like you'd never guess. Habitats are impacted, and that's before we get on to the electro-magnetic fields that bugger up navigation, predator detection and the ability of fish and shellfish to find mates.'

It's a breathless mouthful, but it's enough to hook the unsuspecting flounder opposite him. Her eyes brim with tears at the oceanic devastation that she, in her ignorance, has helped to bring about. 'I never realised,' she confesses. 'I've been too focused on above the waterline, so to speak.'

'Yeah, well,' says Tony, 'it's an easy mistake to make.' Growing in confidence he adds, 'Out of sight, out of mind and all that.'

'You're so right,' she agrees. 'But I don't suppose you could have a better event than this to get your message across. Nobody has ever been as interested in offshore energy islands as they are this week.'

Encouraged, he loosens the grip on his cuffs, pulled down tight to cover up his magic square of tats (18, 2083, 28 and 1488) and continues. 'You'd think so, but it's a thankless task. Nobody seems to be bothered about the poor little fishies at all.'

'Tell me about it,' Eclipse sighs. 'A plastic lawn is the nearest most of this lot get to nature. To be honest, they make me sick. All of them. The fans, the organisers, the band. It makes my blood boil. *Let's promote our green agenda with a gig by Oasis on an energy island in the North Sea* – what cant. Conspicuous consumption at its height, an orgy of waste, the epitome of capitalist exploitation… I could scream.'

Cody is struggling to follow her argument but deduces she's not a happy bunny. He nods sympathetically. 'You obviously feel very strongly about it.'

She collects herself. 'Sorry. Bit of a rant there. Let's just say that the role I was promised hasn't exactly lived up to expectations. I wanted Be Here Now to be a celebration of sustainability and environmental protection, but it's anything but. End of story.'

The fierce young eco-warrior breaks off to tackle her tapioca at last. Cody has spent most of his life laughing at earnest tree huggers like her, waving their 'No Planet B' placards in people's faces, but must admit she looks very pretty fired up like that. She's a bit of a diva, very posh, and obviously went to a private school – even more surprising in that case she should have fallen for all this climate hoax shit. What did they teach them in those places? He'd love to take her to one side and explain, as Bryan had to him, how science would provide the solutions as it always did, how climate change was natural and had happened before with no ill-effects. No, remember he's on a mission, and must close on his objective.

'Do you think you could help us at all?'

Eclipse shrugs. Help them? She can't even help herself, not even with all the power supposedly at her disposal. 'In what way?'

This is it. Cody is in the box, the keeper is off the line, and he has a clear shot. 'Could you get us a backstage pass?'

She slumps. A backstage pass? She thought she'd been speaking to a serious environmental activist looking for advice, but no, he's just some fan boy trying to butter her up for access all areas. 'No. Definitely not,' she blasts. 'I have to say this isn't what I expected. I thought you wanted help with your campaign, not freeloading.' She picks up her bag. 'I'm going.'

Panicked, Cody blurts it out. 'I want get on stage to disrupt the concert, to wave a banner promoting our message.'

Eclipse lets out a shriek of laughter. 'Are you mad? You'll not get within fifty yards of that stage. Nobody will. They've got the SAS on duty.' She softens and lowers her bag. 'But I admire you for thinking you could.'

The SAS? Crestfallen, Cody is wondering how he's going to report his failure to Bryan. 'Well, it was worth a try,' he says gamely.

She fixes him in a long, cool stare. 'Are you serious about disrupting the concert? Like, really serious?'

Cody nods.

A thought fans the ember of resistance within the cold ashes of her campaigning heart. Could she? Should she? No sooner does the idea form, it bursts into flames. It's all they deserve. A wicked smile plays across the cupid bow of her lips. 'Well, you're not going to get very far with a stage invasion and fluttering a flag. There's only one way it could possibly be done.'

22

BRING IT ON DOWN

Jez and Cleo's producer has ordered them to the heliport at the rear of the arena to report. They're not allowed inside for the sound check, but even a muffled approximation of a recognisable song in the background will send viewers' pulse rates soaring. A gaggle of fans watch on as they set up, interested in the recording as well as what might be happening backstage. One of them is Sifter, intent on some up-to-the-minute updates for his followers.

Jez spots him and points him out to Cleo. 'There's the twat who started the *Liam has a sore throat* rumour.

'He posted the video of Amanda Teale as well,' she reminds him. 'We should get him on.'

Jez disagrees. 'No, sod him. Get some normal punters instead.'

Cleo, not for the first time, is about to question her co-presenter's sense of news when the producer breaks in: *No way are we having that dipshit on. We've got an exclusive instead.* Before he can explain further, they spot Amanda Teale, game face on, marching resolutely towards them. The minister for CLEAN could be forgiven for lying low given she's now the number one meme in the UK, but no, here she is to front it out, a strategy heartily endorsed by her media team. She hasn't so much agreed to an interview as insisted on being the face of tonight's news coverage. However, behind the sober clothes, the business air and the rictus grin, Amanda is dying inside. The humiliation has hit hard. The cruel joke played on her isn't only potentially career-ending but has also delivered a real blow to her self-esteem and pride. Being unfamiliar with the comedown effects of ecstasy, Amanda doesn't realise she's fighting a feeling of depression as much as anything else. Nor does she know that anxiety, impulsivity, irritability and aggression are common bedfellows of the downer she's experiencing (not to mention the potential loss of interest in sex). She has been advised to rest, but she cannot wrestle back the agenda lying down. This is what she must do.

As if on cue, a live clattering emanates from the arena as she arrives – perfect for the report.

Jez kicks them off with an enthusiastic, 'The wait is almost over, people. Oasis have arrived. And we are here to make sure you don't miss a thing.'

Cleo joins in, ear cupped in hand. 'You can probably hear them sound-checking in the distance.' She pauses. 'Can you tell what it is yet, Jez?'

Can he heckers like. It's just random bass notes booming over an intermittent kick drum. 'No spoilers now for our viewers, Cleo. What they'll be playing later is a closely guarded secret.'

'But I think we can all guess, don't you?'

He moves swiftly on. 'Joining us now is someone who's had a very big part in making this evening possible, the minister for CLEAN, Amanda Teale. How are you feeling, Amanda, now that we're only hours away?'

To nobody's surprise, she ticks the first square off her bingo card. 'Mad for it, Jez, is the only way to describe it.'

First question – the video.

'And you were mad for it last night, Amanda, judging from the video we've seen online.'

Fuck's sake, Cleo. Gently does it.

Fortunately, all Amanda picks up on is the word 'video', the tee-up for her prepared soundbite. 'Oh that,' she laughs. 'How can you not dance to all the brilliant music we've been hearing this weekend? And the best is yet to come.'

Mindful of the conditions set by the minister's team for this interview, the producer moves it along: *Her department's role in making this weekend happen.*

Cleo picks this up. 'So, Amanda, why exactly are you here this weekend?'

Jez nips in to clarify. 'Ha ha. I think what viewers are interested in knowing is what government has got to do with the greatest rock 'n' roll event of the century. Are you planning to nationalise Oasis?'

Amanda snaps this up. 'They're already a national treasure, Jez, but maybe we should look at that idea.' Not bad, but time now for her earnest face: 'No, seriously, the UK is now the world's leading exponent of green, renewable energy. Where we are standing, on Holm Island in the middle of the North Sea, will power millions of homes and industry across the nation and bring down the cost of energy while contributing to our net zero objectives at the same time.'

It's a shameless lift from the manifesto, delivered without a wobble. But it's still not enough for Cleo who's just been struck by a curious thought. 'Does that mean taxpayers are footing the bill for this weekend? Underwriting Noel and Liam's golden payday?'

Fuck's sake, Cleo. This isn't Newsnight.

Amanda feigns astonishment at the very suggestion. 'Absolutely not. What we have done is work closely with BRITE to ensure this unique location could host the comeback, showcasing to the world the best of British in every sense. The commercial aspects of the weekend are purely self-funding.'

'And of course, Oasis have contributed millions of pounds to the exchequer over the years with their tax contributions,' Jez reminds her. 'And they'll pay tax on what they earn this weekend.'

Amanda, wary of validating either of those statements, smiles inanely in lieu of a response.

Enough of that. What does she want to hear tonight.

'Now, we've all got a favourite Oasis song,' Cleo trills. 'Which one are you most looking forward to tonight?'

It's a simple enough question, but one that afflicts Amanda with a sudden brain freeze. Her team should have anticipated this and prepped her with a slick answer, but she's on her own now. Any Oasis track will do, but she's buggered if she can recall one. 'They're all brilliant tracks in my view,' she stalls. 'Whatever they play tonight is going to be special for everyone, both here and at home.' Can she go now?

Last question, the weather.

Jez obliges. 'Finally, Minister, the question on everyone's lips. Do we need to worry about the weather?'

Amanda is confused. It's beautiful out. No, wait a minute, she has a vague recollection of addressing Salt on this subject last night. What was it he said? *Nothing that would interfere with our plans.* He swore it on his dear, dead mother's grave. Nor has her team mentioned the weather, and quite frankly, she's had rather a lot on her plate to contend with today. 'Well, as long as people remember their sunblock and drink plenty of water, I don't foresee any problems.'

Now it's the presenters' turn to look puzzled. 'No,' Cleo clarifies for the sake of the minister, 'The storm that's been forecast for this evening. It's not going to cause a postponement?'

The wide-eyed minister tries her best to disguise a double take and searches for a diplomatic answer to this unexpected enquiry. Failing to locate one, she fires from the hip: 'I can assure everyone watching that nothing, but nothing, is going to stop tonight's show. You can take my word for that.'

***

Interview concluded, Amanda Teale has a further action on her immediate 'to do' list – get to the bottom of what happened last night. She knows exactly where to start, which is why Martin and Eclipse have been summoned into her presence. In fairness, both knew she'd find a way to lay the blame at their door.

Amanda, like all kangaroo court judges, is prepared to review the evidence in full before sentencing, as long as the accused get on with it: 'So, which one of you was it? Or were you in it together?'

Martin looks horrified at the charge, but it's only an act as he couldn't give a stuff. He wishes he had spiked her. 'I can assure you, Amanda, neither Eclipse nor myself had anything to do with the unfortunate events of last night.'

Eclipse enters the fray. 'I really resent the accusation if I'm being honest. Why would we do something like that, even if we had the means? We were actually concerned for you.'

'Oh, really? But not enough to report my disappearance to anybody or make sure I was OK,' Amanda tartly replies.

That's a harder one to bat off. 'We assumed your security detail was taking care of you,' Martin says. 'Really, this has nothing to do with us, and we didn't see anything suspicious.'

Eclipse, however, isn't finished. 'Funny that, isn't it? Nobody saw anything. Maybe you weren't spiked. Maybe you just fancied popping an E and need a scapegoat now you're all over the news and social media.' She looks to Martin for support and is met with a nod of agreement – *a perfectly plausible theory.*

Amanda (well into the anxiety, impulsivity, irritability and aggression stage of her comedown by now) explodes. 'How dare you. I have never taken a controlled substance in my life. You are pushing your luck here, Miss.'

The 'miss' in question knows that. So what? Do your worst. 'Who's to say?'

'It's inevitable,' Martin wryly observes, 'that you're upset with how you've been ridiculed in the media, but I think you should be really careful throwing baseless slurs about.'

Ridiculed? Slurs? Amanda is taken aback – when did these two suddenly grow a pair? She's unaccustomed to having her authority undermined, it's unsettling – and maybe she is barking up the wrong tree. 'I'm not accusing anybody,' she says in contradiction of her earlier indictment, 'just trying to establish the facts.' She backtracks, 'You must realise I have a lot riding on the success of this event.'

If she's looking for sympathy, she's come to the wrong place. They know exactly how important Be Here Now is for the minister and can hardly suppress their glee at her present discomfort.

Eclipse twists the knife. 'Can I ask, Amanda, what emboldened you just now to guarantee the show would go on tonight, come what may? I didn't realise you had control over the weather.'

Amanda's wits are struggling to keep up here. That British obsession again – the weather. Those stupid interviewers had raised it too, but hadn't she laid the matter to rest? And since when did she claim to have power over the elements? What's Eclipse driving at? 'I don't know what you mean. Why would the weather be a problem tonight?'

The two mutinous underlings snigger. She doesn't know. 'You've not seen the latest weather forecast, have you?' says Eclipse.

Well, no, Amanda has been rather busy, thank you very much, what with having responsibility for the country's energy needs and making Be Here Now happen, not to mention the almighty downer she's coping with. She has a faint recollection of the weather being discussed yesterday, but nobody has briefed her that there is anything to worry about. Or have they? It's impossible to order her thoughts; all she wants to do is lie down, but that's impossible as without her the entire undertaking would fall flat. She needs to check what the situation with the weather is, yes, but not with these two subversives. Don't admit to being on shaky ground. Ignore the question and move on. Regain control.

In this vein she scrambles to put a question directly to Martin. 'Where are we on the Gallagher brothers' endorsement of our green energy agenda? Done, finally?'

It's a crude diversion, and she fully expects another 'the dog ate my homework' response from the marketing maestro but he instead surprises her with a delirious cackle. He's past caring. 'God, Amanda, you can be so thick at times. Do you really think Noel and Liam Gallagher would go on the record to endorse the government's green energy policies?' Both women gasp at his audacity, but he's not finished. 'The entire Be Here Now shindig has been one big jerk-off for you, hasn't it? Granted, an expensive one at fifty million quid to the exchequer. The whole world is laughing at you and, you know what? So am I.' It's an outburst he's been dying to make for months – may as well get it off his chest before it's too late.

Despite her shock, Amanda maintains her dignity. 'Right, you've done it now, you dipsomaniac dipshit. You're fired, you hear me? Fired.'

This amuses him. 'I don't work for you, Amanda, so fire away.'

This is a mere technicality as far as the minister is concerned. 'You might not work directly for me, but I'm telling you, you're finished.'

Martin is unperturbed. 'Fine. Will I be confined to barracks in the meantime? Or are you going to have me forcibly exfiltrated by helicopter?'

That triggers Eclipse again. 'May as well. It's busier than Heathrow Airport around here.'

Amanda is having immense difficulty dealing with this dual onslaught on her authority, on her senses. She'd called the bloody meeting as well. Her own energy reserves are now so depleted it's going to take the national grid to reboot her.

'Just go,' she hisses at Martin, 'and stay out of my sight.' She turns to Eclipse. 'As for you, I'll deal with you in my own good time.'

Martin performs a mock bow. 'My pleasure, Minister.' Turning to Eclipse, 'Fancy a drink before the main action? I certainly do.'

The eco-warrior smiles sweetly at the minister as they sail out of the room. *Just you wait…*

23

I HOPE, I THINK, I KNOW

For anyone wishing to get away from the crowd, the small island offers few retreats. Dave and JJ, however, have found their way to the far end of one of Holm's fish-tailed groynes, a pier-like sea defence designed to dissipate wave energy. They sit peering at the horizon, imagining they're castaways. Given their outlook it's not long before their thoughts turn to musical selections of a desert island variety, JJ posing the question: 'What do you think they'll start with tonight?'

By rights, this game should be played by the four of them drawing on their many years of collective experience and knowledge, so excluding Ent and Stoggy is a punishment of sorts.

Dave, of course, has been boning up on Setlist. 'We've got to assume it'll be a greatest hits set. Stands to reason – live album, movie and all that. Plus, it's got to reflect their career.'

This much JJ knows. 'OK, we'll get on to that, but opening track. Come on.'

'Easy. "Fuckin' in the Bushes". Bookies' favourite.'

JJ gets his phone out to make a list. 'That's a walk-on track, a recorded intro. Does that count?'

This is news to Dave. He assumed they played it live. 'Of course,' he says. 'Forgot that.'

'So, what's second – first live – song then?'

Dave only needs to reflect on this for a few seconds. 'Got to be "Rock 'n' Roll Star". Nailed on.'

'Ah, but,' JJ counters, 'Liam used to start a lot of his solo gigs with that, so maybe not. I'm going for "Acquiesce". They share lead vocals on that – rare. And they've started with it in the past. Plus, it's a banger.'

Dave realises, despite his secret swotting up, he's not going to better JJ's knowledge. 'It's a possibility.'

They meander through various selections, but it doesn't feel the same just the two of them speculating. 'Ent and Stoggy would have been good on this, especially Stoggy,' JJ offers once they've run out of steam.

Given his earlier ruminations on the nature of friendship Dave is reluctant to acknowledge this but ultimately can't disagree. 'Sifter too. Although if you consider his inside info regarding Liam's sore throat, maybe not so much.'

'I wonder where they are. It's a bit quiet without them.'

'Hmmm.'

As they continue to look out to sea, the silence is suddenly shattered with a cry of, 'So this is where you've been hiding, girls.' They turn to see Ent and Stoggy advancing down the break towards them. 'Thought you'd shaken us off?' Ent laughs. 'No chance.' They sit down on the compacted rock surface. 'Thought you'd be in need of a beer,' he says, thrusting two chilled cans into their hands.

Peace restored, it doesn't take long… 'We were just trying to work out what they'd be playing tonight,' JJ informs the newcomers.

'Piece of Piss,' Ent says and reels off "Hello", 'Some Might Say", "Roll with It", "Cigarettes & Alcohol", "Supersonic", "Wonderwall", "Rock 'n' Roll Star", "Cast No Shadow", "Don't Look Back in Anger", "Morning Glory", "Champagne Supernova", 'Live Forever", "Acquiesce" and "I Am the Walrus".

'In that order?' Dave says drily.

Stoggy takes a sip of his beer. 'Don't you think you're missing the obvious there?'

They strain to work out the omission until JJ pipes up, 'Of course. "Be Here Now". They have to play that.'

'There's bugger all from their later albums there,' Stoggy points out. '"Lyla", "Hindu Times". What about "Go Let it Out"?'

'They're not even "late" late albums,' Dave notes. 'Tonight's setlist might basically be a confirmation they only made two decent albums, the first two classics, and everything after that was sloppy seconds.'

They want to disagree with him, but it's a hard argument to counter. 'They can't play everything, can they?' JJ reasons. 'They'll do two hours max, probably not even that. Say, twenty songs if we're lucky. It is sort of self-selecting.'

'No, it's not,' Stoggy dissents. 'First of all, you've not factored in whether Noel will do an acoustic section to slow it down mid-set – "Half the World Away" is a contender there. Then, what about tracks from their solo careers? "If I Had a Gun", "Wall of Glass". And what about special guests joining them?' He's clearly given this some thought.

'No chance they'll do solo stuff,' JJ says. 'Forget that.'

'They had John Squire guest at Knebworth,' Ent recalls. 'Except they edited him out afterwards.'

They nod in unison. *Unlikely then.*

'Here's one,' Dave says. 'Will they acknowledge each other, or will they keep to opposite ends of the stage? Imagine the two of them embracing in front of millions.'

The boys become dewy-eyed at the thought until JJ pulls up a distant memory. 'Yeah, but remember Pink Floyd at that Live 8 reunion? Dave Gilmour looked like he'd gladly kill Roger Waters on the spot.' They shake their heads sadly. *Please don't let it be so.*

Oasis predictions complete, there is a further item Ent feels obliged to raise, specifically for Dave's sake. 'Did you see that MP bird laughing off the video? Couldn't admit what happened, see. Told you there was nothing to worry about.'

Dave shrugs. *Like who was worried anyway?*

The main items on the agenda attended to, Stoggy contemplates his empty can and moves a motion. 'It's fucking baking out here. Head back to the beer tent?'

It's the official starting gun. It's show time.

The boys are back in the saddle.

***

Bryan runs through the details with Bob and Cody one final time before they synchronise their watches. This is it – they're going in. Their plans have radically altered following Cody's meeting with Eclipse. On his return, the young agitator had been of the opinion Plan B offered even less chance of success than storming the stage, but their leader had seized upon the intelligence he bore as if this course of action was ordained all along: *I knew something would come up.*

Cody is further miffed Bob has it easy again. While he has to go on dangerous manoeuvres, his fellow protester must simply post a video at the appointed hour. Where's the fairness in that? They could have at least tossed for it, but Bryan wasn't having it – *you're the one with the intel.* Of course, Bryan was going, that went without question.

As they make their way to the other end of the island, Cody continues to harbour concerns. 'I still think this is a bit rash,' he moans.

'Nonsense,' comes the reply from a bullish Bryan. '*He who is prudent and lies in wait for the enemy who is not, will be victorious.* The Art of War,' he adds (unnecessarily).

Cody rolls his eyes. 'But if we get caught, we'll be in real bother. Far more serious than a stage invasion.'

Bryan stops and grips him by the shoulders. 'We have an important message to deliver, you agree?'

'Well, yeah.'

'And what is that message? Tell me.'

'*Green Energy is Whistling in the Wind. Stop Climate Hoax Now.*'

'Correct. Remember that. We are standing up for our country, we are fighting for jobs and this action is justified and necessary. Time to step up.'

They set off again, Cody still looking for a get-out. 'Shouldn't we at least wait until later? We have hours yet.'

'No. We go now. Establish our position.'

The unwilling recruit has another thought. 'We should have packed water and food. Rations. We've still time to get some.'

Immaterial to Bryan. 'Is that all you can think about? Your stomach?'

'It's baking hot, and I suspect even hotter once we get there.'

'You've got a bottle of water. You'll be fine. We're not turning back now.'

Bryan can't understand Cody's reticence. This opportunity has dropped like manna from heaven. Credit to the young lad for playing the green goddess along but he needs to show some backbone now they're manning battle stations. If they pull this off, they'll be heroes.

Cody at least seems to know where's he's going, and it's not long before they reach a sunken walkway, out of sight of the rest of the island.

'You sure this is it?' Bryan whispers.

'Definitely.' He indicates the icon of a giant wind turbine stencilled on the wall. 'She said we couldn't miss it.'

'And there's nobody working down there?'

'Not today, according to her.'

Bryan takes a last look around. Happy they are not being overlooked they slip out of the sunshine and into the shadows of the ramp. Reaching the solid steel door at the bottom, Cody thrusts out his arm where the digits of the passcode are scrawled in biro. 1-9-6-6-4-2. Bryan smiles. Set by a true patriot, obviously. He punches in the numbers and the door swings open. Within seconds they are inside the underground processing plant.

If only Eclipse had known, in light of Amanda's walkabout, that an unscheduled change in security arrangements had led to the deployment of a small SAS unit down there.

***

Rachel and Justine hit on the perfect spot to avoid the Mancs: a small corner of the island dedicated to healing and connection, where those of a spiritual bent can explore – and hopefully expand – their outlook on life. Entitled 'Re-gen', the attractions here tap into the fountainhead of the 1960s counter-cultural dream (provided your wristband has sufficient credit remaining).

Re-gen nearly didn't make the cut in the planning stage. *Hippy nonsense* according to Salt. *A waste of space* (quite literally) to Martin when every square foot on the island counts. Eclipse, of course, was in favour – *our own Healing Fields* – while the final decision went to Amanda, who greenlighted it after concluding people with an elevated consciousness were more likely to vote for her. (Ironically, Re-Gen is probably the place where Amanda should be recuperating right now after her wild night.)

It's not exactly busy (endorsing Salt's view that Oasis fans and patchouli oil don't really mix) but despite the pressure on space, Re-Gen isn't short of things for the two friends to see and do. Breathing in the incense they wander beneath the Tibetan prayer flags, past the giant Buddha and the firewalk pit, until they're approached by an earnest young man: 'Our gong workshop is starting in five minutes. Would you like to join?' Despite the promise of an immersive sound bath and the powerful vibrations that will be unleashed, they decline the opportunity to release their energy blockages, for now at least. 'Maybe the five o'clock one,' Rachel says over her shoulder as they retreat, so as not to appear a stranger to her inner consciousness.

'Fancy the yoga?' Justine asks as they study the list of free participative events taking place during the afternoon.

Rachel shakes her head dismissively. 'God, no. I tried it once at the leisure centre. It was supposed to be meditative but all I could think about were the jobs I had to do when I got home.'

'Well, how about Tai Chi in that case?'

'Isn't that a cocktail? I could be up for that.' It's a crap joke, and Rachel knows it. 'Sorry, I'm useless, aren't I? Boring. I suppose I get plenty of exercise walking the dogs. You do a lot more of this stuff than me, don't you?'

'Well, I suppose I have more free time. I love yoga, and Pilates too. You should try it. Good for the mind as well as the body.'

Rachel reflects, not for the first time recently, how conventional and unadventurous her life has become. Same old, same old, while everybody she knows appears to be doing new and exciting things. But hang on, she's at bloody Oasis on Holm Island. How many people are doing that? That's not being boring or stuck in a rut. No, she's as game as anyone. Up for it. 'I tell you what,' she says, 'how about we get a tattoo?'

Justine laughs. 'Seriously?'

Rachel points to a distant stall. 'Yes. Over there.'

Justine is immediately circumspect. 'I don't think a tattoo is the sort of thing you should rush into. And what about the risk of infection?'

'I just feel like doing something, I don't know, rebellious.'

'It will hurt like hell, especially depending on where you have it. And what would you have tattooed anyway?'

'Come on, let's at least take a look,' Rachel says, dragging Justine along by her un-inked arm.

They approach the stall only for Rachel to let out a disappointed cry as the signage becomes clearer: 'Oh, they're not real ones.'

Justine squints and reads the heading from the display poster: '*Choose from six celebrity-designed temporary tattoos and help combat climate change.*'

Rachel chafes. 'I was going to have one done, as well.'

Justine's sense of relief is palpable. 'Thank goodness you can't. You'd have regretted it.'

Crestfallen (in the way you convince yourself you would have gone through with something if you hadn't been stopped), Rachel examines the six illustrations on offer. 'They're all Oasis themed.'

Secure in the knowledge no needles are in prospect, Justine is positivity itself. 'I don't mind something that washes off after two or three days. Which one do you fancy?' They study the designs. A series of badly executed doodles and poor puns in dayglo colours knocked out by a coterie of C-list musos (or their offspring) during a tea break. Justine pulls a face. 'Then again, maybe not. They're crap, aren't they?'

Are they? Rachel hadn't really noticed. She'd been thinking which one Matthew might like, or whether she should buy him all six because they wouldn't be readily available off the island. But Justine is right – these are tat tattoos, and at £20 each, or £100 for the set (for char-i-dee), a rip-off. She can't disagree. 'You're right, I'll pass.' In the space of sixty seconds she's gone from Mrs Doubtfire to Xena: Warrior Princess and back again. What's wrong with her?

Rachel does a double take. Right next door is a sign welcoming festivalgoers to a *Get to Know Your Vagina* workshop. 'It says men are welcome too. I'm not so sure about that.'

That's off the agenda for Justine too. Thankfully, she's spots something altogether more suitable in her opinion – a small tent bearing a sign: *Tarot Readings by Anastasia. The Cards Never Lie.* She points. 'There's something we can do.'

Now it's Rachel's turn to be diffident. She's never had a Tarot reading. In fact, she's never 'dabbled' in what she considers to be the 'occult' – seances, Ouija, crystal balls. Nevertheless, she allows herself to be drawn over for a closer inspection, whereupon Anastasia herself materialises, seemingly out of nowhere, to ensure they don't leave without crossing her palm with silver. Anastasia doesn't look strikingly Romany or mystic to Rachel – she looks like a pub landlady – but it's not wise to judge a book by its cover in this game.

'You go, and I'll wait,' she says to Justine.

No chance – Anastasia isn't having that. 'I'll do a special price for the two of you,' she growls, with the insistence of a mugger wielding a blade. It's quickly agreed, and neither of them is inclined to cavil that the 'special price' turns out to be the single fee multiplied by two. Anastasia weighs them up – 'You, first,' she barks at Rachel, a clear escape risk. Within seconds she's inside, sitting at a small table, her eyes adjusting to the dark interior after the bright sunshine outside.

Anastasia gets straight down to it. 'Welcome to this voyage of self-discovery. What is on your mind that the cards may help you with?'

Rachel wavers. That's direct. It was her understanding that fortune tellers simply fed back to you whatever information you gave them, and it was best to volunteer zilch, but there's no doubt that question was on the nail. She capitulates. 'Er, my relationships, I suppose. Relationship, that is.'

Anastasia nods sagely, like she had already guessed that. She solemnly shuffles the pack of cards and fans them out across the table. 'Pick three cards and lay them face down,' she instructs.

Rachel studies the arc of cards, urging them to speak to her. Then, remembering it's all a load of baloney, plucks three cards from the middle of the spread and places them side by side.

'First, the past,' Anastasia intones as she turns the first card over. 'Ah, the Ten of Wands.' She scrutinises the image carefully. 'You are a driven individual, with many accomplishments. You take responsibility but sometimes feel the weight of these burdens. Am I right?

Rachel starts. That's remarkably accurate. She'd set up her own business, after all. And people always admired how organised and on top of things she was. And, yes, true, she often wished somebody else would help out – *Why do I have to do everything around here, Matthew?*

Anastasia takes that as a yes and moves on to the second card. 'Now, the present.' Her eyes widen briefly. 'Oh. The Tower. A Major Arcana card. Significant.'

That piques Rachel's interest. 'Is that good or bad?'

Anastasia closes her eyes searching for the right words. 'Life changing, with a long-term effect. The Tower signifies sudden upheaval, broken pride… or disaster.'

'Disaster?'

'The cards are not always literal,' says Anastasia, citing the Tarot Card Union's standard get-out clause. 'But this should not be taken lightly.'

Rachel contemplates the implications of this card. Upheaval. Apt given what she's going through with Matthew. Broken pride? She wouldn't have expressed her current feelings in quite those terms. Disaster? No, that's wrong. Whatever you could say about her life right now, it's not as if she has an appointment with Armageddon scheduled in her diary. Still, best be on guard.

'The final card, the future,' Anastasia says dramatically (and with one eye on the clock). Rachel bolts upright as The Lovers is turned over. Surely that's a fix? 'Another Major Arcana card, that's unusual to get two out of three.'

'Is it?' She doesn't know what Major Arcana means, but still. 'Should I be worried?'

Anastasia makes a calming gesture with her palms. 'Major Arcana cards indicate seismic shifts. There are only twenty-two Major Arcana cards out of the full Tarot set of seventy-eight, so to draw two out of three has resonance.' She returns to The Lovers card again. 'This signifies union, physical intimacy and attraction. Choices. It tells me you are in a place to receive and share love.'

Rachel feels the tears well up. 'Yes, but who with?'

The seer is careful not to over-commit on this one. 'That is up to you. It is time to contemplate what you truly desire so you can manifest it.'

It's more than Rachel can bear.

Seconds later, Justine is astounded as her friend dashes from the small tent in a flood of tears. As she dashes after her, the sky turns black, and she feels the pitter-patter-plink of large raindrops falling on her bare shoulders.

24

FORCE OF NATURE

Sifter's up-to-the-minute post contains tidings millions would rather remain unfamiliar with:

Sifter's blog:

Disaster! Three hours to stage time and the entire fucking island has been hit by a cataclysmic storm. You couldn't make it up. It feels like we're getting the area's annual rainfall in a single dump, whipped up by a vicious wind that's driven everybody under cover.

It's hard to imagine the band going on in conditions like this.

The weather has been amazing for days, but this was always an accident waiting to happen. Whoever decided an energy island in the middle of the North Sea would be a good place for Oasis to make a one-off appearance after twenty years away needs horse-whipping.

From what I hear, the boys were already unhappy with the sound check, complaining it wasn't loud enough.

That might be a technicality now unless the weather relents sufficiently to allow them to play. They're currently holed up in their dressing rooms, and I can only begin to guess how they're feeling with the whole world watching.

Whatever happens, there needs to be an in-depth post-mortem into the planning and preparation of this so-called 'gig of the century'.

More as I get it.

PS: If you know any 'stop the rain' spells, now's the time. Maybe a human sacrifice of the twats who assured us 'optimum weather conditions' would prevail.

***

Nobody wants to say it out loud, but the consensus of the hastily arranged crisis meeting isn't dissimilar to Sifter's: *It's a fucking disaster.*

Martin and Eclipse slip into the room, not out of a sense of duty as much as curiosity – what are *they* going to do about this? Amanda is so pre-occupied she doesn't eject them – her focus is elsewhere, specifically on Salt and Ross. 'So, what's the plan?' the minister demands.

Ross, still smarting from the sound check (*It should have been louder, man! Slide the fuckers up),* nevertheless remains calm under pressure. 'The first thing is, let's not panic. The weather is unfortunate but could pass as quickly as it arrived. That's the forecast. The site and staging will survive the conditions – they're designed to – so this could be just a temporary setback. If – and I stress the word if – it calms by eight, then I'd say we would be good to go live with Oasis by ten, one hour late, but still doable.'

It's a cool assessment and encouraging under the circumstances, but not good enough for the minister. 'Fine. But what if the weather doesn't relent? What then?'

It's left for Ross to pick up the pieces again. 'Well, in that case, we'd have to implement the reserve day and do it tomorrow. That's the contingency plan.'

Salt is stirred into action. 'That would be an extreme eventuality, of course. I'm sure it won't come to that.'

'No,' says Amanda firmly. 'It had better not.'

Ross bites his lip. The reason they have contingencies is to deal with the expected unexpected, like the weather for example. It's standard stuff. Can't do A, so do B instead. Keep calm and carry on. But these two appear to be ignoring what's in front of their noses with their bland assurances and fruitless demands. They're losing it. He feels compelled to speak up again. 'I appreciate the pressure we're all under but *wishing it to be so* is a bit different from being able to *make it happen*. If this weather doesn't blow over in the next hour, we're stuffed, and it'll have to be tomorrow.'

Salt, who appears to have aged ten years in the past few minutes, shakes his head. 'It has to be tonight. Everything is lined up, the punters, the broadcast, the band. It's only a bit of rain. We've done shows in worse.'

The entire group looks at him like he's lost his marbles. *Only a bit of rain*? It feels like the worst storm at sea since the Spanish Armada sank.

'We've done shows in the wet, yeah,' Ross wearily reminds him, 'but not in this wind.'

'It has to be tonight,' Salt repeats.

Ross looks around for support. Martin is glassy-eyed, struggling to keep up, while Eclipse is sporting a crooked smile like she's enjoying the exchange. He tries again. 'If it's of any interest – and it surely is – I've checked the forecast for tomorrow and it's going to be fine.'

'We have to go tonight,' insists the impresario once more.

The head of production changes tack. 'Can I ask what the band is saying? They may prefer to wait until tomorrow given the momentous nature of the gig. Has anybody actually asked them?'

All eyes are on Salt, who doesn't look at all well. 'They do what I tell them. I'm the one who's paying them.'

Objection. Amanda isn't having that. 'I think you'll find that it's me who's paying them, Salt, not you. The final decision should rest with me.'

Martin's and Eclipse's ears perk up at that. Is Amanda really equipped to make that call? She may as well toss a coin. (But given momentous political decisions are often made on that basis, why change now?)

The lights flicker as another broadside of wind and rain buffets the green room, prompting Amanda to take control. 'We will reconvene at eight sharp, assess the situation, and I will make the final decision. Understood?'

Happy to escape, they each file out nursing their thoughts:

Ross is mystified as to Salt's reckless insistence on going ahead in such conditions.

Amanda is calculating how her reputation might be restored if she repels the waves and delivers Oasis for the people.

Martin, buoyed by a warm glow of *schadenfreude*, could do with another vodka.

Eclipse is wondering what this means for the Conserve Aquatic Reserves Partnership.

Salt is kicking himself for not taking out the extra 'second night' weather cover from his insurers. *It'll never happen. Why waste money? Better off in my pocket than in theirs.*

***

The four Mancs had watched in amazement as the sky turned black and the rain began to teem. At least they were already under cover in the marquee when it started but that consolation was soon dashed as thousands of Supernovas, with nowhere else to shelter, invaded their space.

'So much for privileged access,' Dave gripes.

'At least we have seats,' Ent is gracious enough to point out.

As the bedraggled horde squeezes into every square foot of available space the tension begins to rise. 'It's like a scene from a disaster movie in here,' JJ observes.

'Yeah – The Poseidon Adventure, if you ask me,' (not that anyone had asked Stoggy).

An announcement comes over the speakers that the bars are to be shut as a safety precaution. That elicits a groan despite the obvious fact there's no room to swing a cat, never mind raise a glass. Whatever Dunkirk spirit briefly held sway soon dissipates as more and more saturated souls try to gain access to the haven of the marquee. Self-appointed bouncers repel all boarders and fights and arguments erupt along the line. Nobody can say where the people who can't get in should go. That's their problem.

Sitting tight as they look to the heavens, it's left to Ent to sum up their present predicament: 'I don't like the look of this.'

'We're screwed,' JJ agrees.

Stoggy shakes his head sadly as Dave ruminates on how much this trip has set him back, the prospect of another twenty-four hours on the island, and what he's going to tell his wife.

A quick read of Sifter's latest blog does little to lighten the mood, so they take to checking any weather forecast they can find for a glimmer of hope.

'The Beeb was right,' Ent says. 'They said the weather might be stormy.'

'I saw that too, but didn't like to say anything,' JJ confesses. 'Didn't want to tempt fate. Bit late now.'

They gaze at the torrents of water cascading off the marquee awnings, and the plastic chairs and bar parasols cartwheeling across the site like tumbleweed. The temperature has dropped twenty degrees, causing everybody – especially the drowned ones – to shiver in their light summer clothes. It's dismal, but Ent suddenly discovers faint grounds for optimism. 'Hang on. The Beeb said there might be a storm *during* Oasis, but it's storming now. So maybe it'll pass in time for them coming on?'

'Positive thinking, Ent. Nice one,' says JJ consolingly.

Dave the meteorologist gloomily disagrees. 'This looks well set to me. Admit it, we've no chance tonight. And what if they can't put it on tomorrow either? What then?' He pulls out his phone to check under what conditions, if any, refunds might come into play.

Stoggy cannot bear such defeatist talk. 'There's no way the boys will let us down. Rain or shine, innit? They'll play, you'll see.'

'They can't play in this, Stoggy,' Ent reasons.

'And the decision won't be theirs, either,' JJ adds. 'It will be a health and safety one.'

'What a bloody mess,' Dave groans.

An already dire situation takes a further downward turn as a second announcement comes over the speakers. 'Can all Supersonic ticket holders please relocate to their accommodation so we can free up more space for people without shelter.'

The four look at each other. 'So, what do we do now?' Ent asks.

They stare balefully into the deluge. 'Well, one thing's for certain,' Dave decides, 'I'm not bloody going out in that. It'll be hailstones next.' They each slide their Supersonic passes under their shirts.

***

Rachel and Justine make it back to their pod just before the heavens fully open. The weather isn't the first thing on their mind, however.

'What's wrong?' asks a concerned Justine. 'What did she say?'

The rain dashes a steady drumbeat on the flat roofs of the plastic palaces as Rachel recovers her breath. Finally, 'Nothing really. Or nothing I didn't already know.'

'So why are you so upset? I was scared for you.'

Rachel shakes her head. She knows she's being irrational, but she can't help it. 'I picked out three cards, one for the past, one for the present, one for the future. She started with a compliment – saying how I had many achievements and stuff like that. Great. Who hasn't?'

That does sound kind of general, Justine agrees.

'Then, I drew the present card. Upheaval and disaster no less. Well, she didn't need to tell me about the state of my relationship because I already know. But what am I supposed to make of "disaster"?'

Justine points upwards: 'Maybe she was referring to the weather. So, what did you get for the future?'

'Guess. The Lovers of course. A bloody fix.'

'I doubt it – there's a lot of cards to go at, after all. But what did she say about it that was so upsetting?'

Rachel shakes her head. 'That's the thing. Nothing specific. She said I'm in a place to share love, but it's up to me. Brilliant, eh? As if I haven't been wrestling with that one for months. But all I could think of, when she said it, was last night, and then Matthew. And that's when I lost it.'

'I'll say you lost it,' Justine laughs. 'I could hardly keep up with you when you ran off. Plus, I didn't get my reading, and I doubt we'll get a refund.'

'Oh, I'm sorry. Should we go back?

'Only joking.'

Rachel feels calmer now. 'I've been such a fool. Telling myself I don't know what I want, when I sort of do really. Or do I?'

It's a brainteaser that would tax anyone, but not Justine. 'I know exactly what you mean. Listen, this is all good. You've taken time apart to decide on your marriage, and you're working it through. You'll make the right choice in the end, I know.'

Rachel squeezes her friend's hand. Two days ago, she was bemoaning having Justine as a companion, her third choice for this monumental trip, but what a surprise she's turned out to be. Not the thing with JJ – although that was, well, unexpected – but her understanding, her empathy, her encouragement. It's made Rachel feel small. Moreover, it's made her feel grateful for her company.

Her appreciation is cut short by a loud bang as a heavy object strikes the door. They can hardly push it open as they go to investigate, the wind doing its best to slam it in their faces. The sight that greets them is as alarming as it is unanticipated. Dark skies, torrential rain, figures scurrying for cover amid flying furniture and debris. They quickly withdraw to the rather impressive protection of the pod.

'Oh my God,' Rachel cries. 'It's like one of those climate disaster movies.'

Justine is equally stunned. 'Where on earth has that come from? We're lucky to be in here.'

Her friend is feeling anything but blessed. Her spirits sag once more. Winning this competition was supposed to be a major landmark in her life, a new beginning, or maybe a validation of what she already had. It was billed as a big adventure, only not the sort of adventure it's turning out to be.

Another item crashes into their pod, making them jump. It must be said the seventy-five per cent recycled water bottle plastic walls are doing a fine job – the international disaster relief charity that's due to receive them next will get good use out of them.

'Well, one thing's for certain,' Justine says, 'you can forget Oasis tonight. We're going to have to sit tight until this stops.'

Rachel groans. All she'd really like to do right now is get back to the mainland.

25

ROLL WITH IT

Deep inside the processing plant, the aircon provides a welcome respite from the heat they left behind. Not only that, but Cody is delighted to discover an array of vending machines in what is clearly a rest area. A quick inspection reveals a problem though. 'Bollocks, they don't take cash. Do you have your credit card on you?'

Bryan is about to point out the idiocy of leaving a direct link to his identity behind when he remembers that anonymity isn't what this mission is about. 'Yes,' he answers, 'but there's only one Twix left and I'm having it.'

Five minutes later they are armed with a pyjama party's worth of energy drinks, crisps, chocolate bars and biscuits. 'I could do with a receipt for my tax return,' Bryan quips. 'We are on a business trip after all.'

'Look at the state of this place, though,' Cody says in disgust, clearing dirty plates and cups from the unwiped table and placing them in the bin. 'It doesn't take much to clean up after you, does it.'

Only thirty minutes prior to their arrival these very seats had been occupied by four off-duty members of the SAS until they were abruptly issued with fresh orders by a jumpy ministerial team. Two had been scrambled 'up top' to provide extra protection for Amanda, while the remaining two had been posted to the centre of the wind turbine hall, the island's 'soft underbelly' in the eyes of the anti-terrorism squad.

Blissfully unaware of this, the two gallant HUTH (Had it Up To Here) members idly commence their wait. 'How long now?' Cody asks.

Their leader checks his watch. 'Just under four hours yet, plenty of time. The main thing is we're in and haven't been rumbled.'

Cody contemplates his Curly Wurly. 'So, they're on at nine, and we strike at ten, yeah?'

Bryan nods. 'Bang in the middle of the set. Optimum impact, maximum exposure. Bob posts the video and we go global, exposing climate hoax for what it is.'

His younger companion puts the chocolate bar aside and rips open a packet of smoky bacon twists instead. 'It's good to be out of that heat,' Cody says as he slumps down in his chair.

'Too bloody right,' Bryan agrees. 'I don't know what's been happening to the weather recently.'

'A few hours to kill, then. Did we really need to come down here so early?'

Bryan reaches for another maxim from Sun Tzu, before opting for: 'Yes, we bloody well did. This is an operation, not an outing. We needed to ensure we are in position, and no one saw us entering.'

'Suppose so.'

'That green bird said no one else would be down here, right?'

'Not until tomorrow, no.'

'You sure about that?'

Cody takes a chug from his bottle of Lucozade Sport before replying. 'Course, I'm sure.'

'Right, so we sit tight here for a bit and then make our move at the right time. Don't go wandering or touch anything in case we set off an alarm or something.'

Cody peels the foil wrapper from his Chocolate Mini Roll and pops it whole into his mouth. 'Do you think this will, like, actually work?'

Understandably, Bryan is a little miffed at his lieutenant's wavering faith in the new masterplan. 'What do you mean, will it work? You're the one who came up with it.'

Cody swallows hard. He's not taking the blame if it goes wrong. 'No, she told me this was the one thing that would stop the entire concert. I was just passing it on. You decided to try it because she also said we'd probably get shot or something if we tried to get on the stage.'

'Well, it makes sense, doesn't it?'

'What?'

'That they can't have the wind turbines turned on while there's ten thousand people on the island. Health and Safety.'

Cody shrugs. Sounds about right.

'So, we switch them on at ten and pow – they have to stop the show.'

'Apparently.'

'One control panel, three switches – it's like it's all been laid on for us.'

Cody nods. Affirmative. It sounds so easy the way Bryan puts it, but he's more interested in the move after that. 'And then we get out of here?'

'Yeah, and then we get arrested, 'cos that's part of the plan too. We'll go peacefully. A night in the cells and a slap on the wrist is a small price to pay for all the publicity we're going to get for the cause. We'll be hailed as heroes.'

'Not by Oasis fans, we won't.'

'You say that, but I suspect a lot of them are on our side anyway.'

'Really?'

'Well, maybe not, but remember our line is we're regretfully taking this action, not to spoil people's fun but to bring this important issue to the world.'

Cody gets it. 'The end justifies the means and all that.'

'Exactly. The end justifies the means.'

A loud rumble suddenly emanates from deep within Cody's guts. 'Christ,' he says, ruefully rubbing his stomach, 'I think I've eaten too much.'

'You know what,' Bryan says, 'we've made a bit of a mistake here.'

Cody views him with alarm. *What?*

'We should have brought a pack of cards. We've got bloody hours to kill here.'

***

Miraculously, five minutes before Amanda's eight o'clock deadline, the storm abates as suddenly as it started.

Salt is beside himself with relief as he charges into the green room. 'Told you,' he brays, as if the devastation of the past three hours was all part of the plan.

Ross, however, has reservations. 'I still think we should postpone until tomorrow. The site is a mess. The rain has stopped but there's still a strong wind, and that will play havoc with the sound balance. Plus, everybody is piss wet through and miserable.'

The impresario falters. Since when did his head of production get so knock-kneed? It must be tonight. *Has to be.* 'Not as miserable as they're going to be if they don't get to see

Oasis in a couple of hours,' he counters. 'And millions around the world too. Rain or shine, Ross, rain or shine. It would be a crime to chicken out now.'

He looks to the group for backing. Eclipse and Martin have somehow escaped the minister's red card again, and sensibly wait for her to speak first. Amanda, for her part, breaks down the challenge into two distinct parts: *she's damned if she does, she's damned if she doesn't.* She needs to reach a decision where she can take the credit if it goes well and be able to blame somebody else if it goes tits up. 'Take me through the downsides again,' she demands of Ross.

All eyes are on him. Where does he start? 'Well, there's still a strong wind and that could play havoc with the sound, and I don't think the band would forgive us if that wasn't bang on. Then we don't have time to double check all the equipment if they go on tonight. It could have sustained damage in the downpour. Then there's crowd safety…'

Salt interjects at that. 'Crowd safety? Seriously? We've had a bit of rain, not a hurricane. It's a bigger safety risk keeping people here for another twenty-four hours.'

Ross is becoming alarmed at Salt's casual dismissals, so falls back on his earlier observation. 'We could really do with the band inputting into this discussion.'

The impresario dismisses this out of hand. 'The band? They'll do what's in their best interests, which is one hundred million smackers being wired into their bank account the second they take to the stage.'

Martin stirs. 'I wouldn't have a problem waiting another day if I knew a hundred mill was going to drop into my lap.'

'Yes, well nobody asked you,' Salt growls. He moves to close the argument. 'Look, we're wasting time here. We can get this show on by ten if we agree to agree now.' He defies anyone to dissent. Nobody does. 'So, I can tell Oasis it's a goer?'

Amanda doesn't like being forced into a corner, but he has a point. They can't sit here all night having a debate.

Eclipse picks this moment to join the discussion. 'If I may, Minister, can I refresh your memory as to what you said on air just four hours ago.'

Amanda's brain is fried. She's said a lot of things and it's hard to keep on top of it all, especially when you're on a huge downer. 'Remind me,' she instructs.

Eclipse smiles widely, only too happy to help. 'You said you could assure everyone watching that nothing, but nothing, was going to stop tonight's show. And you added, *You can take my word for that.*'

The minister freezes. Did she? But even if she did, 'But I didn't know there was going to be a storm, did I?'

Eclipse clears this up for her. 'The interviewer asked you specifically about the storm forecast.'

Salt sees his opening. 'I think, Amanda, it would reflect very badly on you if we were to postpone. You've given your pledge it will go ahead tonight; you don't want people saying politicians never keep their promises, do you?'

There's silence as Amanda lets this sink in. She is a representative of the people, respected for her candour and honesty (or so it said on her election handout). Part of the new breed of politicians who underpromise and overdeliver. Did she really assure everyone tonight's show would go on? Well, in that case: 'We go tonight,' she says. 'Let us meet the expectations of the people both here and at home.' Such is the weight of responsibility thrust upon the shoulders of a minister of state. Thank goodness, Amanda reminds herself, she isn't afraid to make the big decisions where others dilly-dally.

Salt wants to punch the air in triumph. Saved by the bell. 'I'll go and tell the lads,' he says gleefully. Turning to Ross: 'Over to you now. Don't screw it up,' and with that he's out the door.

The stoic head of production shrugs – *On your head be it* – and follows him out.

The minister still has one more decision to make – her planned outfit for the gig. Perhaps, given last night's unfortunate events, it would be wise to leave the rock chick in the red despatch box. It's such a shame, but the shine has well and truly come off the entire event for her at this juncture. Best to get it over with as soon as possible and go home. They say don't mix business with pleasure – so true. The vital thing now is getting through it without any further mishap. An hour's rest before it starts wouldn't go amiss either.

'Right, everybody,' she says, before realising that 'everybody' comprises Martin and Eclipse (*didn't she sack them?*). 'Action stations.' As she exits, she glances over her shoulder: 'Let's hope nothing else goes wrong,' she half laughs.

Eclipse smirks. *Yes, let's.*

26

DON'T GO AWAY

It's left to Cleo and Jez to deliver the glad tidings to the world from the damp arena floor. Both are wrapped up to the eyeballs, she in a fetching Barbour waxed jacket, he in a parka with a fur collar he'd dug out of his wardrobe as a tribute to tonight's act. The picture doesn't exactly suggest fine sunlit summer evening.

'The news is tonight's concert is very much on,' Cleo beams.

'Fears were raised earlier when Holm Island was swept by heavy downpours and high winds,' Jez says. He holds his upturned hand out and looks to the skies, 'But thankfully, the rain has now stopped.'

At that exact moment a gust of wind blows Cleo's gaily coloured felt trilby from her head, skimming it like a frisbee towards Blighty. Professional as ever, she continues, 'But as you can see, we still have a bit of wind to contend with.'

'Well, we are on a wind farm, so maybe that's to be expected,' Jez smiles. He then switches to serious face: 'But nothing that will get in the way of the show, we are assured.'

'I'm so excited,' Cleo squeals. 'I've never seen Oasis before. It's such a thrill to be here.'

'Were you even born the last time they played, Cleo?'

'I believe I was. It was the same year you retired for the third time, wasn't it?'

Jez moves it on. 'The countdown has commenced so let's update you on that important stage time.'

'Oasis will be on stage at ten o'clock – one hour later than originally scheduled.'

'But after a wait of twenty years, what's another hour?

'And remember, here on the Oasis livecast you won't miss a single minute of tonight's show.'

'Are you ready, world?' Jez exclaims.

Cleo turns to her co-presenter. 'Are you ready, Jez?'

'Always,' he cracks. 'I was brought up on Baden-Powell's *Be prepared* motto.'

Cleo looks confused. 'What century was that then?'

He ignores her. 'We're hearing the show may run to two hours. Plenty of time for your favourites to be played.'

'And all being well, we're hoping to get some backstage reaction once the show wraps.'

'It's really happening, folks.'

'Stay tuned.'

***

The news isn't as welcome in some quarters as Jez and Cleo anticipate. A puffy-eyed Rachel is gobsmacked that the show is going ahead. 'In this weather? It's going to be miserable.' At least the conditions will match her mood.

Justine is more upbeat as she rallies her friend. 'Come on, it's going to be better than being cooped up in here. We're seeing Oasis – that's what we've come for. And it will take your mind off things for a while too.' She doesn't need to spell out what 'things' she's referring to.

They look outside to inspect what's going on. There's still a stiff wind blowing but it's not raining anymore and, remarkably, due to the artificial drainage, it's firm underfoot. People are emerging from their shelters and making their way towards the arena. There's no doubt it's on.

Rachel pulls from her bag the outfit she'd so carefully planned for tonight. It feels wrong now, not just mood-wise, but in practical terms. 'I'm going to freeze in this,' she concludes.

'I've got a spare cagoule,' Justine offers. It's gratefully accepted.

Minutes later, both are decked out as if they're about to embark on a coast-to-coast hike. After all, there's no such thing as bad weather, only the wrong clothes.

As they join the line of fans making their way to the entry gates, Rachel has to remind herself that this is the biggest thing to happen in music this century, because it certainly doesn't feel like that at this precise moment. Would Matthew be feeling this same sense of anticlimax if he were here? She reproaches herself yet again for not fully entering into the spirit of the event. *Focus on the gig. It will be great once it starts. Enjoy it. Don't be a mardy arse.*

She also knows she can't put off a decision about her future for much longer. Time's nearly up. Maybe, just maybe, she'll get some sort of sign to help make her mind up.

***

The four Mancs don't know whether to be happier that the gig is going ahead, or that the bar has re-opened. With less than two hours to the start they have some serious catching up to do on the drinking front.

Stoggy downs his first pint of the evening with a chaser of smugness: 'Never in doubt.'

The group's health and safety expert is still scratching his head. 'I must admit I'm very surprised. After a storm like that you'd imagine there'd be all manner of checks they'd need to do.'

'Sod that, JJ,' Ent blares. 'It's on, and it's going to be the best moment in my life since *Aguerooooo!*'

Dave, however, is unable to refrain from voicing some misgivings. 'It's still a bit damp. And blowy. I'd envisaged it being a perfect summer's evening.' The sort of weather to match his investment in other words.

This is a trifling consideration as far as Ent is concerned. 'Doesn't matter, it's going to be epic. Outdoor gigs aren't always sunny – it pisses it down at Parklife every year.'

'Yeah, but you never go to that, do you,' JJ reminds him. 'You may think differently if the rain starts up again.'

'No, I won't,' Ent replies. He takes a swig of his beer. 'Waterproofing inside and out. Nothing is going to spoil tonight for me.'

'Are we going to get changed?' Dave asks. Like most people he's planned his attire for the night.

'You can if you want, you big tart,' Stoggy snipes, 'but we're staying here. No time to waste. It's not a fashion show. It's Oasis.'

Ent nods his agreement as Dave and JJ give up on the idea of a wardrobe change. They're still dressed in shorts and T-shirts, but at least they're dry.

Fortified with a double double round, their thoughts turn to the optimum time to enter the arena. The original plan was to get in early, get a good spot, and soak up the atmosphere, but the storm has thrown a big spanner into that stratagem.

'There'll be a massive queue already,' JJ observes.

'Valuable drinking time lost in my view,' according to Stoggy.

'But we don't want to be at the back,' Ent says anxiously. 'Not after all this time. We have to be at the front.'

Dave envisages them missing the gig altogether at this rate. 'I think we should go now, and queue up with everyone else. Really.'

Stoggy is not for turning. 'Nah. Stay here until everybody is in and make a late run inside just before they come on.'

'But then we'll be at the back,' Ent repeats. 'I don't want to be miles away.'

Stoggy shakes his head. 'No, we won't. We'll do the pincer movement.' They look to him for further explanation. 'Get inside, hare down the side of the crowd to the far corner, then push back at forty-five degrees into the middle. Nobody ever stops anybody coming away from the stage, and fuck 'em if they try.'

This seems to put Ent's mind at rest. It sounds Napoleonic and Northenden at the same time. 'I'm in,' he shouts enthusiastically.

Dave and JJ exchange glances, and it's left to the host to express what they're both thinking. 'I don't know, lads. I think we'd rather head in now, to make sure.'

Stoggy shrugs. *Do it the hard way if you want.*

Ent decides he's sticking with the late crew. 'If you're sure. We'll see you down the front, yeah?'

The two eager beavers finish their drinks and stand up. 'Right,' says JJ, 'down the front it is.' They all know this won't be happening.

As they exit the marquee Dave turns to JJ and asks, 'Do you think we've time for a quick change?'

Inside, their two friends are holding court in the rapidly emptying bar. 'I guarantee we'll be nearer the front than them,' Stoggy jests. He fishes a small plastic bag of white powder from his pocket. 'And there'll be more of this for the two of us at the same time.'

Ent chuckles. 'Let the festivities begin.'

27

HEY NOW!

The fans file into the arena, hardly daring to believe the weather has relented. As if to eliminate any lingering doubts the skies lighten beneath the cloud cover, the setting sun creating a dazzling sunburst finish of yellows, reds and blacks on the west side of the island. The crowd divides itself into three distinct tiers on the arena floor: the frontline crushers, the halfway housers, and the comfort seekers at the back with a poor view. Those in the elevated tiers congratulate themselves on having secured a seat, despite the stiff breeze parting their hair. As it has been decreed no other band can perform alongside Oasis, it's been left to Mr Scruff to knock out a few piscine-related toons to entertain the waiting masses. At least he can be relied upon to fill in for hours if needs be.

Ross is paying a visit to the sound booth, no doubt with a reminder, as if needed, to make sure the volume for the show is turned up to eleven. Although he'd earlier been in favour of holding everything over for twenty-four hours, he's relieved it's going ahead. He realises now, looking at the weather, the stage, the arena and the gathering crowd, he'd been over-cautious. He's done shows in far worse conditions. Thankfully, he'd been in the minority in the crisis meeting, with Salt, Amanda and Eclipse all pushing hard not to delay. Well, nothing lost. He was only doing his job in pointing out the factors that needed to be taken into consideration. Decision made, get on with it. They look all set, a tribute to meticulous planning. Plus, the sooner it's over, the better really. He'll be home by this time tomorrow.

Curiously, the atmosphere is unlike many of the festivals Ross has done in the past, which are generally full of high spirits, joy and anticipation. Here, it's the crowd who seem to be having butterflies, a tense undercurrent filling the air. Perhaps it's the earlier threat to the evening, the dampening effect of the tempest, or the sheer disbelief they're about to see Oasis after twenty years away that's weighing on people. Or possibly it's the consciousness of the large amount of money they've paid to be here. Ross remembers reading somewhere about the leisure pressure phenomenon, where simply doing something pleasurable isn't enough. The afflicted worry an event won't be as good as they anticipate, have misgivings over how much they've paid for a ticket, or question whether a superior seat or view would have made their experience better. Crucially, they fear someone else will have a better time than they do. Ross smiles to himself at these first world problems and it reminds him this is nothing compared to what would really have tipped these people over the edge – no mobiles at the show. Incredibly, it had been discussed, with the argument being made that it was better to enjoy the experience live rather than through the screen of a phone. Artists like Bob Dylan, Jack White and Guns N' Roses, who made fans lock their mobiles in Yondr pouches for the duration of their shows, were cited. Fat chance. The whole point of people paying all this money to be here *was* to show off to their friends and acquaintances, and what better way to do that than via a jerky and out-of-focus live stream of something occurring half a mile away? The head of production reflects, as people check the battery levels on their devices all around him, how close they came to being forced to watch the actual show. Satisfied all is on track, he heads off to the main stage.

***

After a panic-inducing queue to get in – *we're going to miss the start* – Dave and JJ manage to penetrate ten metres onto the arena floor before deciding 'this is far enough'. They nod to each other – no point getting mangled at the front. Dave is fine as he can see over the heads of most people, while JJ is on tiptoe already. Still, he'd be on tiptoe at the front as well as being flattened, so this will do.

'Look,' Dave says taking in the stage set-up, 'Sifter said they'd keep it simple.'

'Cheap, you mean? He wasn't wrong, was he?' There's no doubt about it, there are few frills to the design – a backline, a drum riser, and a string of microphones sit beneath a Jumbo videowall.

'What's that at the back?' Dave says, pointing to a large shape covered in tarpaulin.

'A portable loo?' JJ deadpans.

Dave, mindful of Stoggy's stinging putdown to his praise of Coldplay's stagecraft, mimics his absent friend. 'Remember, *It's all about the music, not the gimmicks.*'

'Stoggy's right though,' JJ reasons. 'It's good they've not succumbed to style over substance, putting up a smoke screen to mask any rustiness or inadequacies. It's a no compromise approach, rock 'n' roll in its simplest and most impactful form. Its roughness, its rawness, is part of the appeal.'

'Bloody hell, JJ. What magazine did you get that from? You said it was cheap a second ago.'

'Not them,' JJ insists. 'You know what I mean.'

This cultural exploration is brought to a rude conclusion with a violent shove in the back from a very animated Ent. 'Is this as far as you've got, you pussies?' he laughs. 'How long have you been in?'

'Not long,' JJ guardedly replies. 'How did you get in so quickly?'

'Strolled in. Told you to let the queue go down,' Stoggy gloats. 'You could have had a couple more drinks.'

'We're fine, thank you,' Dave tersely assures him. 'In perfect shape for the performance.'

Ent excitedly bounces up and down. 'So are we. We've been treating ourselves,' he says, theatrically wiping his nose. They don't need to ask what they've been treating themselves to.

'C'mon,' Stoggy says, already tired of this exchange. 'Need to get a wiggle on down the front.' The directive clearly doesn't extend to Dave and JJ (for which they're grateful).

As they make to move, Dave spots both of his friends have large coffee cups in their hands. 'Hang on. You're drinking cappuccinos?' he mocks. 'Really rock and roll.'

The two accused exchange conspiratorial looks.

'Not exactly,' Ent admits.

Not coffee? They've disguised their drinks. Dave is less than impressed. 'You could have at least sneaked us a beer in, even if you weren't sure of bumping into us.'

'It's not beer,' Stoggy confides, and they both start to giggle.

It's JJ who catches on first. 'Oh no, you're not going to throw that, are you?'

'Laters, boys,' is the only response they get as Ent and Stoggy disappear into the throng.

'What was all that about?' Dave innocently asks.

JJ sorrowfully shakes his head. 'You really don't want to know,' he sighs. 'You really don't.'

Dave lets it pass as he's beset by another thought, one he's had a few times today. 'It's weird we've not seen Rachel or Justine anywhere. Do you think they're avoiding us?'

JJ shrugs. 'Hard to say. There's ten thousand people here, after all. Forget them – Oasis are on in a minute.'

This Dave knows, but still, it's a bit of a coincidence they've not seen the two women today. 'I think you must have scared Justine off, JJ.'

His friend objects to such a charge. 'I think you'll find, Dave, that your stalking of Rachel might be a bigger factor in their low profile.'

Dave is visibly stung at this accusation. Did his attentions to Rachel amount to nothing more than pestering? JJ's comment strikes deep, not least because he'd been experiencing a growing paranoia all day over how Rachel had put an abrupt stop to his advances last night. Had he misread the situation? Whatever he thought about JJ and Jus getting it together, at least they'd clearly been on the same page. 'Do you really think so?' he asks shakily. 'It's because of me?'

JJ looks to the heavens and blows his cheeks out. 'Christ, will you stop obsessing? Priorities. Oasis. Focus. Be here now, like it says on the poster.'

***

Justine doesn't want to say it, so Rachel does: 'You'd have thought as competition winners we would have been a bit closer.'

They can barely see the stage proper from where they are, on the back row, at almost ninety degrees to the stage, looking at a screen mounted on the side.

'Well, at least we didn't pay,' says Justine charitably. 'But these other people must be well miffed. They might as well have watched it at home on the telly.'

Rachel nods. 'And they'd have been dry. And able to go straight to bed afterwards.'

'And get nachos and beers from the kitchen in between songs.'

Rachel falls into a reverie again. Matthew would have given anything to have this view. What he wouldn't have liked is all this mithering, that's for sure. The first thing he'd have done is tell them off for sounding like a couple of old women, that's what. Buck up now. You're here, on Holm Island, to see the only show by Oasis in twenty years, and millions of people would kill to swap places with you. What was that old saying? In the land of the blind, the one-eyed man is king. Well, they're only going to see half of what's going on from here, so one-eye would be just about right. No, that's the wrong attitude. Better to regard this vantage point as the royal box and she the queen. (In which case, should she have brought her king along too?)

Justine is surveying the crowd on the arena floor. 'Do you think they're in yet?' There's no need to clarify who 'they' are.

Rachel stares blindly at the gathering mass and feels another stab of guilt. Had she led Dave on last night, acting like a randy teenager before turning tail and running? He must have been confused. Forget that, she was confused. They'd avoided them all day, but why? Was it her, or Justine, or both playing hard to get?

'Do you want to see JJ again?' she asks, a genuine question.

Justine considers this. 'Do I want to see JJ again? Not particularly, no.' She smiles: 'He's served his purpose. Scratched an itch – that'll do me for a while.'

Rachel snorts in admiration. How strait-laced she feels compared to her free-spirited friend. 'God, Jus, I wish I was more like you.'

'Well, you've still got a chance later, but only if you really want to. But I'm not so sure you should be using me as a role model.' She pulls the hood of her cagoule up tight. 'How much longer do you think? The sooner they start the sooner we can get back inside again.'

***

Sifter's blog:

We're on! Whoever did the rain dance, massive thanks!

I confess, I thought we were buggered for tonight, but we are definitely go, go, go. Kick off time is ten o'clock now – a sixty-minute delay, which is a miracle given the conditions earlier. It's starting to get dark now which can only help with the lighting from the outset of the show. The arena is crammed already – nobody wants to miss the magic moment we see the Gallaghers together again after all this time. Me? I'm down the front (as you'd expect), pinching myself that, yes, it's really happening. I knew in my heart I'd get to see Oasis again, even if it is only one more time. It's emotional! The time for talking – and blogging – is over. I'm diving in. Cum on feel the noize. (Full report later, natch.)

***

The great and the good have gathered on the VIP gantry overlooking the stage, emitting well-practised *what's the big deal?* vibes. The guest list had become an instant nightmare for Salt the moment Be Here Now was announced, with the world and his wife (especially the wives) pleading for a pass. The list of family members supplied by the Gallaghers alone was enough to warrant a redesign of the stage, so the impresario hit on a novel idea: charging for the remaining spaces at an extra £25,000 each. The first thirty went so quickly, he upped it to a £40,000 premium for the next fifty. In the last two weeks he could only squeeze somebody in (*we're full, mate*) for a £50,000 top-up. The sole condition was nobody was to know money had changed hands, so the 'guests' could hang out and milk the association as if they were an especial friend of the band. Some agents baulked at first, but as Salt quite rightly pointed out, you can't put a price on street cred. And it was all going into his retirement pot. He takes in the scene below and out front and congratulates himself on how he's managed to fit a quart into a pint pot, using every available inch of space (helped partly by insisting all bars, toilets and merchandise stalls be located outside the auditorium to increase capacity). This had caused a huge degree of disgruntlement, but Salt was adamant punters had plenty of time to get in the mood and would just need to plan better if they didn't want to knot their legs. There's a backstage bar, of course, which the guests have been availing themselves of since being admitted. None more so, Salt notices, than BRITE's Genie of What If, Martin, who is openly necking vodka as if he's heard the Russian wheat harvest has failed. *There's a man with a death wish,* he thinks. He looks for other familiar faces – yes, the rest of the gang's all here. Amanda, decidedly uncomfortable and out of place, is being ignored by everybody present while Eclipse is holding court as if it's a debutante ball. He glances at his watch. Nearly showtime. Thank Christ he won't have anything to do with any of these people ever again after tonight.

***

Bob is still outside, walking to and fro in a distracted state. He's tried his best to message Bryan that the gig is delayed, but there's obviously a problem with the signal. The founder of HUTH (Had it Up To Here) may even be unaware of the weather that's battered the island since he went underground. The plan is to hit the show halfway through, but there's a good chance now that Bryan will make his move before Oasis come on stage. Bob is in a quandary. They should have set up a contingency. Still, not much he can do about it; he might as well go in and see the concert now he's here.

28

LOCK ALL THE DOORS

The two SAS soldiers locked securely inside the turbine hall can't believe their luck at being given this doss of an assignment. Used to doing nothing for long periods, they've occupied themselves all evening by playing cards, kicking off with gin rummy before moving on to hands of whist, blackjack and pinochle. As the hour approaches ten o'clock, however, they're feeling a little peckish, and cut the deck to see who will go back to the vending machines in the rest area for some emergency rations.

At around the same time, having calculated Oasis are well into their performance, Bryan and Cody are making their move deeper into the processing plant after a patient five hour wait. At the next steel door they encounter, Cody checks his arm for the scribbled passcode. 'No need for that,' Bryan says as he taps merrily away.

As the door swings open, Cody is impressed. 'How on earth did you remember the numbers? I forget my own PIN.'

Bryan grins. 'Easy. The only time we ever won the World Cup.' Cody is none the wiser, so he elucidates. 'Wembley Stadium, England versus West Germany for the Jules Rimet Trophy. The year, 1966. The final score, after extra time, 4-2 to the Three Lions. Therefore: 1-9-6-6-4-2.' He breaks into a snatch of song – *It's coming home, it's coming home* – as Cody shakes his head in bewilderment. 'Nice of the geezer who set it to use it for all the doors too.'

'That's pretty dumb, I know that much.'

'Yeah, well, he's a very helpful chappie. A true believer. I must buy him a pint if I ever bump into him.'

Cheered by this jingoistic diversion, they turn their attention to the huge chamber they've just entered. 'What the hell is that?' Bryan asks, staring at the giant centrifuge dominating the space.

Cody is shaky on the detail – he had a lot of info to take in quickly from Eclipse. 'Haven't a clue. She said we'd pass through bioenergy before the turbine hall, whatever that is.'

Bryan doesn't know what that is either. 'Everything is bloody bio these days. It's probably a yoghurt making machine.'

They proceed across the hall slowly and carefully. With the machinery turned off the dimly lit space has a ghostly air, the faint hum and blinking lights of the three control panels the only things stirring. They reach the next door and Bryan punches in the six numbers with aplomb, citing a name for every digit: 'Moore, Hurst, Peters, Charlton (Jackie), Ball, Stiles…'.

Nothing happens. 'What the hell?'

'Did you put it in right?'

'Of course I did.'

'Do it again.'

Bryan lingers over the keypad. He knows he put the numbers in correctly, but he's not giving way to panic just yet. 'You watch me this time, OK?' He taps in the numbers again, ever so carefully. 1-9-6-6-4-2. Nothing. Scratching his head,

'We have a problem. Are you sure this is the only code she gave you?'

'Yeah. One code for all the doors. She said so.'

'Well, she was either mistaken, you heard it wrong, or somebody has changed it.'

'It isn't my fault,' Cody tetchily replies. Then, on a more practical note, 'So, what are we going to do now?'

Bryan takes control of the situation. 'First, we remain calm and assess our position.'

On the other side of the door, Trooper B freezes in his tracks on hearing muffled voices. Nobody is supposed to be down here but him and his mate. He immediately withdraws to cover the entrance with his C8 Carbine, while radioing his colleague for backup. It could be that whoever is on the other side of that door is entirely legitimate, but he's not paid to take chances (wisely, the military training manual doesn't cater for assumptions). Within seconds he's joined by Trooper A and a brief conflab takes place. They radio command for instructions.

Back on the other side of the door, Bryan is thinking hard. 'It's obviously a different combination,' he deduces. 'What could it be?'

Cody can't believe what he's hearing. 'Seriously? You're going to try to guess a six-digit code? There must be millions of permutations.'

Bryan is unfazed. 'There might well be but remember the chap that set these is on the right side of history. Let's see…' He closes his eyes tight in concentration. 'Right, how about this.' He carefully punches in 0-8-0-5-4-5. Nothing.

'What was that?' asks his incredulous sidekick.

'VE Day. Worth a punt.'

'This is madness.'

Bryan can't disagree, but he's no quitter. 'OK – one more for luck, eh?' He strains yet again for inspiration. Then he has it. 'I know. Totally random, but here we go.' Tongue hanging out in concentration, he enters 2-3-0-6-1-6. Nothing again.

'For fuck's sake, can we head back now?' says Cody, shrinking under the pressure of engagement.

'Not yet,' asserts the master strategist. 'There's an old Chinese proverb that says *A crisis is an opportunity riding a dangerous wind.* We've drawn a blank here, so we improvise.'

Cody's spirits slump. They've tried and have been defeated. It was a hare-brained plan in the first place, one he should never have reported back to his messianic leader who is now clearly on a divine mission. Surely, it's time to retreat. 'Improvise how, exactly?'

Bryan casts his gaze around the large bioenergy chamber. 'We'll think of something,' he says defiantly. But before they can set their minds to a new challenge, Cody needs to ask: 'So, go on then. What was that last number you put it?'

Bryan is slightly surprised it wasn't obvious to him. 'The date of the Brexit Referendum,' he says reprovingly. Then, 'Come to think of it, whoever set the codes might just have been a keen footie fan rather than one of us.'

Cody rolls his eyes and curses Bob on the surface again for getting the easy ride.

Beyond the steel door, it has been established that whoever is in the bioenergy chamber is neither friendly nor authorised. The battleplan is quickly prepared – a pincer movement with two SAS men entering via the main entrance as Troopers A and B close from the rear. Watches are set to five minutes.

29

UP IN THE SKY

Salt receives the news from the different dressing rooms that he's been dreaming of for months. The boys are ready. The impresario grabs his laptop and heads backstage for his one final job of the night.

Ross gives the word for the lights to go down and to run VT, and they're off, a three-minute video tracking the band's career appearing on the Jumbotron, a clock in the corner of the screen counting down the seconds to curtain up. Spotlights play on the crowd as they pinch themselves. The stars have aligned. The great wait is over. Be Here Now is happening and they, the chosen few, are present to see it, smell it and touch it like no other.

Such is the fever pitch all around, few notice the elderly promoter and the band's accountant huddling over a laptop in the wings. But this is how it's all become possible. Money. Guarantees not being worth the paper they're written on, even if signed in Gallagher blood, the usual contractual protocols bit the dust early on in negotiations. Money. An agreement struck that the second Oasis physically take to the stage they're to be paid in full. Money. The responsibility falling to Salt to wire the transfer the instant two pairs of boots – one size eight and one size nine – tread the boards. Money. One hundred million pounds.

The countdown on the screen reads one hundred and fifty seconds.

***

Ent and Stoggy have pushed all the way to the front, leaving hundreds of fans to curse them as they barged past with nary an apology. Still, they're in prime position near the barrier as the video starts up – perfect timing. Ent is so excited he fears (despite recently emptying his bladder) he might soil himself, but nothing is going to make him move from this premium spot.

Stoggy is shouting something at him over the deafening soundtrack. He points at the coffee cups they've safely toted to the front. 'Chuck these as soon as they come on, yeah?'

His fellow flinger spots a flaw in their plan. 'Hang on, we're at the front. We can't chuck them at the band, can we?'

Unabashed, Stoggy has the solution. 'Hoy them backwards in that case. With any luck we'll hit Dave and JJ.'

The countdown on the screen reads one hundred and twenty seconds.

***

Down below in the bioenergy chamber, Bryan has alighted on the three control panels in the corner. 'What do you reckon these do?' he asks, mainly to himself.

Cody has forgotten everything Eclipse and Sun Tzu said and has only one thing on his mind. 'I really think we should get out of here. Before we get into trouble.'

Bryan isn't listening but rather running his thoughts aloud. 'Let's think about this. We can't get into the wind turbines chamber, but could this somehow be part of the process?' He studies the switches and lights flickering in the gloom. 'Looks pretty simple. It's got to do *something…*'

Cody looks on with trepidation. 'I wouldn't…'

Too late. Bryan's hands play over the controls of the first panel like a concert pianist playing "Flight of the Bumblebee". As he stops (no encore) the silence gives way to a giant whirring sound from within the centrifuge.

'Now you've done it,' Cody wails.

Yes, but done what?

The countdown on the screen reads ninety seconds.

***

As the roadies remove the tarpaulin from the object adjacent to the drum riser a cheer goes up from the crowd. 'Look,' JJ giddily reports. 'It's the phone box! They're going to come out of the phone box. Be Here Now – of course.'

Dave hadn't seen that tour, nor had he watched it on YouTube, so is none the wiser. He also can't understand why a man dressed as a circus ringmaster is whipping up the crowd in front of the box. 'Yeah, thought so.'

'Talk about recycling,' JJ shouts over the din. 'Love it.'

Dave, mindful of having something to show for his fifty grand (memories not counting as currency) grabs his mobile and primes the video setting. He's not alone – thousands of other mobile phones are already high in the air, ready to capture the moment of arrival. (The Space Station later releases an image of the light emitting from the collective screens.) This isn't just any walk-on, of course, but one of sacramental and venerable significance. The Second Coming. If the Pope was still awake in the papal bedchambers at this hour, he'd sense the change in world order and a shiver would run down his spine.

Amid the gathering maelstrom the ever-grateful JJ squeezes his benefactor's arm warmly and shout in his ear. 'Cheers, mate. Thanks for bringing me.'

'No problem. My pleasure.'

The countdown on the screen reads sixty seconds.

***

On the gantry, manners go completely out the window as the too-cool-for-school mob makes a mad scramble to get on the rail. The minister for CLEAN, who has occupied the best spot for the past thirty minutes, is rudely shoved aside by a young man sporting a monobrow. Her protestations meet with little success – it's every man – and woman – for themselves. Looking around to find someone to intercede on her behalf – she has paid for all of this, you know – she alights on Martin *(didn't she sack him?)*. However, it's apparent he's not going to be much use to her because he's acting in a most peculiar way. Eyes tight shut, he's swaying backwards and forwards as if in a trance. Perhaps he's tuning into the vibe, but given his past record she suspects other factors may be in play. She edges away – best give him a wide berth – but there's little respite. This is nothing but an unruly bearpit – better arrangements should have been made for her, consistent with her status. Wait until she sees Salt and gives him a piece of her mind. She then spots the only other person on the gantry she recognises: Eclipse. Curiously, the eco-warrior is looking in the opposite direction to everybody else; while all eyeballs are drawn to the stage, she's staring out to sea at the wind turbines as they lose their battle to be seen against the gloaming. What's suddenly so interesting about them? Or maybe she's on helicopter watch again. Amanda reflects that the oddballs she has been forced to work with on this project have been off-the-scale nuts. It will be a relief to be back at Westminster among normal people come Monday.

The countdown on the screen reads thirty seconds.

***

In the bioenergy chamber the noise from the centrifuge has cranked up from a whirr to a rumble, and from there to a deafening roar. Standing on the runway at Heathrow would be quieter.

The two agitators look at each other in alarm. This suddenly doesn't feel like a good idea anymore. What have they done? More accurately, what has Bryan done?

'Turn the bloody thing off,' Cody screams over the racket.

Cold sweat springing from every pore, Bryan punches randomly at the controls in a bid to reverse the start-up. The sound and intensity only increase. Abandoning the first panel, he works his magic on the second, whispering a blessed incantation of *Charlton (Bobby), Hunt, Wilson, Cohen, Banks* under his breath as he does so. Sadly, the victors of 1966 fail to bring him any luck; instead, the giant sphere in the middle of the hall begins to pulsate violently.

Barely feet away, the two SAS men are rocked by the vibrations and deafened by the racket behind the door and instinctively understand they can't afford to wait any longer for their colleagues currently scrambling from the backstage area to the entrance hall – they need to intervene now. A quick nod is exchanged, and Trooper A punches in the door code: 0-4-0-7-2-5 (the date Elsa, the head of security's dog, was put down). Nothing happens. He punches the digits in again but to no avail. Confused, they call for further orders. Whatever you do, they are told, don't input any more numbers as the system becomes frozen for ten minutes after three incorrect entries.

Unaware his earlier wild guesses have bought them more time, Bryan is desperately trying to kill the noise emanating from the centrifuge. Under these trying circumstances he does the only thing he can do – he turns his attention to the third panel. This has only four large black push buttons to choose from so, being a completist, he depresses all of them simultaneously. A sudden lull in the general agitation gives them temporary grounds for hope until, like a bawling baby who has paused only to draw breath, the sphere kicks up another gear and resumes from where it left off. And then builds some more. Just as it seems the clanging, banging and shaking can't possibly get any worse, the hall lights begin to flash, and the sound of a loud and insistent Klaxon adds a distressing top note to the clamour.

Cody has seen enough. 'It's going to blow,' he screams. 'Run.'

Bryan doesn't need telling twice.

The countdown on the screen reads one second.

***

Noel is the first to emerge from the bright red phone kiosk, to be greeted by frenzied cheers of devotion from the ecstatic crowd. He's followed by Bonehead, then some other musicians nobody really knows the names of and can't be bothered to learn. But no Liam. There is little in the way of preliminaries or an attempt to address the crowd, just a few waves and mock bows. Without further ado, the older Gallagher brother straps on his iconic Union Jack Epiphone Sheraton and they're straight into the first number, a plodding jam played at ear-splitting volume.

Down at the front, Ent and Stoggy blindly hurl their urine-filled receptacles back over their heads and start to bounce in unison with everyone else.

A sudden fear grips Ent. 'Where's Liam?'

Stoggy shouts in his ear. 'Coming on, just wait. It's Maine Road '96, see? "The Swamp Song". Watch.'

Also watching in the wings are two people with important business to attend to. 'Shall we?' says the accountant, indicating Salt's laptop.

The promoter eyes him warily. 'Not until Liam is on that stage.'

The suit makes light of his concern. 'Just the old showbiz tradition of making an entrance, Salt. I thought you'd have known that. I can wait.'

On cue, the younger Gallagher sibling emerges from the red box, and strolls on as if he's nipping out for a newspaper. The hunched figure grabs a tambourine and heads front of stage to milk the adulation. The insistent beat continues behind him as he prowls, nods, postures and points. Not a word has been sung, yet the crowd is putty in his hands.

Salt opens the laptop, pulls up the bank app, enters his password and keys in a figure which he shows to the accountant. He nods and the key is pressed. Send. One hundred million pounds. The accountant checks his phone to ensure receipt. Done. They shake hands – transfer complete, everybody can relax now and enjoy the show.

Up on the gantry, Amanda can't see the stage clearly, but it doesn't matter. She can hear and palpably feel the euphoria gripping this little piece of England and instinctively knows it's a success. She has made Be Here Now possible. She has put Britian on the map. She has showcased the nation's green energy credentials like no one before her. It's a proud moment for the minister, especially after this morning's spot of bother. Who's going to be the first to congratulate her on her magnificent achievement? Not Eclipse, who is still peering out to sea as if she's checking for icebergs. Very strange.

Further along, Martin remains comatose, slumped against a pillar. It's remarkable how he's able to sleep amid all this noise, even allowing for the vodka. Suddenly, however, he opens one eye. He's listening intently, but not to the band. A subterranean rumbling has reached his feet that, unless you knew better, would be easy to confuse with the stomping of the crowd and the general rapture breaking out in front of him. He grips the rail to confirm the seismic ripples he feels are indeed emanating from deep below. There's no doubt about it, the centrifuge…

That's as far as his scattered thoughts get as, a nanosecond later, there is a massive eruption beyond the arena, followed by an avalanche of effluent raining down on every square inch of Holm Island. Nobody is spared a coating of shit and piss as a tsunami of toilet offerings from the east coast of England engulfs the tiny area. The biomass plant has blown, and with it, the hopes, dreams and aspirations of the Supersonics and the Supernovas, not to mention the greens and the red, white and blues. It's a mini-Pompeii. As a tidal wave of crud catches the wind and blankets all in its path, one could hazard a guess as to what any future archaeologists excavating the site might conjecture: what strange rite was taking place on this spot;

who were the false idols being worshipped; what angry god has wrought such vengeance upon the debauched and the profane?

30

WHERE DID IT ALL GO WRONG?

As Holm Island falls into chaos the live feed to the world is suddenly cut and replaced with a re-run of Oasis at Wembley Arena 2008. The polluted performers scurry back to their dressing rooms as thousands of frenzied fans bolt for the exits in a disorderly retreat. A bomb? A terrorist attack? An industrial catastrophe? Nobody knows, and few want to hang about in case there is more to follow. But where can they go? They're on a bloody island for God's sake.

Given the gravity of the crisis, it's fortunate that a government minister is on hand to take charge, secure the site, and direct operations while ensuring people's safety. Except Amanda has legged it too, perhaps for a quick shower and a change into something clean and dry (maybe not the unused 'rock chick' outfit).

Martin snorts foul-smelling faecal matter from his nostrils as he tries to make sense of it all. He may be befuddled, but a clear chain of evidence – Eclipse's disenchantment, the midnight tour of the processing plant, his revelation that turning the wind turbines on was the only thing that could interrupt the concert – suggests the heavily soiled eco-warrior who is currently throwing up at his side has gone rogue. But that doesn't explain this inundation of impurities. It's impossible. How on earth has this happened?

Shocked, horrified and mystified in equal measure, Eclipse catches his accusatory stare and realises he knows she somehow has a hand in this. God knows what though – she didn't intend this to happen. Seriously, how could turning on some turbines for five minutes result in this? She shakes her head in frantic denial, as good as a confession in Martin's eyes. His reaction is unexpected as he breaks into a full-throated whoop of jubilation at the realisation of what's just happened. Talk about a shitstorm: the soon to be rechristened minister for SHITE can stick that up her manifesto and smoke it, *poop, poop, de doop.* In fact, it's beyond genius – it's poetic too. He grabs a startled Eclipse in a bear hug and pulls her tight against his turd-encrusted body. 'Bravo,' he gasps. What happens next is even more bizarre – he tears at his soiled clothes until he's stark bollock naked, and shins over the gantry rail to the stage below. Grabbing the still live mic the Genie of What If announces to the rapidly emptying auditorium: 'Ladies and Gentlemen, tonight's show has been brought to you in conjunction with our sponsor, Scrape-It arse wipes. Don't forget your free sample on the way out.' He swings around to mime a thorough application of said product. Still having the freedom of the stage, he throws himself onto his back and waves his arms and legs back and forth in the slime. 'Look, I'm a shit angel,' he shouts up at Eclipse. It's more than she can bear. She turns and runs. Anywhere will do.

***

Given their proximity to the rear of the arena, Dave and JJ are among the first to escape the dung discharge. Covered from head to toe in slurry, they make a sorry sight as they dash for their pod, the only place they can think of to shelter. In common with the rest of the crowd, thoughts of Oasis are far from their minds. 'What the hell just happened?' cries a shellshocked Dave when they think they're out of danger.

Sniffing his palm to confirm it is effluent, the group's health and safety aficionado pronounces: 'I'd say the main centrifuge blew.' At least he'd been paying attention to the island's processes and infrastructure. 'Pressure build-up in all likelihood. I suspect the flues were flooded with all the rainwater, although why somebody was trying to vent it during the concert I'll never know. Someone is going to get a real arse kicking for this.'

'You can bet on that,' says the personal injuries lawyer, sniffing an altogether different type of ordure. He counts the opportunities on his fingers. 'Full refunds. Damages. Trauma. Distress. The works.' He regrets not having brought business cards with him – it would have been useful to hand them out.

'Well, let's hope it's no worse than that. If some poor souls were in the plant when it exploded, they may not have made it out alive.'

The thought *double-bubble* crosses Dave's mind but he restrains himself from saying it out loud. 'Do you think Ent and Stoggy are OK?'

'They're as indestructible as cockroaches those two, so I reckon so. I doubt there's any fatalities in the arena – we just got the shower of shit. Very unpleasant.'

Dave goes further. 'Unpleasant? Bit of an understatement there, JJ. It's an outrageous attack on innocent people, a toxic threat to our health and well-being, a disgusting trauma-inducing...'

JJ stops him in his tracks. 'OK, Dave. You're not at work now. We get it.'

The lawyer stops thinking about business openings and reflects for a moment. 'When you come to think of it, Ent and Stoggy getting covered in piss and shit serves them right. Hoist by their own petard.'

'You can hardly equate chucking two cups of urine, deplorable as that is, with the forced discharge of a million litres of untreated sewage.'

Dave thinks about that for a second. 'Fair point,' he concedes.

JJ has a practical suggestion. 'Shall we go and look for them. Rachel and Justine too?'

Dave nods. 'Try the girls first.'

However, there is no answer from the adjoining pod, so they head out again, the night sky lit by blue and red emergency beacons. The Supersonic marquee has already been turned into an emergency hospital, home to hundreds of dazed and distressed fans wrapped in silver space blankets like they've just run a marathon. No recognisable faces there either, so they press on.

***

Ent and Stoggy have indeed survived the discharge, although they now resemble two chocolate soldiers left by the fireside. Even if they don't know the how, they have at least gleaned that something has gone terribly wrong and dipped everybody in doodoo. Under the circumstances, it's to their credit that their first thoughts are for the Gallaghers rather than themselves, having had a grandstand view of the brothers receiving a direct hit just as they were about to go into "Acquiesce".

They hover outside the auditorium as it empties. 'Noel looked furious,' Ent observes.

'It's hard to tell with him, but yeah. Liam just looked dazed – they had to help him off.'

'Do you think they'll come back on?' Ent asks, somewhat optimistically.

'Don't be soft. No chance. That's it, I tell you. We're never going to see them again.'

Stoggy's brutal assessment causes a tear to fall from Ent's eye, cleaving a clear channel through his new foundation. 'I can't face that, I can't. I'm serious. I'll kill myself if we don't get to see them play.'

'No, you won't, you idiot.'

They've managed two minutes of Oasis, got covered in shit, they stink like polecats and that's their lot. *Finito.* They let it sink in for a minute or two, their self-pity curdling into anger.

'People are going to laugh at us,' Ent gripes. 'It's not on.'

Stoggy, too, begins to bristle at the injustice and humiliation of their situation as his cack-infused clothes begin to stiffen. 'Fuck it,' he spits. It's then that he notices the merchandise stalls have been left abandoned. He points. 'Let's get our own back on the twats.'

Ent takes in the piles of unattended swag begging to be liberated. 'We can't nick all that. We'd never get it back on the boat.'

Stoggy shoots him a malevolent smirk. 'Who said anything about looting it?' And with that he flicks open the lid of his Zippo.

***

Amanda is just about to strip off for a shower when she is interrupted by her head of security. Having established she isn't injured, he has but one question for her. 'What instructions, Minister?'

'Get off the island as soon as possible,' is Amanda's obvious reply.

'Affirmative, but I mean the developing situation here.'

'Is this a terrorist attack?'

'Early indications are that it's an explosion in the processing plant. There's nothing at the moment to suggest it was intentional. No fatalities reported but there are thousands of traumatised people to deal with and certain unruly elements of the crowd, angry the performance has been curtailed, are engaging in rioting, arson and looting.'

Amanda feels like flushing herself down the toilet. This is on her watch. 'What do you think we should do?'

He's grateful to be asked, as she clearly doesn't have a clue. 'We are essentially dealing with a disaster area. The first thing to do is establish order – forcibly, if needs be. We need to evacuate the island without delay – get everybody on the boats and to the mainland. We need to determine what's happened here and confirm that an inquiry is already under way. And you need to do a brief media appearance reassuring everybody on the above.'

'What?' Amanda objects. 'Looking like this?'

'If it's any consolation, Minister, the fact that you look as much a victim as everybody else should play well with viewers.'

Amanda looks in the mirror. She's a mess, but the same sort of mess Joan of Arc tied to the stake would cut, or that girl on the Les Misérables poster. Heroic. Valiant. Unbowed. 'I'll do it,' she says without hesitation. 'But tell me, where are Oasis now? I'd better say something about them too, hadn't I?'

'Left already. First off the island. By helicopter.'

This isn't what Amanda wants to hear. How dare they? She should have been the first to leave. 'Is there a helicopter for me?'

'There was. It came but took off again. I'm sure it will be back soon.'

***

Bryan and Cody emerge from Hades to a scene of devastation. The island resembles a child's painting where too many colours have been applied; what started out as a vivid landscape is now one giant canvas of brown sludge.

'Oh, Christ,' Cody wails. 'They're going to lock us up and throw away the key for this.'

Bryan maintains his composure under pressure. 'No, they won't. This has nothing to do with us. It's just a coincidence.'

Cody can't believe what he's hearing. 'A coincidence? Try telling MI5 that when they're waterboarding you.'

'Don't be daft. The British don't do that sort of thing. Let's not hang around here though – we need to find Bob and mingle.'

They head off in the direction of the arena, their hearts sinking with every step. What have they done? A spluttering press of dung-doused demons stagger aimlessly about the barren landscape as a foul-reeking miasma assails the senses and stings the eyes. In the distance, flashing lights, the sound of sirens, and what looks like a serious blaze catching hold. Never mind a five-year-old's daub, Hieronymus Bosch would have been hard-pressed to come up with something as hellish as this.

It couldn't get any worse. Or could it? 'What if we've killed somebody?' Cody whispers.

'I think you'll find we were nearest to the blow-out and we're in one piece, so stop stressing, will you?'

Remarkably, they discover Bob in the rendezvous spot they'd agreed earlier. He looks a sorry sight. 'Did you do that?' he says balefully, pointing skywards.

'There was a bit of a problem,' Bryan concedes, 'but I'm not sure all of this is down to us.'

'So how come you two are the only people on the island not totally covered in shit?' Bryan and Cody check themselves out. Totally turd-free. Remarkable. 'You stick out a mile.'

'Should we smear some on, to fit in?' Cody suggests.

Bryan thinks about that for a few seconds. 'No bloody way. Look, we need to get our ducks in a row here. A strategic retreat is called for. We've not been here, nor undertaken any action, and we'll live to fight another day. Agreed?'

'Hang on,' Bob protests. 'We didn't only disrupt the gig – we totally stopped the bloody thing. Surely that's mission accomplished, in spades.'

Their general is already mounting his horse. 'No, not this time. We have to accept that the fallout from this might be problematical. Unintended consequences and all that.'

Cody seizes on this slim chance of avoiding chokey. 'Retreat under cover. Seconded.'

Bob shakes his head in dismay. 'What about the cause?'

Bryan doesn't intend discussing orders with his subordinates. 'Stand down, Bob, you hear? Now is not the time.'

'And we'd better destroy that video as well,' Cody chips in. 'You know, get rid of the evidence.'

Bryan agrees. 'Good thinking.'

Bob gives his clean-cut colleagues a mutinous stare. 'A bit late for that. I've just posted it. You should have said.'

***

Salt has seen enough. As soon as the cascade of crap calls time on Oasis, he knows it's curtains for him as well. It doesn't matter how it's happened, what should have been the crowning glory of his career will now form his epitaph: *Could always be relied upon to put on a shit show.* Reputational damage is one thing, but what about the financial implications of this disaster, especially for him?

What should he do first? Attend to the band or seek out the minister? Or perhaps find the dependable Ross, who normally knows what to do in any emergency. Whatever he does, he senses all paths will lead to accusations, anger and antagonism towards him personally, not that any of this is his fault. As the arena empties, he makes some quick calculations and determines a course of action. Within minutes he's heading out of the backstage area in the direction of the helipad. Ahead of him, he can just about make out a gang of shit-stained musos in the gloom – the band has beaten him to it. They pile into the waiting chopper in an undignified heap, a scene vaguely reminding the seasoned impresario of the Rolling Stones' retreat from Altamont (and to think people used to say that was the most disastrous festival of all time – well, they won't be saying that after tonight). Salt gesticulates wildly at them to wait but the door is slammed firmly in his face – all he can see is somebody's arse pressed up against the window, and two fingers flashing him a V-sign. The bastards. With that, the pilot throttles up, the rotors strain, and the overweight eggbeater rises slowly from the floor, leaving Salt to shake his fist angrily at them in an unfond farewell. Rooted to the spot, clutching his laptop, he watches the white taillight of the helicopter recede. He knows he can't go back, not now; he must get off the island. That's when he hears a faint *phut-phut-phut* in the distance and spots two lights, one green, one red, growing ever closer. They're coming back! The chopper heads for the H and lands, but it's empty. What's happened to Oasis? Then he realises it's a different chopper.

He rushes to pull the door open and clambers inside. 'You're a godsend,' he gasps to the pilot.

The birdman at the front shakes his head. 'For the minister, mate. Hop it.'

Without a pause, Salt puts him in his place. 'I'm the promoter. Under strict instructions from the minister herself to be airlifted, as a priority, on security grounds.' He brandishes his laptop authoritatively as evidence of his claim. 'It is of national importance this is removed to a place of safety without delay.'

The pilot is hesitant, but Salt ploughs on. 'She won't thank you for fucking about. You're to come straight back for her after this.'

'Shouldn't we…'

He's cut off by the impresario. 'Didn't you hear me? Orders. Or do you want to be sent to the Gulf for your next tour of duty?'

Salt hears a sigh, followed by the sound of rotors revving up. He slumps in relief in his seat and buckles up. As the chopper clears the wind turbines and heads away from Holm, his mind is in overdrive as to his next move. Finally, he decides. Opening his laptop, it takes him several minutes to key in a succession of passwords and security questions, until he finally accesses the Be Here Now RFID account. The balance, mid-point between receiving the payments made into ten thousand wristbands and before paying out to concessionaries, isn't quite Oasis fee level, but it'll do for the impresario's trouble. As the pilot whisks the whirligig towards the coast, Salt wings a cool six million pounds into his Swiss bank account. By morning, he'll be half the world away.

31

LET THERE BE LOVE

The retreat from Holm Island is conducted in brisk fashion by the Royal Navy. Punters are unceremoniously dumped willy-nilly onto whatever craft is docked, and no possessions are allowed to be taken on board. The contracted cruise liner owners initially refuse to transport the effluent-encrusted excursionists, arguing it would take them years to refurbish the facilities, but a compromise of sorts is finally reached in only allowing passengers on deck. Yet more misery for the afflicted.

As dawn breaks, the mini-Dunkirk reveals the full extent of the dusting of crud each passenger has received. 'Just look at the state of us,' Rachel cries tearfully. 'This is the worst weekend of my life.'

Justine is made of sterner stuff. 'At least we're on board. Just pretend you're a pig – they roll in shit on purpose. We're going to have a real glow-up after this. *Oink*.'

Rachel isn't persuaded. 'We could catch all sorts. Diarrhoea for a start, never mind hepatitis or E. coli.'

Justine remains upbeat. 'They're going to give everybody a full scrubdown and inoculation boosters once we get to Hull. They're bringing in those disinfection tunnels they have for epidemics – we'll all be going home in white forensic suits. Very stylish.'

Rachel shakes her head. 'I wish I'd never won that bloody competition,' she laments.

The pair are squeezed into the bow of the ship, prompting Justine into another attempt at lightening the mood. 'Look,' she says, 'we could do that Jack and Rose thing from Titanic if we weren't covered in shit.'

At last Rachel allows herself a faint smile. Under the circumstances she couldn't have asked for a better companion on this trip. Justine has been unflappable and unflinching throughout, especially after the disaster struck; she's the one who's pulled them through. From their vantage point in the stand they'd seen the tidal wave of gook sweep the arena, swallowing everything in its path before engulfing the stage. Like everybody else they'd ducked for cover, but to no avail – nobody was spared a dousing. As people around them reacted in shock and horror, it was Jus who'd yanked them away from the cesspool, pushing their way through the throng and out of the auditorium, back to their pod. There, they'd locked the door and hunkered down, in fear of the wayward mob raging outside. As things quietened down, rudimentary attempts at a clean-up at least bore some results – make-up removers, tissues and hand wipes clearing most of their faces and hands. When a sailor arrived in the early hours with an instruction to head to the dock and take the first boat available, Justine listened intently and didn't kick up a fuss when told to leave their luggage behind. Getting off the island was what mattered. Once on the jetty the crowd was anything but orderly, fights breaking out among the frenzied hordes desperate to board, catastrophe having unleased a dog-eat-dog mentality among normally sane people. Justine had bobbed and weaved, never letting go of Rachel's hand, until they reached the top of the gangplank. The worst behind them, they were heading back to the mainland.

Composure returning, Rachel squeezes her friend's hand in gratitude. 'Thanks, Jus. I don't know what I'd have done without you.'

'We're going to have a tale to tell, that's for sure. Probably better than actually seeing Oasis if you ask me.'

'If I'm being honest, I probably saw more of them tonight than at Benicassim. It's maybe time I gave up on concerts. I never liked Oasis that much anyway.'

'Me neither.'

The journey is taking an age, but surely their ordeal is almost at an end. It's then they are discovered. 'Rachel, Justine!' comes the shout.

They turn to confront two creatures from the black lagoon, who despite their unnatural tans are easily identifiable as Dave and JJ. 'What are the odds of that?' Dave gets to utter for the second time that weekend. It is, indeed, a remarkable coincidence among all these people.

The two men move in to swap war stories. 'Thank God you're OK,' JJ gushes. He means it, as well.

'Oh, you know us,' Justine breezes. 'Hardy souls.'

'Are you alright?' Dave asks, looking directly at Rachel. It's as if he has reason to suspect otherwise.

Within seconds they've paired off into two separate conversations. Dave is full on from the off. 'This is going to be the biggest damages claim in history. I'm going to take this lot to the cleaners, you just wait.' He catches her studying his soiled garments, and adds, 'No pun intended.'

'I'm just glad we're in one piece and safe,' Rachel replies. 'That's all that matters.'

Dave remembers JJ's rebuke about not acting the lawyer 24/7. 'Yes, absolutely. Of course you're right.' He leans in and lowers his voice. 'Can I ask you something, Rach?'

Here it comes… She ignores his use of the familiar and nods warily.

An earnest entreaty: 'Did I do something wrong?'

'In what way?'

'Well, you know. We were getting on so well last night, and I felt we had a real connection. But then you just suddenly… stopped.'

Her heart skips a beat. She can't deny she did a runner. But why? Did he do something wrong or did she, letting it go that far in the first place? She can't answer him directly. 'It was a nice evening, that's all.'

Nice? Dave thought it was more than that. He outlines his case as if it's a whiplash claim. 'We seem to have so much in common. The personal situations we're both in for one. Marriages going nowhere.'

Ouch. Is her marriage going nowhere, or is it merely on hold? Isn't that what she's here to decide in the first place?

'I was hoping that maybe we could meet up again.'

Oh, My Lord. Does she want to see Dave again? It's a simple enough question. He has a certain charm, and he didn't push it last night, which is to his credit. He appears to be successful in his job although incapable of ever switching off from it. As for their domestic situations being the same, she's not sure she agrees with that assessment, and what would it matter if they were? This is all her fault – she embarked on this matrimonial break, this big adventure, to evaluate her future, but is this really the holy grail she was seeking?

She takes a deep breath, then, channelling her inner-Justine, replies. 'I don't think that would be a good idea. We had a bit of a flirt, that's all. And now we're on our way home, no harm done. Best leave it there.'

Dave searches for a counterargument, but all he can come up with is a deflated, 'Oh'.

Having got that out, Rachel feels empowered to go further. 'Can I say something?' she asks. She doesn't bother to wait for an answer and says something anyway. 'If you're really unhappy with your wife, maybe you should speak to her about it. Maybe she's unhappy too. A marriage can be fixed if both sides put their minds to it, and if it can't, then at least you can agree to part. It doesn't need to be hostile if that's what you both think is for the best.'

Dave doesn't look entirely convinced at this homily, so she continues.

'This weekend has been a blast from the past – a festival, Oasis, "having it large". But face it, we're not teenagers anymore. Boring, I know, but there it is. Time to grow up and leave it to our kids to chase after rainbows.'

Is Dave chastened or humiliated at this knockback? It's hard to tell. He forces a strained smile: 'At least you have a very eloquent way of saying no.'

The awkward silence that follows is interrupted by Justine. 'Toilet?' she beckons to her friend, girl-code for 'let's split'. They leave the two men with a cheery 'bye then' and a backward wave.

'Lifesaver,' Rachel giggles as they scurry away.

'Likewise,' Justine snorts. 'He wanted my phone number. It was time to go.'

'JJ? You didn't give it to him, did you?'

'Yes and no. I made one up and told him my phone was flat, so he didn't try and ring it there and then. He'd served his purpose; that's good enough for me. No need for a sequel.'

'You brazen hussy,' says Rachel admiringly. 'Meanwhile, Dave was telling me about the special connection he felt with me. I couldn't help it, but I just had to burst his bubble.'

'We'd better not stop at the service station on the way home in that case. Wouldn't want to bump into them again.'

They nudge their way down the deck until their progress is halted by a knot of people watching a film crew – it's the dynamic presenter duo conducting vox pops. (It's a hard transition from entertainment to news reporting, but needs must.)

'The weekend hasn't turned out as hoped,' Cleo says brightly to a a pair bearing a remarkable resemblance to Ent and Stoggy. 'Tell us how you're feeling right now.'

'Great,' admits the beanpole. 'It was top.'

'Seriously?' Jez harrumphs. It's hard to tell if the interviewee has PTSD or if he's as high as a kite, but in any case, it's not the answer the viewers at home – the ones who couldn't get tickets – want to hear. *Schadenfreude* demands a first-hand declaration of disappointment, deprivation and the revelation *I was in fear of my life* at the very least.

'Yeah, seriously,' his overfed mate pipes up. 'We've had a ball. A proper Oasis gig; piss and wind with a bit of ultraviolence thrown in. It was like being sixteen again.'

Cleo knows what to do even before she hears the instruction in her ear. 'Ah. That famous Mancunian wit.' She turns swiftly to another face in the crowd, a man wearing a baseball cap, polo shirt and cargo pants. 'At least you've managed to clean up a bit, sir,' she observes. 'Could you describe for our audience that dreadful moment when disaster struck?'

Bryan thinks about it for a millisecond before bolting, knocking people over in his haste to escape.

Jez is immediately empathetic to his plight. 'The anguish and emotional strain this accident has inflicted is still raw. Thankfully, we understand a specialist team of trauma counsellors is on standby at Hull to greet the boats. They're going to be busy.'

'Absolutely,' Cleo concurs. She calls after the fleeing figure, 'Take care, sir.'

The two women inch away before they're ensnared. 'Wherever we go, those bloody Mancs pop up,' Rachel complains. 'I'm half expecting one of them to jump out of the bushes on my dog walk tomorrow.'

'Or be driving the next Uber we book. But what did you make of what they said? *It was top?* They were taking the piss, surely?'

'It's hard to tell. Couple of wackos.'

'And what about those interviewers?' Justine says. 'I don't think much of their bedside manner. That second guy looked totally shell-shocked by what's happened – it's crass to stick a microphone under somebody's nose like that when they're so clearly distressed.'

'I know. Poor fellow – him and the rest of us. It's going to take an awful long time for folk to recover from this.'

Their exchange is suddenly broken by a sound not dissimilar to a swarm of bees –mobiles springing to life as they approach land. Justine has one message:

CatsWhiskers – Justine via Metuyu Messaging:

> *Luna and Coco say hi.*
>
> *All nicely fed (and pooper-scooped) and looking forward to your return. I'll call in Sunday morning – with treats! – for the final time as arranged.*

Let me know if you're delayed, but all being well will see you next time.

X

PS: It's a definite no to those cat cameras. They don't like being watched.

PPS: Hope Oasis was good.

Hope Oasis was good? 'Under what stone has she been hiding?'

Rachel's phone has only just stopped buzzing. 'Twenty missed calls and forty-three messages. I'm in demand.'

'I'm not,' her friend reports. 'Are you going to answer them all?'

Rachel stares at the screen. 'No need,' she says, 'a call will be quicker.' She punches ICE in her favourites.

Justine can't help but hear one half of the conversation, but it's enough to make sense of it:

'Yes, in one piece thankfully.'

'Landing in Hull soon.'

'I'll tell you all about it when I get home.'

'Yes. Home home. Our home, Matthew.'

'Love you too.'

32

DON'T LOOK BACK IN ANGER

Sifter's blog:

Is it really a year since the Holm Island debacle? (Time flies slowly when you're trying to remove sewage from every crevice in your body.) Still, after this passage of time it's instructive to look back, not so much in anger, but relief.

I'll get flak for saying this, but I'll say it anyway: I'm glad it all turned to shit.

Am I being serious? I am.

I spend my life writing about Oasis. I live and breathe the band. Did I want to see them reform? Yes. No. Maybe.

The fact is, Oasis should never have agreed to legitimise this overblown, greenwashing junket in the first place. That it blew up (quite literally) in everybody's faces was, on reflection, the best possible thing that could have happened.

A carrot worth one hundred million quid for two hours' work would test anybody's resolve, but rock 'n' roll isn't – and shouldn't be – about the money. Oasis have a stature worth far more than gold. Trotting out two hours of under-rehearsed greatest hits for an audience of corporate wankers and privileged weekenders would have devalued that far more than a tsunami of turds ever could. Going through the motions indeed.

Undoubtedly, Be Here Now was an 'event', stirring the blood and rebooting the memory banks, but to what end other than to set the cash registers ringing? I ask, is that honestly a good enough reason? We'd certainly have seen nothing new on Holm Island. Nobody, including the band, would have dared claim it was as good as the first time around. I guarantee fans and critics alike would have panned the performance because it didn't live up to the glory days.

Rock 'n' roll is alchemy – the white-hot heat of creation, discovery and sharing. Once it's out of the test-tube and mass-marketed, it's a 'product'. Personally, I don't want my Oasis stacked high and sold at a premium.

Holm Island was promoted as the 'ultimate' festival. And you know what? I'm glad it was such a disaster 'cos it might stop others following suit. I wish I'd been around when festivals were all about the music, not the online scramble for tickets, the pre-sale, the sponsors, the merch, the VIPs and luxury accommodation, when tickets were affordable as well as accessible. You may say that's rosy nostalgia, misplaced idealism, but wouldn't you prefer that too?

Another thing that still stinks as much as that night is the so-called enquiry into what went wrong. Still 'ongoing', and no doubt it will be a complete whitewash when the findings are finally slipped out at 5pm on a wet Friday evening three years from now. Two hundred protest groups claimed responsibility, yet we're supposed to believe the thing just blew up of its own accord. Pull the other one, surely?

In fact, the sweetest thing about Holm Island was how it backfired so spectacularly on those on the make. Sacked ministers, a promoter absconding with £millions (hilariously still on the run – way to go), and polluted eco-warriors. As for the punters who paid all that loot to attend? Well, good luck with the compensation claims.

Remarkably, and pleasingly in my view, the only people it ***didn't*** *tarnish were Oasis themselves. Because, in* **not** *playing, Oasis preserved their reputation and cemented their legacy. And, better still, managed to bank a hundred million without putting on a show (always check the small print, folks).*

The greatest rock 'n' roll swindle since Malcom McLaren?

Now there's a story that will live forever.

ACKNOWLEDGEMENTS

Most of us have festival memories to fall back on – I hope *Be Here Now* stirs yours.

As a callow youth, my first ever rock three-dayer was The Yorkshire Folk, Blues and Jazz festival, Krumlin, near Halifax. It quickly descended into farce (clue – it was declared a disaster area after only two days). If you search for it online, you'll fall about laughing. Pink Floyd and The Who were scheduled to appear. Neither did. Elton John, at that time entirely unknown, did turn out and mentions in his official autobiography how he avoided festivals for decades afterwards.

Getting *Be Here Now* into print wouldn't have been possible without the help and support of some very special people, who each deserve a shout out:

The Brian Epstein award to my brother, Patrick Carroll, for input, encouragement and meticulous editing, and for being alongside the realisation of the novel every step of the way.

Not forgetting Nathalie Bagnall and Liam Ferguson for pointing out the bum notes in earlier drafts and insisting on further takes. Ditto David Baboulene, for your story crafting suggestions. I was wrong, you were right.

Thanks to beta readers Catherine Barrett, Martin Carroll, Neil Fox, Brendan Gore, David Hargreaves, John Kelly, David

Lomax and Gerry McLaughlin for valuable feedback (more buzz, less hum). It all went into the final mix.

Take a bow, Mark Beaumont of dinosaur.co.uk for another 'collector's item' cover design.

A big thumbs up to Glenn Jones, Suzanne Darke and Lucy King for the www.paulcarrollink.co.uk website.

Finally, props to Edward J Marsh, of publishers DreamEngine, for keeping an eye on the budget (*what do you mean, we've made a loss?)*

ABOUT THE AUTHOR

Writing that puts the 'stab' into establishment

Paul's novels consistently let fly at the latest social trends in an entertaining mix of cutting observation, human drama, dark humour and compassion.

Born and brought up in Leeds, Paul has a degree in English Language and English Literature from the University of Manchester and worked in PR for many years before becoming a full-time author. Paul lives in Altrincham, Greater Manchester.

A marketing gamekeeper-turned-poacher, Paul is to be found peering behind the curtains of 'the next big thing' when he's not writing.

Website:	www.paulcarrollink.co.uk
X:	@paulcarrollink
Instagram:	@paulcarrollink
Facebook:	@paulcarrollwrites

PREVIOUS NOVELS BY PAUL CARROLL

Shaking Hands with Elvis (2024)

When assisted dying is legalised in the UK following the sell-off of the NHS, where does the killing stop?

Don't Ask (2021)

A DNA ancestry test opens up a Pandora's Box of secrets. Two families become reluctantly entwined as inconvenient truths and long suppressed memories resurface.

Trouble Brewing (2017)

A celebrity chef whose star is on the wane is enlisted to help save a small Yorkshire brewery and its 'miracle' ale from closure.

Written Off (2016)

Don't be fooled into thinking that writing a book never killed anyone as four wannabe authors dream of getting their work into print.

A Matter of Life and Death (2012)

In the new zeitgeist of conspicuous public mourning the government's 'bereavement czar' single-handedly puts the 'fun' into funerals.

Published by DreamEngine